D1260766

Democracy Unchained

Democracy Unchained

How We Should Fulfill Our Social Rights and Save Self-Government

Richard Dien Winfield

Deeds Publishing | Athens

Published by Deeds Publishing in Athens, GA
www.deedspublishing.com

Printed in The United States of America

Cover design by Mark Babcock.

ISBN 978-1-950794-13-3

Books are available in quantity for promotional or premium use. For information, email info@deedspublishing.com.

First Edition, 2020

10 9 8 7 6 5 4 3 2 1

To Ady Barkan

In admiration of his courageous fight to unchain our democracy

Contents

Introduction — America at the Crossroads: Why We Need a Social Bill of Rights

The Unfulfilled Promise of Our Democracy

We stand at a crossroads where our democracy will either fulfill its promise or succumb to shortcomings that already imperil American self-government. What we do in the next few years is critical for the future of the United States, as well as for the prospects of all humanity. As members of the country with the world's largest economy, most powerful military, most dynamic scientific establishment, most influential culture, and greatest impact upon the global environment, we face national challenges of an importance second to none.

Grounding these opportunities and perils is our constitution, the oldest continuously operative one in the world, which continues to wield enormous influence upon world politics.

Despite its longevity, our constitution retains an unparalleled brevity. This reflects persisting omissions that have put our freedoms in jeopardy. Although the United States Constitution lays down the basic framework of our representative democracy and secures our political and civil liberties, it says virtually nothing about our family and social rights. This silence conforms to the truncated vision of freedom of classical liberal social contract theory, which identifies liberty with property rights and restricts the task of government to protecting person and property with the consent of the governed.[1] Political freedom, however, cannot operate on this basis alone. Unless family and social rights are recognized and enforced, relations of domination in the household and society will obstruct self-government.

The dependence of political freedom upon family and social self-determination is easy to see. If spouses do not have equal opportunity to co-determine their joint household property and welfare, but face discriminating hierarchies of gender and sexuality in the family, they cannot participate as free and equal members of society and state. Whoever lords over the family will dictate household responsibilities and what participation other family members may have in economic, social, and political activity. Without spouses wielding equal say in the household, social and political engagement becomes a privilege instead of a right. Finally, with heterosexuality exclusively ruling the household, those with other sexual orientations will confront obstacles that carry over from the home to the world outside.

Similarly, if social opportunity is blocked by hierarchies of wealth and occupation, those who are disadvantaged will lack sufficient resources and time to engage in self-government on a par with those who are socially privileged. Individuals wielding significantly greater wealth and power will be able to pressure those who depend on them, as well as disproportionately influence political opinion and who gains political office.

For these reasons, our democracy is in jeopardy if we cannot secure the family and social rights on which political freedom depends. Like any rights, these deserve constitutional protection so that we do not ignore them with impunity. The absence of any authoritative provision of our fundamental household and social rights in the United States Constitution is a problem that we citizens need to address if government of, by, and for the people is to prevail.

Our history has largely been preoccupied with struggles to give consistent fulfillment to the civil and political rights that our Constitution does mandate. Although the United States Constitution notoriously made room for slavery, it does not explicitly differentiate between the rights of men and women, or of individuals of different sexual orientations, or of members of different races and ethnicities, nor require property qualifications for voting or holding office. Nonetheless, our Republic began its career by conferring civil and political freedom exclusively to white men who owned a substantial amount of property. Instead of fulfilling the political equality promised by the Declaration of Independence and the Preamble of our Constitution, American "democracy" made its debut as a White Supremacist, patriarchal oligarchy, privileging heterosexuality. Our founders and too many of their immediate and not so immediate successors accepted that full participation in civic and political activity should fall to none other than adult white males. Although some local exceptions existed, non-white free men could not vote or run for office throughout the land. States restricted voting rights and office holding to those who met a property qualification. Slavery was tolerated, Native Americans were barred from citizenship, and Chinese immigrants and newly conquered Mexican Americans were deprived of equal political rights. Homosexual relations were outlawed, gay marriage was prohibited, and discrimination based on sexual orientation pervaded society.

The true spirit of our democratic project has still never been completely dormant and stubborn recognition of the glaring inconsistencies marring the American experiment has ignited waves of civil rights struggles. Spanning nearly two and a half centuries, these efforts have achieved undeniable progress towards fulfilling the universal opportunity basic to civil and political right. Through judicial decisions, statutory reforms, constitutional amendments, civil disobedience, and the convulsions of civil war, we have largely freed the formal exercise of civil and political freedom of restrictions based on wealth, race, gender, and finally, sexual orientation. With the elimination of property qualifications and the extension of citizenship, legal equality, and voting rights to women and non-whites, as well as the legalization of gay marriage and adult consensual sexual relations of any orientation, the narrow provisions of our constitution have become much more consistently realized than our founders either desired or anticipated.

Nonetheless, these very triumphs of civil rights movements have made increasingly obvious that consistent interpretation and enforcement of the United States Constitution is not enough to secure our self-government and the family and social freedoms on which it depends. The Preamble may promise to “establish Justice”, “promote the general Welfare, and secure the Blessings of liberty to ourselves and our Posterity”, but our Constitution rules over a nation of such growing social disparities as to undermine family welfare and the political equal opportunity of its citizens.

Today, the United States is the most economically unequal developed nation. Our most wealthy 1% have nearly twice as much wealth as the bottom 90%, a quarter of our population has no or negative net worth, three out of four Americans have less than $700 in reserve to meet any emergency, nearly half our children are impoverished, and we have less social mobility than anywhere else in the developed world. In this most wealthy nation in human history with the world’s most productive agriculture, families suffer malnutrition, not to mention homelessness and unhealthy substandard housing. A whole generation sees its future slipping away as more and more public schools fail their students while increasingly unaffordable higher education lies out of reach. Alone in the developed world, we Americans find that healthcare remains a privilege rather than a universal right, with medical costs driving more of us into bankruptcy than any other cause.

The American Dream is supposed to offer anyone who lands on our shores the opportunity to reward hard work with a decent livelihood.

Instead, we still face unemployment, underemployment, and stagnating wages, whose share of national wealth is at an all-time low. The days when one 40 hour per week job could support a whole family are fading into oblivion, as more and more households struggle to make ends meet with two providers working more than one job each. Meanwhile, full time employment, to which all too many benefits remain tied in the United States, is itself under accelerating assault. Jobs in every sector face growing threats from automation and the exploding "gig" economy, in which internet connectivity enables employers to outsource work to free-lancers anywhere and anytime, with no guaranteed hours or benefits. Finally, we find ourselves increasingly politically disempowered, as the money of powerful interests uncontrollably inundates our political process, while most citizens lack enough resources to run for office.[2]

Nor have we escaped the toll of our past inconsistencies. Compounding all the above difficulties, racial and gender disparities in opportunity remain entrenched, despite the elimination of legal discrimination and the introduction of affirmative action.

Three Salient Junctures in U.S. History Highlighting the Need for a Social Bill of Rights

At three salient junctures of our history, each of which affirmed our civil and political liberties, the need to recognize and enforce our neglected social rights has come to the fore, challenging our nation to fulfill its defining mission as a bastion of freedom.

The first of these moments of opportunity took place after the Civil War, as Reconstruction got under way. In every former Confederate state, the newly emancipated slaves put forward two primary demands. On the one hand, they insisted that the restored democratic government give each of their families "forty acres and a mule" with which they could win economic independence and security. On the other hand, they demanded that each state establish public education open to all and funded by state taxes.[3] In advancing these demands, the former slaves expressly recognized that the Thirteenth Amendment's abolition of slavery, the Fourteenth Amendment's mandate of legal equality, and the Fifteenth Amendment's enfranchisement of citizens, regardless of race, were not enough to make them free. If the emancipated slaves lacked the means to support themselves and their families, they would have scant opportunity to exercise their formal civil and political liberties and would face new forms of economic bondage to stave off looming destitution.

Without access to education, which the Confederate states had outlawed for their slaves, the newly emancipated citizens would be unable to make full use of their new legal and political rights, nor have any equal opportunity to earn a decent living. Since Southern slave plantation society had severely limited opportunities for free labor, the former slaves had good reason to seek their economic independence in small holdings of land and livestock with which they might subsist as independent farmers. Even this option, however, could hardly guarantee prosperity, if the former slaves remained condemned to illiteracy and deprived of an education that would become ever more crucial as a bulwark for freedom in a fast modernizing democracy.

The Constitution did not then and still does not now guarantee a decent livelihood or education to Americans, so the fate of the emancipated slaves hung in the balance, awaiting some national or local remedy. Neither federal or state governments met the demand of "40 acres and a mule," leaving the freed slaves little escape from a new peonage as share-croppers, landless hands, and "outsourced" prison laborers, often working the reborn plantations of their former enslavement. The Reconstruction state legislatures did succeed in initiating free public education for the first time in the South. Although public education remained in place after Federal troops withdrew from the South ending

Reconstruction, public schools became separate and more and more unequal, leaving genuine educational opportunity an unrealized dream. As for the civil and political rights ushered in by the 13th, 14th, and 15th Amendments, they too fell victim to a century long reign of White Supremacist terror, which would not wane until the Civil Rights movement ended the regime of Jim Crow.

Admittedly, the dual demands of the former slaves addressed the particular challenges of people newly granted legal and political rights, but possessing nothing but the scars of enslavement and the clothes on their back. Nonetheless, their demands raised the call for the fundamental social rights to livelihood and education crucial to the political emancipation of all Americans and any other population striving for democratic freedom.

The failure to recognize and enforce these rights came to the fore once more seven decades later, when the United States was emerging from the Great Depression, the greatest economic crisis of our history, through total mobilization for World War II, the greatest war in human history. As victory was finally coming into sight, Franklin Delano Roosevelt addressed Congress for the last time and issued a call for a new bill of rights. Although the impending triumph over Fascism represented the saving of our democracy, Roosevelt recognized that his fellow citizens needed to confront the limitations of this victory. In this 1944 State of the Union Address to Congress, Roosevelt put the nation on notice that the civil and political liberties protected by our Constitution and secured through military triumph were not enough to provide for freedom in the face of modern social conditions. Our democracy needed to extend constitutional protection to the social rights on which family welfare and self-government no less depend. Roosevelt's words retain their urgency still today:

"This Republic had its beginning, and grew to its present strength, under the protection of certain inalienable political rights – among them the right of free speech, free press, free worship, trial by jury, freedom from unreasonable searches and seizures. They were our rights to life and liberty. As our Nation has grown in size and stature, however – as our industrial economy expanded – these political rights proved inadequate to assure us equality in the pursuit of happiness. We have come to a clear realization of the fact that true individual freedom cannot exist without economic security and independence."[4] We therefore need "a second Bill of Rights under which a new basis of security and prosperity can be established for all regardless of station, race, or creed."

Roosevelt went on to list eight new social rights, starting with the true right to work, "the right to a useful and remunerative job in the industries or shops or farms or mines of the Nation." Whereas not all people have the capital or credit to get by as an entrepreneur or landlord, the entitlement to gainful employment can anchor the economic independence and security of anyone who is able and willing to work. To liberate individuals from destitution or welfare dependence, this right to work must guarantee employment at wages sufficient for a decent standard of living.

Consequently, Roosevelt adds the corollary "right to earn enough to provide adequate food and clothing and recreation." Since some breadwinners may be independent farmers and entrepreneurs, Roosevelt calls for two additional rights of livelihood, "the right of every farmer to raise and sell his products at a return which will give him and his family a decent living" and "the right of every businessman, large and small, to trade in an atmosphere of freedom from unfair competition and domination by monopolies at home or abroad."

Further, Roosevelt recognizes that a Constitution, which promises to "promote the general Welfare, and secure the Blessing of Liberty to ourselves and our Posterity," must not fail to acknowledge "the right of every family to a decent home." The rights to livelihood and decent housing, however, still leave our freedoms at risk if we cannot maintain the well-being on which all our activities depend. Roosevelt thus insists that we supplement our Constitution with "the right to adequate medical care and the opportunity to achieve and enjoy good health."

Moreover, since all these rights may still leave us vulnerable to the effects of aging and unforeseen disease and accidents, Roosevelt adds "the right to adequate protection from the economic fears of old age, sickness, accident, and unemployment".[5] Lastly, Roosevelt echoes the vision of the emancipated slaves, calling for constitutional enshrinement of "the right to a good education", as necessary to engage in the pursuit of happiness and participate equally in self-government.

During the Great Depression, Roosevelt tried to implement some of these social rights through such programs as the Works Progress Administration and the Civilian Conservation Corps, which put millions of unemployed people back to work, building innumerable public facilities and providing countless human services, art works, and performances contributing to our national well-being. To win the support of Southern Democrats and gain passage through Congress, Roosevelt allowed his New Deal Programs to contain restrictions that excluded the participation of African Americans.[6] Moreover, many of these programs were introduced as emergency measures contending with the economic crisis. When war production and enlistment overcame much of the remaining unemployment, the New Deal public works initiatives were disbanded. Roosevelt, however, understood that the social rights agenda outlined in his 1944 Address to Congress was not a disposable emergency mandate, but a standing commitment to furnish perennial essential conditions of the "pursuit of happiness" in a democracy, which should be provided to all.

Roosevelt died before being able to implement any of his new bill of rights, and to this day, our Constitution still fails to guarantee the right to employment at a fair wage, to food and clothing, to decent housing, to health care, and to education. Nonetheless, all of Roosevelt's proposed social rights received international recognition by being enshrined in the Universal Declaration of Human Rights, which was drafted by a United Nations committee headed by Eleanor Roosevelt and adopted with overwhelming support by the UN General Assembly in 1948.[7]

The Preamble of the Universal Declaration of Human Rights proclaims the wider scope of its affirmation of right. It invokes the Four Freedoms with which the Allies of World War II promised to follow the defeat of Fascism with "the advent of a world in which human beings shall enjoy freedom of speech and belief and freedom from fear and want".[8] Whereas the rights to freedom of speech and belief echo the First Amendment of the Bill of Rights, the freedoms from fear and want suggest a commitment to respect not just person and property, but family and social welfare as well.

The Universal Declaration of Human Rights does incorporate in its Articles 1 through 15 and 17 through 21 the fundamental property, legal, and political rights that the United States Constitution and our Bill of Rights protect.[9] In Articles 16, 22, 23, 24, 25, 26, and 27, however, The Universal Declaration of Human Rights breaches the narrow limits of our Constitution and gives international affirmation to all of Roosevelt's new social rights, with a few important additions.

Article 16 initiates the extended reach of the Universal Declaration of Human Rights by addressing family rights, which receive no mention in the United States Constitution, nor any explicit affirmation in Roosevelt's new bill of rights. Article 16 confers upon adults the "right to marry and to found a family", with marriage "entered into only with the free and full consent of the intending spouses", and with spouses entitled to "equal rights as to marriage, during marriage and at its dissolution".[10] In addition, Article 16 maintains that the family "is entitled to protection by society and the State", a right that requires social and political institutions to accommodate family welfare and respect family rights and duties.

On this basis, Article 22 sets the stage for the social rights agenda by broadly upholding "the right to social security" of every member of society, mandating its fulfillment "through national effort and international co-operation" enforcing "the economic, social and cultural rights indispensable for his dignity and the free development of his personality." The cornerstone of Roosevelt's new bill of rights is then introduced in Article 23, which affirms the right of every adult "to free choice of employment, to just and favorable conditions of work and to protection against unemployment." These conditions entail the corollary rights of each adult "to equal pay for equal work" and "to just and favorable remuneration ensuring for himself and his family an existence worthy of human dignity, and supplemented, if necessary, by other means of social protection." Since fair opportunity in employment depends upon evening the power and options of employee and employer, Article 23 further acknowledges a worker's "right to form and to join trade unions for the protection of his interests."

Articles 24 and 25 make explicit important aspects of Roosevelt's recognition of the right to work, with due account of what concerns family welfare. Article 24 insures that work does not extend so long as to conflict with family and political engagement, mandating that "everyone has the right to rest and leisure, including reasonable limitation of working hours and periodic holidays with pay." Article 25 spells out Article 23's mandate for "just and favorable remuneration," guaranteeing to every bread winner "a standard of living adequate for the health and well-being of himself and of his family, including food, clothing, housing and medical care and necessary social services, and the right to security in the event of unemployment, sickness, disability, widowhood, old age or other lack of livelihood in circumstances beyond his control." Article 25 further acknowledges that this injunction for a decent livelihood requires "special care and assistance" for "motherhood and childhood", including the "same social protection" for "all children, whether born in or out of wedlock."

Article 26 and 27 complete the international enactment of Roosevelt's social rights agenda by affirming access to education and the fruits of culture. Article 26 guarantees everyone the education they need to develop their autonomous agency and respect the rights of others, whereas Article 27 mandates that "everyone has the right freely to participate in the cultural life of the community, to enjoy the arts and to share in scientific advancement and its benefits."

Taken together, the family and social rights specified in the Universal Declaration of Human Rights provide an agenda for fulfilling on a global scale Franklin and Eleanor Roosevelt's ambition to extend the architecture of freedom beyond the all too narrow confines of civil and political rights. In the wave of post-war de-colonization, many of the new nations adopted constitutions incorporating the agenda of the Universal Declaration of Human Rights. Nonetheless, that agenda remains largely ignored and unenforced in much of the world. This is particularly true in the United States. Despite our ratification of the Universal Declaration of Human Rights, for which the Roosevelts played such a seminal role, we have adopted neither the constitutional amendments nor congressional statutes that would fulfill its call to enforce family and social rights.

Two decades passed before a third moment of opportunity arose. This occurred at another juncture of liberation, when the Civil Rights movement finally succeeded in getting Congress to pass legislation extending to every American the civil and political liberties that Jim Crow legal discrimination had taken away from African Americans, despite the 13th, 14th and 15th Amendments to the Constitution. Martin Luther King could have basked in the glory of that moment to which he had so decisively contributed. Instead, he recognized that the reestablishment of civil and political rights, important as it was, could not remove the glaring social disadvantage in which African Americans remained entrapped. Suffering from disproportionately high rates of unemployment and impoverishment, African Americans could not make equal use of their newly granted access to buses, trains, planes, stores, restaurants, hotels, theaters, clinics and hospitals, and colleges and universities. Nor could they expect their reestablished voting rights to change their circumstances in a political climate in which freedom remained primarily identified with property rights and unencumbered free enterprise.

As Martin Luther King succinctly stated in his very last month, "if a man does not have a job or an income at that moment, you deprive him of life. You deprive him of liberty. And you deprive him of the pursuit of happiness."[11] He recognized that the Civil Rights movement had unfinished business to address, the business of supplementing the retrieval of civil and political freedom with the economic emancipation of a social rights agenda. In 1968, Martin Luther King accordingly launched his Poor Peoples Campaign. It renewed the call for a social bill of rights anchored in a Federal Job Guarantee that would end unemployment and poverty wages by offering decently paid jobs to everyone willing and able to work, as well as by providing fair replacement income to those who cannot work.[12] Before this campaign could gather steam, Martin Luther King was shot down in Memphis, where he had gone to support the striking sanitation workers. Although the Poor People's Campaign soldiered on through the early summer of 1968, marching on Washington and setting up a protest camp on the Mall, the nation did not respond to its summons.

Instead, the social rights agenda languished in political limbo for another six years. Then, in 1974, Coretta Scott King co-founded the National Committee for Full Employment/Full Employment Action Council to launch a new campaign for guaranteed jobs at fair wages for every United States resident.[13] She hoped that this campaign could move Congress to adopt legislation to secure a Federal Job Guarantee. Despite rallies and protests in three hundred cities drawing more than 1.5 million participants, the movement failed to spur Congress to enact anything more than a watered down law, the 1978 Humphrey-Hawkins Full Employment Act. Instead of providing legal enforcement of the right to a well-paid job, the bill limited itself to setting goals of lower unemployment rates.[14]

Since then, the call for a new social bill of rights, anchored in a Federal Job Guarantee, has fallen on deaf ears and virtually disappeared from our political agenda.[15] Now, fifty years later, the United States, the richest and most powerful nation in human history, leads the developed world in wealth and income inequality, mass poverty, employee disempowerment, ill health, educational failure, mass incarceration, and barriers to social mobility. Racial and gender disadvantage remain deeply embedded, while political disillusionment, "nationalist" resentment, and authoritarian appeals are intensifying. The time to save our democracy is growing short.

Philosopher for Congress

In Plato's *Republic*, Socrates suggests that the simplest, most direct way for justice to come into existence is for philosophers to rule or for rulers to become philosophers.[16] Once we recognize justice to consist in the reality of freedom, philosophy can have no direct rule. Citizens have a right to engage in self-government whether or not they have a philosophical understanding providing the rational justification for the institutions of freedom. Individuals must know what their rights are so that they can exercise their freedoms and respect those of others, but this knowledge does not require any engagement in philosophical reasoning. What philosophy can provide are the concepts of the different institutions in which self-determination has its reality. These philosophical ideas specify the general norms of property rights, moral conduct, family co-determination, the social freedom of a civil society, and self-government, but not the concrete policies by which we can bring our institutions into conformity with them.

Nonetheless, philosophy has an essential role to play. Whereas historical investigation can uncover how humanity has lived in the past and social sciences can describe how given conventions operate, no examination of facts can determine what our institutions ought to be. What is need not be just and it may be up to us to achieve the fulfillment of right that human history has yet to bring into being. Religion, for its part, may prescribe norms of conduct grounded on faith. When belief wavers or becomes called into question, the help is needed that has led religions to enlist philosophers to provide rational justification for their dogmas.[17]

Fine art may represent our fundamental ethical conflicts and make us more receptive to the demands of justice. Nevertheless, only the tribunal of reason can firmly establish how we should lead our lives and order our households, society, and state. Without philosophy, we cannot uncover and justify the principles of what ought to be, and without the guidance of these principles, we cannot judge whether our policies are right. Still, unless we immerse ourselves in the facts of our particular conditions, including the history from which we have emerged as well as the current condition of our mores, society, constitution, and global conjuncture, we cannot determine what policies will best fulfill the norms of freedom.[18]

For four decades, I have devoted my time to the philosophical investigation of truth and justice. In teaching university classes and in writing works of philosophy, I have sought to understand why it is that the good life consists in the exercise and respect for self-determination and to develop in thought the institutions of freedom that give our rights their due reality. To do so, I have had to cast a wide net, for we cannot truly conceive what ought to be without having answered other fundamental questions. To escape dogmatism, we must establish the valid categories of thought with which we can lay hold of the true nature of reality. To insure that freedom is not an illusion, we must conceive how nature can contain organisms with minds, including rational animals who can think and converse. We must further conceive how our psychological endowments of representation and thought and our use of language do not rob our reason and will of autonomy, but rather provide the enabling conditions for thinking and acting freely. With this, we have all we need to think systematically the institutions of freedom and conceive what our rights should be.

In more than a score of books, I have attempted to work through all of these challenges and finally detail how self-determination achieves fulfillment in property relations, moral interaction, the emancipated family, civil society, and self-government.[19] The results of these labors may be sitting in all the great research libraries of the world, but they remain unknown to most of the public at large and to no small part of the academic community.

After the 2016 elections in the United States, it was apparent to me that our nation stood at a turning point, where our failure to fulfill our household and social rights and secure equal political opportunity had paved the way for a political leadership jeopardizing the future of our democracy. I stood at a turning point as well, when the time had come to leave the Ivory Tower and try to transform the political agenda of the nation by running for office, advancing a bold social rights agenda anchored in guaranteed jobs at fair wages.

An opportunity beckoned for doing just this in precisely the most challenging and unlikely of locales. Since 1982, when I began teaching philosophy at the University of Georgia, I had been living in the large university town of Athens, a predominantly "liberal" bastion that had voted by 65% for Hillary Clinton in the 2016 election.[20] Athens, however, was divided up into two Congressional districts, Georgia's 9th and 10th, whose voters have been supporting Republican candidates by supermajorities for more than a decade. The Republican dominated state legislature had repeatedly redrawn district boundaries to insure these electoral outcomes, submerging the two slices of Athens within far larger conservative landscapes of small town rural counties and outer metropolitan suburbs, where Republican candidates have won by huge margins.

A former radio evangelist, Jody Hice, represented my congressional district, Georgia's 10th, and Hice was planning to run for a third term. A socially conservative Republican and Trump loyalist, Hice had run unopposed in his last election. He had succeeded the equally conservative Republican, Paul Broun, who had also run unopposed in the last of his three terms. On the occasions when Democrats had dared to oppose either, the Republican incumbent trounced them with more than 60% of the vote.[21] The indomitable challengers received no appreciable assistance from the national Democratic Party and little from the state Democratic Party, both of which concentrated what resources they had on more competitive contests.

Nevertheless, the option of running for Congress in Georgia's 10th District seemed promising on two accounts.

On the one hand, the real solutions to fulfilling the social rights agenda require action at a national level. Whereas municipal and state governments have comparatively restricted resources and options, the United States Congress can mobilize the full power of the federal government to tackle our national problems. Running for Congressional office presents an unparalleled opportunity to raise the bold measures that can remedy the omissions of our Constitution, fulfill the unfinished business of the Civil Rights movement, and renew our democracy by securing family welfare and the economic independence on which self-government rests. If the race for Congress could garner enough attention, it had the potential to bring into our national political discussion the full social rights agenda that we have ignored for so many decades at our own increasing peril.

On the other hand, the past dominance of Republican candidates in the 10th District made it possible for a political unknown like myself to have a real chance to become the Democratic nominee for Congress. No established political figures with deep pockets and name recognition were likely to enter a race where a Democratic candidate seemed so unlikely to win and so unlikely to attract meaningful support from the national or state Democratic parties, let alone from any other major players. There was even a chance that no one else would dare undertake the quixotic ordeal of challenging the Republican incumbent. My hope was that I could run a shoestring primary campaign and, whether unopposed or facing another political unknown, gain the Democratic nomination for Congress in Georgia's 10th District. With that nomination in hand, I might then have a chance to win state-wide and national attention for a most unusual Congressional contest, pitting an extremely conservative, Evangelical Republican incumbent against a philosophy professor advancing a bold social rights agenda anchored in a Federal Job Guarantee. If I could gain that breakthrough, my candidacy and its message might make it to the national stage. That would allow me to attract sufficient funding and media coverage to reach all the voters of the 10th District and sway enough independents and former Republican supporters to turn the tide.

Soon after Thanksgiving, 2016, I astonished my wife and three grown up children with the news that I was planning to run for Congress in the 2018 election. Skeptical at first, they all soon accepted my resolve, if not without some wary apprehension of the adventure to come.

I faced the "small money" problem, which impairs our equal political opportunity no less than the "big money" problem of unlimited campaign support spending by corporate interests, unleashed by the 2010 Supreme Court decision in *Citizens United vs FEC*. Although all United States citizens who meet residency and age requirements now have the formal right to run for political office, hardly any employees, who make up the vast majority of American breadwinners, can afford to exercise that right. Any serious campaign, particularly for national office, requires a full-time commitment for the duration of the race. Without any public guarantees to provide all candidates the resources to get their message to the entire electorate within a limited period, our campaigns are extending longer and longer, for the sooner candidates can start running, the better their chances of gaining the exposure needed for victory.

Under these conditions, employees face a three-fold disadvantage. First, they must leave their jobs to run for office and during the campaign they and their dependents must somehow survive without the income they lose. Secondly, during this period they must forego all the benefits attached to their employment, including healthcare coverage and pension contributions, which their employers may have been paying in part. Thirdly, under most circumstances, employees can hardly expect their job to be waiting for them when the campaign is over, nor hope to retain whatever seniority they have achieved. Due to these hardships, it is virtually impossible for most United States citizens to run for office. Not surprisingly, our Congress is packed full of millionaires, who are independently wealthy or self-employed entrepreneurs or professionals who can continue to earn during and after campaigns.

As a tenured full professor at the University of Georgia, I faced only two of these "small money" difficulties. State regulations require university employees to go on unpaid leave when they run for statewide or federal office. Ordinarily, university employees can go on unpaid leave for at most one full year and still have their job waiting for them. Unlike most other employees, I could thus at least count on having my job back after an unsuccessful campaign. I would still have to deal with the suspension of pay and of healthcare and pension contributions from the University during my unpaid leave. With the help of a home equity loan, retirement account distributions, and my wife's income, we could survive unpaid leave. I faced, however, one further hurdle due to my employee status. Since I could receive unpaid leave for only a year, I would have to wait until the beginning of January 2018 to announce my candidacy for

Congress and play catchup with the competition. Then I would go on unpaid leave for at least the 2018 Spring academic term, which extends from January into May. If I won the primary, I would continue on unpaid leave for the remainder of the academic year. If I lost either race, I would return to the Ivory Tower and resume my teaching position.

As I prepared to lay the groundwork for the coming campaign, it was becoming apparent that this midterm election would unfold in a very different environment from the last. Since the election of Donald Trump to the presidency, Democratic Party county monthly meetings in the 10th Congressional District were attracting much larger attendance than ever in recent memory. I had been a member of the Athens Clarke County Democrats for some time and our monthly meetings were swelling from a score of attendees to new throngs sometimes topping a hundred. Among Democrats throughout Georgia, the sentiment was growing that no Republican incumbents should run unchallenged, as had happened to a dispiriting degree in past elections.[22]

Unlike the 2016 election season, this time the Republican incumbent would not only be opposed, but face the winner of a Democratic primary contest. In July 2017, Chalis Montgomery, a white music teacher at a Christian private school, announced her candidacy for Congress as a Democrat. She ran on the Democratic Party platform and stressed her identity as a woman, a mother, a Christian, and a small town resident, all of which, she claimed, would make her the most effective challenger to incumbent Jody Hice.

Six months after her announcement, I officially began my campaign for Congress, stressing not my identity, but my bold social rights agenda, anchored in a Federal Job Guarantee.

The Social Rights Agenda as an Electoral Platform in a Deep Red Georgia District

The whole point of my congressional candidacy was to put the social rights agenda at the center of political debate in the United States. To do so required applying philosophical knowledge of the rights constitutive of household and social freedom to the historical conditions of our nation today. I needed to formulate legislative measures and eventual constitutional provisions that could fulfill in a manageable way the family and social rights on which our political freedom depends. I had to leave behind the heights of philosophical speculation and descend into the depths of our historical, contingent existence. I had to gain enough familiarity with the facts of our situation to come up with feasible solutions for securing the economic independence and security on which our family welfare and equal political opportunity depend. Only then could my campaign contribute a program providing a genuine recipe for a new birth of freedom.

The opportunity to forge a social rights campaign program was freely open due to our primary system of selecting party candidates.[23] Most other contemporary democracies have parliamentary governments, where party organizations directly control the selection of candidates and campaign financing, enabling the party to compel candidate fealty to the centrally determined party platform. The United States, by contrast, has come to adopt primaries, which allow prospective candidates to appeal directly to voters. Primaries enable self-selected candidates to become the party nominee and thereby establish what the party stands for, at least in the following general election. My campaign could thus attempt to change not only our national political debate, but the direction of the Democratic Party. This opportunity, however, comes at a cost. Primary candidates having to finance their own campaigns, since during the primary, the party pledges itself officially to neutrality.

In bold departure from the current Democratic Party establishment policy, I advanced my platform as one that renewed Roosevelt's call for a new social bill of rights and would fulfill Martin Luther King's later parallel campaign to complete the unfinished business of the Civil Rights movement. To do so, the platform proposed comprehensive, concrete solutions to the glaring social inequities that endanger our family welfare and obstruct our equal political participation.

The anchor of my social rights agenda was a Federal Job Guarantee, which would enforce the true right to work by offering public sector employment at a fair wage to any resident adult willing and able to take a job. Although markets offer the opportunity to earn a living as an entrepreneur, a landlord, and an employee, guaranteed employment is the foundation of economic independence and security in a civil society. Whereas only some individuals have the wealth and credit to support themselves through a business or rentable property, all adults in a civil society, where slavery has been abolished, are at liberty to fall back upon their capacity to work and seek employment to earn a living. Competition makes the employer-employee relation the overwhelming basis of livelihood since enterprises must grow and concentrate to remain competitive, leading to increasing demand for employees by a much smaller number of enterprises. Since competition has winners and losers and enterprises must continually transform their production and marketing to stay afloat, the market can never insure full employment. Consequently, if we are to uphold the freedom to earn a living, government must step in as employer of last resort and put to work at a fair wage those who are ready to take that opportunity. Instead of competing with existing private enterprises, the Federal Job Guarantee would offer jobs producing goods and services serving the public that the market is not providing. By eliminating unemployment, the Federal Job Guarantee would transform the situation of all those who are struggling to find work, as well as those who have jobs. It would put a brake on the school to prison pipeline and much of the rest of our mass incarceration by providing every ready and able adult a legal opportunity to earn a decent living benefitting our community. The Federal Job Guarantee would lift the fear of firing, so that employees would be more at liberty to stand up to employer abuse, sexual harassment on the job, and work place discrimination. By providing the tightest of labor markets, the Federal Job Guarantee would put employees in the strongest position to improve their wages and working conditions. Moreover, the private sector would benefit from the increased consumer demand produced by full employment, whose elimination of fluctuations in employment levels would also shield us all from much of the threat of depressions and recessions. Finally, our nation would benefit at large from all the constructions, products, and services that the Federal Job Guarantee would furnish for the public good. Among the most important public undertakings that it should tackle, my platform insisted, are building a new green energy infrastructure, extending broad band to all, widening the network of public transportation, and offering childcare and eldercare.

My platform advanced two other measures that need to accompany the Federal Job Guarantee. The true right to work involves not just employment, but employment at a fair wage, insuring a decent standard of living on which all other freedoms can rest. The platform therefore supplemented the guaranteed jobs program with a national fair minimum wage. A fair minimum wage, providing genuine economic independence and security, is not a living wage, which just provides subsistence. The basic income of a living wage is insufficient for individuals to exercise their family, social, and political freedoms on a par with others. A minimum living wage is a recipe for continued poverty, as well as for increasing inequality of wealth as wages continue to fall as a share of national income. If we are all to benefit from our national prosperity, we need to establish a fair minimum wage that increases with productivity gains as well as inflation. Then all boats will rise with the growing wealth of our nation.

My platform accordingly called for a new minimum fair wage, starting at $20 per hour, with adjustments for productivity and inflation. This figure modestly represents what the minimum wage would be if we raise it from 1968 levels in line with the subsequent growth of our national productivity.[24]

Secondly, if every United States resident is to enjoy the fundamental social right to a livelihood allowing for life, liberty, and the pursuit of happiness, we need to supplement the fair minimum wage with a guarantee of equivalent replacement income for anyone who cannot work, due to disability and retirement. This requires substantial increases in benefits above what Social Security currently provides to some of those in need.

Together the Federal Job Guarantee, a fair minimum wage, and equivalent income replacement for those unable to work wipe out unemployment, poverty wages, and much of the welfare dependency of many who could, if given the chance, be economically independent. These three measures, however, do not balance the playing field between employee and employer. That playing field has been progressively tilted to the disadvantage of employees by the concentration and consolidation of enterprises, globalization, automation, and the rise of the "gig" economy, in which internet connectivity allows employers to farm out work at any time and place to "contingent", "contract", "zero-hour" employees.

To remedy this growing imbalance, my platform advanced two measures of employee empowerment to insure that all interests receive fair due, as social right requires. On the one hand, my platform called for mandatory collective bargaining in all enterprises with multiple employees, including part-time and contract workers. On the other hand, my platform advocated fair representation of employees on corporate boards of directors, so that employees would have equal input in key business decisions on out-sourcing, automation, environmental policy, and consumer rights. Together, these measures could forestall the advancing disempowerment of employees that is threatening social and political justice.

Transformative as the above policies are, they do not suffice to guarantee family welfare or fulfill the fundamental social rights to healthcare, decent housing, education at all levels, and legal representation. Still more is required to secure our pursuit of happiness.

To begin with, my platform additionally offered several key policies to overcome the lack of balance between work and family. This lack of balance plays a huge role in the economic and political disadvantage of women that persists despite decades-old equal pay for equal work legislation, prohibitions of gender discrimination, and affirmative action. To enable employees to fulfill their family responsibilities without hampering their careers in the economy and politics, I advocated measures that many other developed nations have long enforced: paid emergency family leave, nine month paid parental leave, one month paid vacations, and the prohibition of mandatory overtime. To enable parents and women in particular to afford to work and politic without caregiving burdens strangling their opportunities, I also called for free public childcare and eldercare.

These measures go a long way to making work compatible with family welfare, but they do not wipe out the scourge of childhood poverty that all too many Americans experience. Since guaranteed jobs, a fair minimum wage, equivalent income replacement, and employee empowerment do not insure that wages take into account how many dependents an employee has, my platform further called for a generous monthly child allowance to cover all the extra expense of childrearing.

To fulfill the fundamental social right to healthcare, my campaign advocated "Super Medicare for All". Unlike Medicare, Medicaid, or the Affordable Care Act, this policy would enforce healthcare as a right by providing a single payer public insurance system covering all necessary physiological, dental, and mental health care needs with no copays or deductibles. With reduced overhead expenses and centralized negotiations with healthcare providers and drug companies, Super Medicare for All could bring down our health care costs to the levels of every other developed nation and save as much as $1.7 trillion dollars a year.

To make decent housing available to all, my platform advanced two complementary transformative policies. On the one hand, it called for using the Federal Job Guarantee to put people to work building an adequate supply of environmentally sound affordable housing. On the other hand, it called for eviction and foreclosure protection to make homelessness a thing of the past. With everyone assured an adequate stream of income through the Federal Job Guarantee, the fair minimum wage, and equivalent income replacement, we can enforce a moratorium on evictions and foreclosures with mandatory rescheduling of rent and mortgage payments, respecting the interests of renters, landlords, homeowners, and mortgage lenders alike.

To fulfill the fundamental social right to education, my platform called for guaranteeing equitable funding of public schools and affordable access to higher education. To overcome the glaring disparities in school district support based on property taxes, I called for national funding of public schools at an equal level for all children, no matter what their zip code. To insure that every citizen has experience in thinking about truth and justice, I called for two years of philosophy studies in every secondary school. Finally, to open higher education to every qualified student, I advocated free tuition and living stipends for attendance at public colleges and technical schools.

Lastly, since none of our rights are secure unless we have equal access to the legal process, my platform advocated Legal Care for All. This novel policy consists in a public single payer legal care insurance program that guarantees every resident comparable legal representation in civil as well as criminal cases. Operating on the model of a single payer public health insurance system, Legal Care for All would enable individuals to obtain personal legal services from any lawyer of their choosing. Legal

Care for All would completely cover the costs of their personal legal representation, while keeping legal fees affordable through national negotiations with lawyers.

Taken together, the above platform policies provide for the enforcement of the fundamental social rights on which family welfare and political freedom depend. None of these policies are or should be based upon means tests that restrict their opportunities to the needy. Doing so divides us into haves and have-nots, jeopardizing general support and obscuring the universality that distinguishes rights from privileges. Like all other rights, our fundamental social rights should be available to all. We follow this approach in our public school systems, which are free, no matter what income and wealth a student's family may have.

Nonetheless, every social right disproportionately benefits those who have most suffered social disadvantage. For example, the Federal Job Guarantee overcomes the racial disparity in unemployment rates by eliminating unemployment in its entirety. So too, the enactment of a fair minimum wage eliminates the disproportionate share of African Americans in the working poor by wiping out poverty wages. Such disproportionate benefit of rights to those who have suffered the greatest oppression led Nietzsche to condemn universal social entitlements as instruments of a slave morality, serving the will to power of the weakest of the downtrodden.[25] Nietzsche falsely understood the unequal benefit of rights to undercut their universality, ignoring how they remain equal entitlements for all.

As transformative as my platform's social rights agenda is, it was not hard to show how we have sufficient means to manage its costs. Many of the policies would more than pay for themselves by making much of our current welfare system expenditures unnecessary, by eliminating the huge social costs of unemployment and poverty, by remedying the deficits in educational opportunity and health, by reducing the expense of our criminal justice and healthcare systems, and by contributing to our national infrastructure and human capital. Whatever costs are not offset by the productive value of the social rights agenda can be fairly met by taxes that target those ablest to bear the expense and that help reduce the inequalities in wealth that hobble our economic growth.[26] My campaign therefore advocated highly graduated income and wealth taxes to finance the investments fulfilling the social rights agenda.

As a whole, my platform laid out the social policies with which we can secure everyone's autonomy in the family, society, and the state. The platform does not serve particular interests at the expense of others, nor make particular identity the basis of any entitlement. Instead, the platform of the social rights agenda advances a universal realization of freedom, which is what politics properly concerns. Because the platform advocates social rights rather than social privileges, it should appeal to all potential voters, irrespective of their race, gender, sexual orientation, ethnicity, religion, or economic position.

Running on a Federal Job Guarantee in Georgia's 10th Congressional District

Could this social rights platform win over the voters of the predominantly conservative, largely rural, small town, twenty-five county Georgia 10th Congressional District? In the 2016 election, they overwhelmingly supported Donald Trump and his fellow Republican candidates, giving them close to supermajority victories in every race. Almost three quarters of the voters in the 10th District are Whites,[27] most of whom have deserted the Democratic Party, as is true throughout the South. Among these voters who are struggling economically, many regard Democrats as elitists, who ignore the plight of White working people at the expense of focusing upon racial and gender diversity issues. What motivated a sizeable part of Republican support may have been the evangelical social conservatism of the Congressional incumbent Jody Hice, as well as the anti-immigrant, White nationalism underlying Trump's presidential campaign.

Nonetheless, an essential part of Trump's appeal to 10th District voters lay in his promise to bring back good jobs to America and reverse the economic decline devastating so much of the heartland. Could another boy from Queens,[28] with as little small town Evangelical credentials as Trump, win over some of his supporters with a real job guarantee platform?

Could they be swayed by a political program that, unlike the timid measures of Democratic establishment orthodoxy, would finally end unemployment, eliminate poverty wages, empower employees, and provide all the other social investments that could make America great, not by being the richest, most powerful bully on the warming planet, but by being the most just nation in human history? If my campaign could bring the social rights agenda to the attention of every potential voter, might the lure of actually fulfilling the American Dream convert enough former independents and Republicans, while energizing the Democratic base, to blaze a path to victory?

The answer to these questions had to wait, because a road to electoral triumph in 2018 first required winning the May 22nd Georgia 10th Democratic primary, a contest entirely different from the following November general election. Whereas African Americans constitute less than a quarter of the population of the 10th District, they made up more than half of the 2018 Democratic primary voters, less than 40% of which were White.[29] Their majority reflects the composition of the Democratic Party throughout the South, which has overwhelming Black support, but has ceded a large majority of White voters to the Republican Party. Georgia's 10th has a higher proportion of White Democratic primary voters than most other Southern districts due to the sizeable liberal university community in Athens, by far the largest town in the district.

Nonetheless, to win the primary, I would have to gain the support of most Black voters.

I managed to put together a small campaign team, with a young first-time campaign manager, a full-time campaign assistant who was a college friend of my youngest son, a part-time treasurer who was a friend trained as an accountant, a part-time outreach coordinator, a part-time volunteer organizer, and a small band of canvasing volunteers.[30] During one of the last months of the campaign, a veteran civil rights activist helped with outreach in the rural counties in which he had grown up and fought Jim Crow.[31]

Throughout, my immediate family played key roles. At the very beginning, my older son, Manas, helped set up the exploratory campaign website. Later in March, my younger son, Rasik, returned from two years of work in India to assist the campaign full-time. From beginning to end, my daughter, Kalindi, the only political professional among us, kept the campaign in some orderly discipline, coming down periodically from her DC job to lend her firm guidance. Above all, my wife, Sujata, was my constant campaign companion, organizing campaign engagements, lending her charisma to my appearances at venues both on and far off the beaten path, and still keeping abreast of her immigration law practice.

My daughter connected us to a direct mail professional, who designed our distinctive campaign materials and, in the closing weeks of the campaign, sent off our barrage of mailings, our biggest campaign expense, which still reached less than half the eventual primary voters. We did manage to raise a respectable amount of money for a District 10 Democratic primary and seemed to be getting our message out more widely than our other competitor.

Campaigning took me through every one of the 10th District's 25 counties, to places I had never visited let alone even heard of before. The rural landscape was dotted with small neglected towns, many of which had never regained the population they had in the 1920's, when agricultural employment began to decline precipitously. Boarded up businesses filled bedraggled town centers and in not a few places the only sizeable employer left was a prison. Even in the growing outer suburbs falling in the district and the booming university town of Athens, where gentrification was gaining steam, it was evident that many residents were living on the edge. The racial wealth gap was on grim display in the glaring contrast between neighborhoods filled with small, often decrepit housing and those on the other side of the divide. Athens was no exception, as should surprise no one who knew it was the poorest city of its size in America.

Every Sunday, I attended a different African American church, where I was usually able to address the congregation about the social rights agenda, always receiving a warm reception. Although not every county had a functioning Democratic Party organization, I spoke at the monthly meetings of those that did. With the exception of Athens, its surrounding counties, and a few outer suburban counties, chiefly African American audiences attend the Democratic Party monthly meetings. They responded well to a Federal Job Guarantee and the other economic rights that I advocated. A positive response also came when I spoke to community groups full of Democrats in Athens and elsewhere in the district. I also attended what candidate forums took place, usually involving only the Democratic candidates. In all of these venues, the audience was full of receptive Democrats, as a primary campaign might hope.

Other occasions, however, presented a chance to reach a wider electorate, whose reactions could give some indication of how the social rights agenda platform might fare in the general election. These occurred at speaking engagements at union meetings, at Senior Centers, and Veterans Groups. I am a member of the Communications Workers of America (CWA) Organizing Local 3265, which is seeking to unionize all the employees of the University of Georgia, Athens' biggest employer. Given my employee empowerment agenda and labor union membership, I hoped for labor support and I spoke to several CWA locals, a Steelworkers Union local, and to UPS drivers between shifts at a nearby trucking facility, at the invitation of the Teamster's local. At these engagements and at those at several Senior Centers and with different Veterans Groups, my message seemed to get a positive response from audiences including not a few likely Republican supporters.

Still, all these activities, supplemented with canvassing on foot and by phone, reached only a small part of the primary electorate, which was itself a meager fraction of voters at large. My hope was that my social rights platform could somehow attract wider attention, which would draw further coverage and support to reach all the voters. Early on, *The Nation* reported on my candidacy, under the title, "Meet the First 2018 Candidate to run on a Federal Jobs Guarantee".[32] I appeared on various Podcasts, some with audiences much larger than I had ever had. Promising as these exposures seemed, they themselves would not reach much of the 10th District electorate.

An auspicious turn took place when Ady Barkan, a leader of the Center for Popular Democracy, took an interest in my campaign. He flew in from the West Coast to Georgia, with a videographer in tow, and spent a memorable day campaigning with me in and around several small towns. We met early that morning in the Town House Cafe in Covington, a venerable African American owned restaurant that was the meeting place of civil rights activists during the long struggle to end segregation and regain voting rights. Former state legislator Tyrone Brooks joined us there and took us to the nearby city jail in which he and other activists were imprisoned during those civil rights struggles. We next attended a meeting of the East Metro for Social Justice organization,[33] where Ady spoke on behalf of the campaign for a Federal Job Guarantee. That afternoon Ady joined me in canvassing a public housing project and a nearby trailer park on the outskirts of Monroe. Navigating the sidewalks and dirt paths in the motorized wheelchair he uses due to advancing ALS, Ady was struck by the positive response of residents in both developments to the social rights agenda. Whereas the public housing project was primarily home to African Americans, the trailer park residents were entirely White and their favorable reaction indicated that likely Republican voters could change their electoral allegiance if given a chance to hear out a message of guaranteed jobs, fair wages, employee empowerment, and the rest of the social rights platform. The day ended with an evening forum with members of several different unions[34] at the Winder United Steelworkers Local 486G Hall, where Ady and I led a discussion on the challenges facing the labor movement and what Congress could do to uphold worker rights.

Thanks to Ady, I was able to get some fundraising help from Shaun King, Alyssa Milano, and Bradley Whitford. I received endorsements from Andrew Young, Jim Barksdale (the Democratic candidate for Senate in Georgia in 2016), Sandy Darity (the Duke University economist who is among the strongest academic advocates of a Federal Job Guarantee), and, in the final weeks of the campaign, several CWA locals, thanks to the efforts of Rita Scott, the head of CWA Local 3204. By and large, however, few political figures, unions, and activist organizations were interested in intervening in a Democratic primary, and many were skeptical about investing their support at any stage in such a deep Red congressional district.

Meanwhile, at the last possible moment during candidate registration in March, just two months before the primary, a third candidate entered the race. She was Tabitha Johnson-Greene, an African American woman from the small town of Sandersville, who had worked as a nurse, but had no known previous political involvements. Her campaign raised hardly any money, seemed to have little in the way of any ground game, and Johnson-Greene herself attended few candidate forums and other campaign events. Hardly anyone had heard of Johnson-Greene or of her campaign, and as primary election day neared, there was little talk of her being much of a factor in the race.

On the day of the election, I felt hopeful that my social rights agenda, anchored in a Federal Job Guarantee, would resonate with enough African American voters to put me ahead of Montgomery, who might gain a sizeable share of the Athens White Democratic vote, particularly among women who wanted to support a female candidate, but knew little about Johnson-Greene. What should have tempered my expectations was a recurring experience every time I went out canvassing, whether in Athens or much more outlying rural counties. Almost always the residents to whom I spoke knew little about the primary election and had heard virtually nothing about the three candidates.

After the polls closed on election day, the first vote counts trickled in, and from beginning to end, Tabitha Johnson-Greene received more than half the votes, with Montgomery and I dividing the rest. There was general astonishment at the outcome. What could explain the result?

Identity politics did not reign completely supreme. In fifteen of the twenty-five counties, I came in second to Johnson-Greene, and these were counties whose Democrats were overwhelmingly African American. Voter turnout, though still a fraction of what the general election would bring, was larger than expected, likely due to the heated race for Governor, in which African American Stacey Abrams's candidacy received wide national news coverage. Did a majority of voters come to the polls with absolutely no knowledge of the three candidates for Congress in Georgia's 10th and make their decision based solely on the three names before them, beginning with Tabitha Johnson-Greene at the top of the listing?

Georgia's 10th Congressional District, like so many other largely rural, small town areas lying beyond metropolitan media markets, is a media desert. Ignored by the network and cable TV news shows and the major surviving newspapers, which all focus their reporting on their metropolitan hubs, local political campaigns operate under the radar. Whatever small town papers remain have largely withered on the vine, leaving them with shrinking readership and little resources to mount any in depth coverage of campaigns. Local radio stations generally have no news staffs of their own and offer hardly anything in the way of serious political discussion of local races.[35] Social media have limited penetration, both because broadband is not available in many outlying areas and all too many residents cannot afford the devices and data plans needed to go online. Moreover, many Democratic voters, especially among the disproportionately impoverished Black community, cannot get to public libraries that offer online access due to the burden of working several jobs, as well as the lack of transportation and affordable childcare.

Compounding the problem is the difficulty Democratic candidates have in such districts to raise sufficient funds to bring their message to most potential voters. The difficulty is most pronounced in primary contests, during which many prospective donors would rather sit on the sidelines. Even in the general election, Democratic candidates in conservative districts are at pains to find supporters who will donate to such challenging races.

Without national campaign finance reform to enable all serious candidates to present their political programs to the voters in a sustained way, citizens in districts like Georgia's 10th have little opportunity to become a well-informed electorate, even if they had the time and means to peruse what candidates might communicate. On the other hand, citizens' lack of sufficient social resources to have the leisure to consider political debate further robs them of the ability to exercise their political freedom in a meaningful way. What then are they to do when they come to the polls and find lists of candidates about whose policies they have heard virtually nothing?

Whatever may have motivated the voters who decided the Democratic primary, one thing is clear. They did not make their decision based on policy differences. The election was not what it should have been, a referendum on a Federal Job Guarantee and the rest of the social rights agenda.

When the general election took place, the Republican incumbent, Jody Hice, trounced his Democratic opponent, winning 63% of the vote. In this final round, the larger electorate made a decision between two names, one with an "R" and the other with a "D" beside it. The incumbent had some degree of name recognition, but the lack of media coverage, the paucity of campaign resources, and the obstacles hobbling the political informing of the electorate all conspired to allow the election to proceed without serious political debate.

Can the Pen be Mightier than a Campaign?

Win or lose, a political campaign should deepen public discussion of the fundamental issues that a nation needs to confront. Whether this occurs depends upon how much candidates focus upon exposing our most important problems and upon formulating solutions that legislative action can implement. Unfortunately, candidates commonly spend most of their public appearances describing their personal and family histories at the expense of any serious policy discussion. Even when a candidate wants to tackle the issues, campaigns offer little opportunity to address much of the public with an argued presentation of political program. Speaking engagements are severely limited in time and rarely can a candidate count on addressing the same audience more than once, which would allow for a series of talks, each concentrating on different parts of the political program. As a result, the same general stump speech gets repeated *ad nausea*. With the media offering less and less sustained political coverage, the wider public encounters little else than recurring sound bites.

Although we cannot fulfill our social rights and preserve self-government without political action, we put our democracy in peril if we restrict political discussion to what campaigns allow. There must be wider and more serious public debate about the solutions to the impairments of our freedoms if our fellow voters and elected officials are to achieve the required remedies. My own campaign did bring discussion of a social bill of rights anchored in a Federal Job Guarantee to more Georgia 10th District voters than ever before. Nonetheless, those who encountered the message were all too few and the message they heard was all too brief and undeveloped. We must supplement political discussion on the campaign trail with thoroughgoing detailed examinations of our road ahead.

More than any stump speech, any podcast, any media interview, any direct mail broadside, any radio or TV advertisements, or any website post of a campaign program, a book can offer the public an adequately comprehensive investigation of why we need a social bill of rights and how we can implement it. This book attempts to provide just that. I hope to prove that the pen can be more powerful than any single political campaign. May many others read what follows and be inspired to take up the social rights agenda and make it a reality before it is too late.

Democracy Unchained

1. Universal Basic Income vs. Guaranteed Employment: Why We Need a Federal Job Guarantee

The Looming Employment Crisis

Today the international order is reeling in the face of growing social insecurity driven by the latest economic developments. In America and abroad, authoritarian "nationalist" populists are increasingly challenging democratic rule, advancing ethnic solidarity while villainizing immigrants and "cosmopolitans" for supposedly imperiling the prosperity of the stressed heartlands. This is a moment calling for bold solutions, but first we must recognize the magnitude of the challenge facing us.

Much concern focuses on how, in every developed nation, manufacturing employment is declining due to the relocation of industry to lower wage regions. Free trade policies have facilitated these transfers by allowing enterprises to globalize their operations to drive down labor costs without fear of countervailing tariff barriers. The enhanced ability to relocate manufacturing wherever lower production expenses beckon has eroded the position of employees in developed nations, weakening the ability of their remaining unions to maintain levels of employment, retain benefits, and keep wages growing in tandem with increases in productivity. Although outsourcing may threaten manufacturing jobs in high wage markets, it does not diminish manufacturing employment worldwide. Particular localities will suffer gains or losses, but outsourcing does not itself threaten global job levels, nor immediately imperil the livelihoods of workers in the lowest-wage nations, for whom globalization provides new opportunities.

Much more ominous for everyone the world over are two accelerating global trends that imperil total manufacturing employment and full time jobs of any kind: the surge in automation and the explosive growth of the "gig economy."

The increasing economic insecurity facing many Americans directly reflects the danger to full time employment posed by automation, which curtailing outsourcing cannot remedy. The mechanization of agriculture has led the way. For most of our history, the overwhelming majority of Americans earned a living from cultivating the land. With the application of automation to agriculture over the last century, food production has risen to record highs in both volume and value while agrarian employment has plummeted to the point where less than 1.7% of the working population earns a living in agriculture.[36]

Manufacturing jobs are experiencing a similar, if not so extreme, decline with the advance of automation. In the last several decades, U.S. manufacturing employment has dropped to no more than 8% of the working population.[37] Although 15% of this decline is due to outsourcing, 85% comes from the replacement of workers by machines. For this reason, the return of outsourced manufacturing to the United States is unlikely to resuscitate anything like former levels of industrial employment, unless employers succeed in depressing wages to such a degree that mechanization loses its cost advantage. Now automation is poised to ravage the service sector, where 87% of U.S. breadwinners earn a living with a human touch.[38] In the next few decades, machines will likely replace nearly half of all service sector jobs.[39]

Compounding the accelerating threat of automation to full time employment is the rise of the "gig economy," enabled by technological developments making it ever easier for employers to replace permanent jobs with part-time, non-standard, contingent, free-lance, contract employment. Thanks to the universal connectivity of the internet and the ubiquity of smart phones, employers can greatly reduce costs by supplanting full time employees with temporary "gig" workers available at any time at any location. These non-standard, contingent, free-lancers can provide goods and services 24/7 at a piecework rate without any of the expenditure on the benefits and permanent overhead of full timers. Working in isolation, the individuals living off the gig economy may think of themselves as entrepreneurs, enjoying flexibility in time and place. They lack, however, all the benefits that full time employment provides, such as paid sick leave, paid parental leave, paid vacations, and pensions. Moreover, they have no opportunity to join with their fellow employees to bargain collectively to improve their job conditions and pay. Employers are not only relieved of the cost of maintaining work places, but they can escape having to contend with any collective action by their employees.

Currently, the assault on the full time job has reached such proportions that only 25% of global employment consists of permanent positions.[40] In the United States, 34% of breadwinners now rely on "gig" free-lance occupation,[41] with that total expected to rise to 50% by 2020.[42]

Further advances of automation and "gig" employment threaten the United States with particularly catastrophic results. This is because we are the one developed nation that has failed to guarantee to all residents the basic social benefits without which we can hardly maintain our economic independence and security. Such crucial factors as health insurance and livable pensions are linked instead to full-time jobs. This connection is not due to any special benevolence on the part of American employers. Rather, it has resulted from the resolute struggles of employees, whose unions have successfully fought for the job related benefits that the United States has neglected to guarantee publicly. Consequently, the assault on the full time job threatens United States employees with more than loss of income. It also imperils all the benefits that are tied to full time employment.

Compounding these looming dangers is the detachment of wage levels from productivity gains that has occurred in the United States and many other nations since the 1970's. From 1948 through 1973, wages and productivity in the United States increased in lockstep, allowing for a significant rise in the standard of living of most wage earners. Starting in 1973, however, American wages have virtually stagnated, while productivity has doubled.[43] Wages have consequently come to comprise a shrinking portion of the national income, reaching the lowest level ever.[44] Wealth has become ever more concentrated at the top, leaving the United States the most unequal society with the greatest poverty and least social mobility amongst all developed nations. Nearly half of all American children are now impoverished,[45] whereas a quarter of all Americans have no or negative net worth.[46] On top of these general inequities, racial disadvantage remains entrenched, with African-American household income averaging just 63% of that of White households,[47] and African-American household wealth averaging just 11% of that of White households.[48]

In face of these accelerating social crises, two bold proposals have been advanced to tackle poverty and the assault on the full time job: universal basic income (UBI) and guaranteed employment. Hardly any current government officials or lawmakers, or any recent candidates for political office in the United States have advocated either of these measures.[49] Nonetheless, these proposals have been gaining increased notice, particularly with Alexandria Ocasio-Cortez and Bernie Sanders advancing a Federal Job Guarantee and Andrew Yang advocating universal basic income as the centerpiece of his campaign for the Democratic nomination for President in the 2020 elections. Now more than ever, we citizens must consider the merits of these competing proposals.

The Promise of Universal Basic Income

Universal basic income has attracted the more attention, drawing enthusiasts from both the right and the left. A century ago, the philosopher Bertrand Russell proposed it as a remedy to poverty and joblessness,[50] as did Martin Luther King decades later,[51] and as do former Secretary of Labor, Robert Reich,[52] and Service Employees International Union President Emeritus, Andy Stern, today.[53] The crux of the universal basic income proposal is that our government should give all individuals funds sufficient to support their basic needs, irrespective of whether they otherwise earn a living. The proposal presumes that the amount each person receives should not suffice to remove all incentive to gainful employment, since basic income will cover no more than the necessities of a conventionally decent livelihood.

Allegedly, universal basic income will remedy poverty by insuring that everyone has the resources to satisfy conventional subsistence needs. This involves not only what is necessary to survive biologically, but what provides a customary sustenance allowing an individual to be fed, clothed, and housed in a decent manner. By providing this income to *every* individual, no one must suffer the indignity of undergoing a means test, nor incur the stigmatization of living on a handout that others do not receive. Moreover, as conservative supporters applaud, universal basic income offers its relief without need of any government welfare bureaucracy to supervise what care the poor receive. Instead of subjection to paternalistic management, every individual simply collects the same amount of universal income funds without any strings attached. Everyone enjoys the unrestricted personal freedom to do with it as he or she pleases.

Moreover, the recipients of universal basic income are not only relieved of poverty while accorded maximum freedom in spending their guaranteed fund. Allegedly, the universal basic income further enables them to engage in all the activities that liberation from the necessity to work might entail. This second emancipation is supposed to inaugurate a new birth of freedom that employment cannot provide. Now, thanks to universal basic income, all individuals are free to do whatever they choose, no longer having to labor to satisfy their basic conventional needs.

Universal basic income thereby provides precisely the same emancipation that the young Marx ascribed to his ideal communist society. There a collectively administered automated economy permits all individuals to consume whatever they need without having to suffer the bondage of wage labor. As far as Marx was concerned, economic activity is a realm of necessity, only beyond which the realm of freedom could begin.[54] That realm of freedom consists in the purely individual license of doing as one pleases, "to hunt in the morning, fish in the afternoon, rear cattle in the evening, criticize after dinner, just as I have a mind."[55] Since politics is, on Marx' account, a disposable instrument of class domination rather than self-government, the communist liberation from economic necessity leaves individuals with nothing more than the same private activity with which the recipients of universal basic income are endowed. This personal liberty can amount to little more than the hobby existence of a premature retirement, in which individuals have no resources to use beyond what their life on the dole provides.

Plato ridicules such emancipation in Book VIII of his masterwork, the *Republic*, where Socrates lampoons democratic man, whose life devoted to freedom consists in doing as one pleases without any necessary regard for what serves the common good. Instead of engaging in production and commerce, in military service, or in office holding, democratic man plays the flute one moment, discourses at another, exercises when the whim arises, "surrendering rule over himself to whichever desire comes along, as if it were chosen by lot".[56] Like communist man and the beneficiaries of a universal basic income, democratic man is free to follow his wishes so long as they involve activities limited to what an individual can do in private, with nothing more than the goods on which personal sustenance depends.

Does this private, hobby existence constitute a genuine liberation, let alone an elimination of poverty? Is poverty a deprivation simply of the means of conventional sustenance or of the resources and opportunities that enable one to exercise one's household, social, and political rights on a par with others? Is freedom a matter of being ruled by one's desires or does it involve participation in the institutions of self-determination, such as the co-determined household of free and equal spouses, a civil society whose members exercise the freedom of occupation in the interdependence of duly regulated market activity, and a democracy whose citizens engage in self-rule? Is universal basic income's celebrated release from economic necessity actually a reinstatement of poverty and a deprivation of social self-determination?

Of key importance in answering these questions is the fundamental limitation upon universal basic income. All its proponents recognize that universal basic income must be significantly lower than ordinary wage levels. This difference is crucial because the funds for universal basic income depend upon the wealth creation of those who are not simply on the dole. Not only must they retain some incentive to earn a livelihood that can support the expense of universal basic income, but their earnings must provide sufficient taxable income to pay for what jobless recipients receive. Admittedly, everyone receives the same universal basic income, so one can subtract from the tax burden on breadwinners the amount that they themselves obtain as universal basic income recipients. Nonetheless, it still falls on their shoulders to pay for the benefits received by those who do not work and enjoy an idle freedom. This burden is hardly insignificant and it threatens whatever equanimity the duly employed may feel with regard to their support of those living entirely on the universal dole.

Out of a current United States population of 325 million, only about 160 million are in a position to be breadwinners. Even if very few potential breadwinners choose to live off the dole, the remaining wealth providers must pay for the support of at least an additional 165 million individuals. If one were to limit the universal basic income to a frugal $12,000 per person per year, doing so would still impose an additional tax burden of nearly 4 trillion dollars. That is equivalent to the entire federal budget for 2016, which means that universal basic income would require more than doubling the tax burden of every breadwinner. Taking into account how these added taxes pay for the universal basic income given to breadwinners, they would receive no net benefit from their individual handout and would have to pay at least an additional $12,000 in taxes to fund the other half of the population living entirely on the dole. Even if this situation were not to generate resentment between breadwinners and those supported exclusively by universal basic income handouts, the divide between these groups is fundamentally at odds with equal social opportunity.

This is because the divide involves both a hierarchy of wealth and a hierarchy of self-determination. Those who have no support other than universal basic income comprise a class of economically disadvantaged individuals, whose consumption and activities are restricted to what resources the dole provides. By contrast, those who receive the dole as well as earn a livelihood possess the economic privilege of enjoying distinctly higher levels of consumption and opportunity that their greater income can facilitate. Whatever these may be, one fundamental divide in opportunity is inescapably operative: those who live on the universal basic income dole do not exercise the economic self-determination of earning a living in interdependence with other market agents, which their supporting counterparts enjoy. The young Marx may regard such earning a living as devoid of self-determination, but as Marx later came to recognize, wage earners are not wage slaves, but free commodity owners who exercise their economic rights in interdependence with others.[57] Without that interdependent engagement of economic right and duty, individuals lack one of the basic realizations of social freedom, together with the self-respect, accomplishment, and service for others it involves.

The Lessons of the Speenhamland Experiment

The corrosive effects of this deprivation are anticipated by the historical experiment undertaken in 1795 in Speenhamland, England.[58] This experiment was instigated by the economic upheaval ravaging the English countryside with the onset of the Industrial Revolution. The leaders of the Berkshire rural district decided to address the growing pauperization of the rural population by enacting the Speenhamland Law, which guaranteed to all country residents, irrespective of any other earnings, a basic living allowance tied to the price of bread. This measure soon became adopted throughout the English countryside under the banner of recognizing and enforcing the "right to live". Although the Speenhamland Law was initially immensely popular, it precipitated a social catastrophe that led to its repeal with the Reform Bill of 1832.

Three consequences stand out as warnings of the drawbacks of a universal basic income policy. First, throughout rural England, the social fabric was noticeably corrupted by the debauchery of an idle populace living on the Speenhamland allowance. The idleness of life on the dole turned out to be "the playground of the Devil", as self-respect withered in the absence of economic independence. Second, the productivity of labor fell dramatically, as those who worked felt always able to relax their efforts and fall back on their basic income. This decline in industry was encouraged by the third consequence of the Speenhamland Law. Employers realized that no matter what they paid as wages, their workers would receive a subsistence income guaranteed by the new universal living allowance. Accordingly, employers lowered wage levels by the amount of the Speenhamland dole. Instead of helping employees, the universal basic income became a public subsidy to employers, who could reduce wages with impunity and pass the expense of supporting their workers onto the shoulders of taxpayers.

The Promise of Guaranteed Employment at a Fair Wage

All of these consequences are avoidable if we reject universal basic income in favor of guaranteed employment at a fair wage. The basic anchor of economic right is recognition and enforcement of the true right to work. This is not the bogus "right to work" adopted by all former Southern slave states, which forbids a "closed shop", where all workers of a unionized employer must pay union dues. The true right to work is rather the essential social right ensuring that all willing and able adult residents can choose full time employment at a wage sufficient to support themselves and their dependents at a level allowing them to exercise their family, social, and political rights.

Admittedly, markets offer other ways of earning a livelihood besides seeking employment. Those with enough capital or access to credit can attempt to make a living as entrepreneurs, earning profits or dividends. Others with rentable property can try to support themselves as landlords, living off rent. The dynamic of competition, however, makes it impossible for everyone, let alone most economic agents, to earn a living as entrepreneurs or landlords. It is pure fantasy to imagine that we can generally gain economic independence as entrepreneurs, just as it is illusory to entertain the corollary notion that small businesses can be the core of livelihood in a market society.[59] On the contrary, competition compels enterprises to grow and consolidate. In order to remain competitive they must produce and accumulate more and more wealth in order to make the investments needed to increase efficiency, develop new products and services, and improve their marketing. Due to the concentration and consolidation of enterprises that competition necessitates, individual firms must hire more and more workers. This means that a growing portion of breadwinners must earn their living as employees, seeking jobs from a diminishing number of larger and larger companies. It is no accident that the overwhelming majority of breadwinners in the United States and every other developed market society are employees.

Moreover, when entrepreneurs or landlords fail to support themselves off of profit or rent, they are left with the one mode of earning a living that is available to every healthy adult in a civil society in which slavery has been abolished. They can fall back on their labor power, the one commodity that every free person owns, and seek a job. Accordingly, the employee-employer relationship is the key to economic justice and the foundation of economic independence and security is none other than the true right to work, that is, the opportunity to have employment at a fair wage. To paraphrase Martin Luther King, without a job and decent income, we have neither any secure life nor liberty, nor the opportunity to engage in the pursuit of happiness.[60]

Markets, however, cannot reliably fulfill the true right to work due to two fundamental aspects of the dynamics of free enterprise. On the one hand, competition always has winners and losers, leading some enterprises to reduce their labor force or collapse, without the winners absorbing all the employees cast adrift or left with diminished employment. On the other hand, the dynamic of competition compels enterprises to reduce their labor costs, introduce ever more efficient production and marketing methods, and develop new products and services, all of which continually roils the labor market, rendering some employees redundant or obsolete. In order to insure that all willing and able adults can exercise their right to earn a decent living through the sale of their own capacity to labor, we citizens must empower government to be the employer of last resort, offering jobs that serve the common good to any adult resident who wants to work. A Federal Job Guarantee will thereby abolish unemployment and secure that key fixture of the American dream, that any of us who are willing to stand on our own feet and work hard should have the chance to support ourselves at a decent standard of living.

The Federal Job Guarantee cannot fulfill the true right to work if it does not insure that the jobs it offers have a sufficiently fair wage to enable individuals to exercise their freedoms without suffering the disadvantage of poverty. Employment itself does not secure economic independence unless no job pays poverty wages. For this reason, the Federal Job Guarantee should not only abolish unemployment but guarantee fair wages as well.

The abolition of unemployment through a Federal Job Guarantee might appear to be unrealizable. As Hegel recognized two centuries ago, if publicly created jobs furnish the same goods and services that private enterprise provides, unemployment will only grow. Public commerce will compete with private enterprise and add to the overproduction that already constitutes market failure.[61] The only solution to this problem is if the employment provided by public authority supplies public works - goods and services that contribute to the welfare of all, but which profit seeking enterprises are either unwilling or unable to provide. These include goods and services whose consumption is not restricted in ways that allow private profits to be made, which are needed but cannot support prices sufficient to attract private investment, or whose scale is too immense to be undertaken by private enterprises.

Besides providing full employment, such public works have important collateral benefits. They provide infrastructure, resources, and care on which economic activity generally depends. Moreover, they inject added purchasing power into the economy thanks to the fair wages that guaranteed employment should extend to all willing and able adults. Since the resulting full employment produces the tightest labor market possible, it will put employees in the strongest position to negotiate higher wages, enhancing effective consumer demand. In these respects, public employment as a last resort tends to diminish the very market failures that call for its enactment. Consumer demand no longer will experience the extreme declines that mass unemployment involves. Instead, the severity of business cycles will attenuate, especially when the fair wage of guaranteed employment keeps pace with both inflation and national productivity gains.

The latter is of key importance, since if wages do not rise with increases in national productivity, the buying power of employees will diminish in proportion to the value of the products and services they provide. This is a recipe for economic stagnation, which has been haunting the United States economy since 1973, when wages began to stagnate while productivity continued to advance.[62] Guaranteed employment will therefore be a mainstay of steady economic growth, provided it pays not just a living wage adjusted for inflation, but a fair wage adjusted for national productivity gains.

Why a Federal Job Guarantee Should be Accompanied by a National Fair Minimum Wage and Equivalent Income Replacement for the Disabled and Retirees

The fair compensation that a Federal Job Guarantee must pay to fulfill the true right to work should and must become a new national fair minimum wage. There is no escape, since all employers will be under pressure to match that wage to retain their work force. Nonetheless, in order for the Federal Job Guarantee to be feasible, we must raise the mandatory national minimum wage to equal the fair standard that public works jobs pay. Otherwise, people employed at lower rates will desert their private sector jobs and flood into the public sector. This will strain public sector resources and leave private employers unable to carry on their operations. To avoid these disruptions, which do not contribute to full employment, we must accompany the Federal Job Guarantee with a new fair national minimum wage. To uphold fair economic opportunity, this national minimum wage should be adjusted to both cover inflation and benefit from national productivity gains.

Aggregate productivity gains reside in how much the national wealth grows in proportion to the number of breadwinners. In order for "all boats to rise" with the rising tide of national productivity, fair wages must be raised in function of national productivity gains, rather than productivity gains in particular occupations. Productivity has risen astronomically in manufacturing, extractive industry, and agriculture, where work has a mechanical character permitting mechanization and automation to increase vastly the speed and volume of production. By contrast, many service occupations have a robot-proof, non-mechanizable nature that resists significant increases in productivity. If productivity gains in each occupation dictated income, income inequality would explode, leaving service workers such as teachers, hairdressers, waiters, police, musicians, actors, directors, visual artists, professional athletes, doctors, nurses, child and elder care providers, and philosophers in extreme comparative poverty. If instead all breadwinners are to participate in the increasing wealth of the nation, we must adjust everyone's income with regard to *national* productivity gains.[63]

Consequently, a fair national minimum wage is not just a living wage, which provides for subsistence. Economic independence rather requires enough income to enable individuals to exercise their rights on a par with their fellow members of society. Only a minimum wage that is adjusted for inflation and national productivity gains allows every employee to escape increasing relative impoverishment. Without taking into account inflation and national productivity gains, the minimum wage leaves its beneficiaries farther and farther behind, deprived of sharing in the growing prosperity of the nation, while intensifying the social inequality that puts our democracy in jeopardy.[64]

When we implement the Federal Job Guarantee and a fair minimum wage in tandem, we abolish unemployment and poverty wages together. Putting everyone to work and pushing all wages above the poverty level, these initiatives increase consumer demand and thereby enhance economic growth. Moreover, these dual policies will enable economic growth to translate into a comparably rising standard of living from the bottom up.

Businesses both big and small will benefit from a new fair national minimum wage adjusted for inflation and national productivity gains. For nearly half a century they have allowed wages to stagnate, appropriating for themselves virtually all the increased wealth accruing from the doubling of national productivity. Since a new fair national minimum wage will apply to all employers, none will be at a competitive disadvantage in raising wages above poverty levels. As with all public regulations that require businesses to do what is just, the fair minimum wage will enable entrepreneurs to do the right thing without compromising their commercial viability. Not only will the fair minimum wage increase consumer demand and help grow business revenues, but it will foster faster economic growth through the multiplier effects of consumer spending, where increased sales lead to further investments in expanded production and marketing, eliciting added growth in income and spending. These multiplier effects will be more pronounced than ever since employees spend much more of their income than do the rich, who can consume only a fraction of their wealth, which otherwise remains hoarded in speculative investments. Businesses will benefit from less employer turnover, since a fair minimum wage will allow employees to keep their job and maintain their own economic stability. Moreover, there will be no nullification of the increases in employee income by comparable increases in consumer goods prices. Labor costs are only a fraction of the costs of production and marketing, since every business must incur additional expenses such as those of fixed investments in building infrastructure and equipment, materials of production, insurance, advertising, and financing. Indeed, as productivity increases, labor costs become a decreasing part of business expenses. Consequently, no business will need to raise its prices as much as it raises the wages of its least paid employees.

Every business, big or small, has four basic options for dealing with paying a fair minimum wage. First, a business that fails to grow its revenue can simply distribute a larger share of its revenues to its employees, without changing the prices on its goods and services. In this way, a business can atone for all those decades in which productivity gains have failed to benefit employees. Second, a business can increase its revenues without enhancing productivity or raising prices by taking advantage of the increased consumer demand provided by full employment and fair minimum wages. Third, a business can maintain or grow its profits by increasing its own productivity and introducing new goods and services, all without increasing prices. Fourth, a business lacking any other initiative can increase the prices of goods and services to maintain its profits. Whether it succeeds will depend upon the business choices of its competition.

In any event, all businesses may find any increase in their labor costs more than compensated by public initiatives we can undertake to relieve enterprises of the costs of pensions and health care.[65]

An important part of such initiatives fulfills the imperative to guarantee those who cannot work the same economic independence provided by a national fair minimum wage. The fair wage of guaranteed employment should equally extend to the replacement income of those who cannot seek employment. We cannot honor the ethical rationale of the true right to work and neglect their economic independence and security. Those who cannot exercise their right to work due to disabilities or age-related infirmity are entitled to an income replacement equivalent to the fair wage they otherwise could obtain. If we fail to provide them comparable compensation, we ignore their inalienable right to a decent livelihood as free and equal members of civil society. Leaving them impoverished, we strip them as well of the means they need to exercise their family and political rights. Adjusting replacement income to the level of a fair wage is essential to the American Dream, which promises to not only give everyone a chance to support themselves decently by their own efforts, but to maintain their standard of living when they cannot or are no longer able to fend for themselves.

Individuals who can work, but choose not to, however, are not entitled to a fair replacement income. This is because they do not lack the opportunity to earn a decent living once we guarantee employment at a living wage through public works. Similarly, any individuals who accept guaranteed employment in some public undertaking, but fail to do the job, cannot expect payment for the work they have not done. They may always try again, but so long as individuals do not fulfill the work they have taken on, they have no right to claim remuneration.

Why the True Right to Work is Basic to All Economic Freedom

The right to work is basic to all economic freedom in two respects.

First, no other forms of earning can secure the economic independence and security of individuals unless we guarantee employment at a fair wage.

Entrepreneurs and landlords are often called the true risk takers and job creators, as if their livelihoods had primacy. Admittedly, a business can always go under, just as rental properties may fail to provide sufficient income. Business owners and landlords, however, can still always fall back on the property that others must rely upon by default to earn a living. This universal endowment is the ownership of one's own labor power with which anyone can seek employment. Those who lack the capital and rental property to live off profits and rent are thus the ultimate risk takers, for they have nothing to rely upon other than their capacity to work. In the absence of guaranteed employment at a living wage, they, unlike entrepreneurs and landlords, stand face to face with destitution. The bedrock against economic risk of any kind is therefore a Federal Job Guarantee for those who can work and comparable replacement income made available to those who are unable to take advantage of guaranteed jobs.

Moreover, wage earners are not just the true risk takers, but also the true job creators. Entrepreneurs must seek profit and accumulate capital to remain viable, since investments must be made in production and marketing to not lose customers to competitors. Profit-seeking is hardly equivalent to job creation, for profit maximization may entail job-destroying automation and free-lance outsourcing. Furthermore, when capital accumulation engenders growing concentrations of wealth, the most affluent individuals can spend a much smaller proportion of their money than do all the others who must spend much more of their wealth upon living expenses. Consequently, wage earners who cannot live off dividends and rent are the true job creators, injecting back into the economy a higher proportion of their earnings, funding the consumer demand on which employment levels depend. For this reason, guaranteed employment at a fair wage, rising with productivity gains, itself fosters job creation by increasing both the amount and proportion of income that individuals plow back into the economy. In all these respects, only guaranteed employment at a fair wage can provide a reliable foundation of independent livelihood, no matter what form of earning individuals pursue.

Secondly, in the absence of guaranteed employment at a fair wage all efforts to make business operate in conformity with household, social, and political freedom will falter if they impose costs that threaten layoffs and reduced employment. How often does one hear the plaint that unemployment will result from the expenses of protecting the environment, insuring employee and consumer safety, and requiring work to accommodate family welfare and political involvement? This common refrain is moot when public authority stands firm as the employer of last resort. Then it becomes possible for business to be ethical and viable without undermining the economic independence and security of its employees.

Consequently, guaranteed employment at a fair wage, supplemented by comparable income replacements for those unable to work, not only eliminates the principal grounds of poverty, but provides a social emancipation that universal basic income cannot supply. As we have seen, universal basic income leaves society divided into two unequal camps consisting of those living solely on the dole and those exercising their right to earn a living. By contrast, guaranteed employment at a fair wage extends to all the real opportunity to earn a decent livelihood through occupation of one's choosing in interdependence with others who do the same. This involves both right and duty, for participating individuals enjoy their freedom of earning while respecting and facilitating the right of others to do the same.

The enactment of guaranteed employment at a fair wage truly amounts to a new birth of freedom, transforming a society all too brutish, nasty, and frustrating. Imagine the altered situation when all persons coming of age can be certain that a full time job awaits them offering a decent livelihood and a meaningful contribution to the common good. Will this not largely shut down the "school to prison pipeline", which consumes so many youth, particularly those who suffer entrenched racial disadvantage? Imagine the new security all breadwinners can have, now knowing that if their hours are reduced or they are laid off, a full time job is always available at a fair wage, providing goods and services that aid their community. Imagine the relief that all returning soldiers can feel, now certain that a worthwhile employment at a fair wage awaits them. Imagine finally the redeeming confidence that all released convicts can enjoy, now knowing that they have the real chance to earn a fair wage in a legal full time job advancing the common good.

Imagine further how Guaranteed Jobs at fair wages saves local communities from impoverishing themselves by giving away tax breaks, subsidies, and promises of low wages to attract employers to their areas.[66] Never again need localities sell themselves short to provide a decent livelihood to all their residents.

Imagine also how a Federal Job Guarantee fundamentally transforms the situation of everyone who has a full-time job. No longer will fear of firing and unemployment discourage employees from blowing the whistle on employer malfeasance, on sexual harassment in the workplace, or on any kind of discrimination at work. No longer will the specter of dismissal put a damper on efforts of employees to organize and wield their common strength in defense of their shared interests. No longer will the presence of an army of the unemployed restrict the ability of employees to bargain effectively for better wages and work conditions. Instead, enterprises that need new workers will have to attract employees from an army of the employed, offering something more desirable than public employment provides.

Imagine how guaranteed jobs at fair wages will facilitate the fastest transition to an entirely green economy, mobilizing vast reserves of labor for public works projects building a new clean energy infrastructure, without any one from the replaced fossil fuel industries left jobless and lacking a decent livelihood.

Finally, imagine how a Federal Job Guarantee makes possible a comprehensive immigration reform that gives our twelve million undocumented residents legal status and a chance for citizenship without undercutting the economic security of anyone else. No longer will unscrupulous employers have so easy a time replacing United States workers with more poorly paid and more easily dominated undocumented laborers, fomenting xenophobia by putting downward pressure on wage levels and throwing some people out of work. The Federal Job Guarantee, combined with a fair minimum wage, will allow comprehensive immigration reform to benefit everyone by insuring that no one suffers unemployment or the scourge of poverty wages.

All this can be imagined, but is guaranteed employment at a fair wage really feasible?

The Practicality of Guaranteed Employment at a Fair Wage

Admittedly, not a single nation today gives capitalism a human face by implementing guaranteed employment at a fair wage through public works. Since 2005, India has introduced a partial fulfillment of the right to work through its Mahatma Gandhi National Rural Employment Guarantee Act (MGNREGA), which provides the countryside with 100 days of paid employment per family per year. Although this measure serves close to 50,000,000 people annually, it only addresses the seasonal lulls in agricultural production, when many rural laborers have no work. A more robust test of the feasibility of guarantee employment at a living wage lies closer to home, if only we remember a bold experiment whose achievements were all too short-lived.

In 1935, Franklin Delano Roosevelt oversaw the introduction of the Works Progress Administration and the Civilian Conservation Corps, which, together with other New Deal initiatives, employed more than 13,000,000 jobless individuals, building some of the greatest public works that our nation has created.[67] This massive effort was accomplished during the severest economic calamity the nation had ever experienced, when the population was only 127 million, less than 40% of what it is today, and when the real, inflation adjusted gross national product was only 5.6% of its current value.[68] Nevertheless, the government managed to fulfill the right to work on a huge scale, employing individuals with the most varied skills. Vast infrastructure projects were completed, including mammoth clean energy hydroelectric dams, expansive electrifications, and national park developments, as well as countless public recreational facilities, roads, bridges, schools, hospitals, post offices, and libraries, often adorned with the murals and sculptures of re-employed artists.[69] In addition, innumerable theatrical and musical performances were provided to the public, together with writings of all kinds designed to serve the public interest.[70] Notably, the overhead costs of all these projects amounted to no more than 1/3 of the wages paid to the re-employed.[71]

As large an undertaking as the WPA and CCC were, they were not sufficient to put all the Great Depression's unemployed back to work. Moreover, these projects were introduced as temporary measures, designed to address the economic collapse, rather than to be permanent fixtures of a just and free society.[72] Accordingly, when the total mobilization for the Second World War engendered its own much larger jobs program in military recruitment and arms production, the WPA and CCC came to an end, with no commitment to renew them at war's end.

Nonetheless, their example demonstrated that even in the most extreme circumstances, it was possible to organize and administer a very sizeable fulfillment of guaranteed employment through public works. Roosevelt recognized this himself and thereby felt confident enough to call for a new economic bill of rights, including the true right to work, in his 1944 inaugural address, as victory lay in sight. Although he died before having a chance to make this a peacetime achievement, Eleanor Roosevelt took up the mantle to the new United Nations. In 1948 she oversaw the committee that drafted the Universal Declaration of

Human Rights, which included a social bill of rights in which the right to work figured prominently. Although every member nation in attendance voted for the Declaration, with the expected exceptions of the Soviet Union and its satellites, the Union of South Africa, and Saudi Arabia, none have since enforced the right to work.[73]

What would it mean for the United States to comply with Article 23[74] and guarantee employment at a living wage? This would be a huge permanent undertaking, but it is not only manageable, but much less costly than a universal basic income.

Granted that the potential number of bread winners is today about 160,000,000 and that un- and under-employment may afflict 10% of this number, let us consider the cost of employing 16,000,000 people in public works serving the common good. Back in 1968, the minimum wage was equivalent to $10 at current prices. If we adjust that figure in line with the doubling of productivity since then, $20 per hour would be a reasonable, but modest starting point for a minimum fair wage, provided we take account of further inflation and productivity gains.[75] Keeping a 40 hour work week, each employee would then receive $41,600 per year. If we multiply this by 16,000,000, the total wages bill for putting the un- and under-employed to work at a fair wage would be $665,600,000,000. If we add a 1/3 overhead cost, in line with the expenditures incurred by the WPA, the total cost of guaranteed employment at a living wage would come to less than one trillion dollars.[76] This compares with the four trillion dollar cost of a universal basic income of $12,000. Admittedly, one could subtract from both totals the social welfare expenditures that each measure supplants. Nonetheless, guaranteed employment involves a much smaller expense, while providing significant additions to the common assets of the nation, as well as an injection of added consumer demand that can spark further economic activity and corresponding growth in tax revenues.

Moreover, the implementation of the Federal Job Guarantee largely pays for itself. Expenditures on unemployment insurance would become unnecessary, as would much of the trillion dollar annual welfare program expenditures of our federal and state governments. In addition, the goods and services produced by giving work to the unemployed should be of a value equal or greater to the labor costs expended in their production, provided their work meets ordinary standards of productivity.[77] Further, the stabilizing and growth enhancing effects of full employment will tend to diminish the need for government to step in as employer of last resort, reducing the magnitude of public sector job creation. Nonetheless, even if we discount all these potential savings, affordability is not a problem.

A government such as our own, which disposes of a sovereign currency that is inconvertible and has a floating exchange rate, need not worry about maintaining reserves of gold or foreign currency. This leaves us with the maximum fiscal policy room to make the public investments necessary to operate a Federal Job Guarantee.[78] Although we can make use of monetary expansion and deficit spending, we can also employ taxation. One trillion dollars of additional taxes may seem forbidding, but there is a fair and feasible way of raising this amount without adding to anyone's economic difficulties. The just approach is to levy a highly graduated wealth tax upon the approximately 95 trillion dollars of United States private assets that make up the greatest accumulation of wealth in human history. The richest 1% of Americans owns considerably more of these assets than the bottom 90% of the population.[79] Obviously, the most affluent can afford to contribute with the greatest ease to the enforcement of the right to work. Moreover, reducing the unequal distribution of wealth helps remedy the stagnation fostered by hoarding assets that are not used to purchase goods or make productive investments. A much higher proportion of the income provided to those employed in public works will be spent on goods and services than that fortune otherwise left in the hands of the most affluent. As a result, wealth taxation will enjoy a multiplier effect, inciting new investment and employment to meet the expanded consumer demand of full employment. This will increase not only national income, but national wealth.

Moreover, full employment will produce the tightest labor market possible, putting employees in the strongest position to negotiate for higher wages, which will further enhance consumer demand and economic growth.

Fears that a Federal Job Guarantee will fuel inflation and currency exchange rate instability are unfounded. The idea that price stability is inconsistent with full employment and that significant unemployment is necessary to prevent a wage-price spiral is, to quote John Maynard Keynes, "a bogy".[80] The fair minimum wage established by the job guarantee will only set the floor for income. Although it may help decrease income inequality, there is no necessity that prices will climb due to its implementation. Rather, the achievement of abiding full employment will act as an anti-cyclical stabilizer, diminishing the fluctuations of booms and busts, as well as the inflations and deflations that accompany such swings.[81] Moreover, since the Federal Job Guarantee will add to domestic income while producing goods and services in the United States, it will not generate a surge in imports that might affect exchange rates.[82] There is little reason to think any damage will befall the dollar's role as the preeminent international reserve currency. On the contrary, the enhanced economic stability and dynamism afforded by full employment will only protect our economy from exchange rate convulsions.

Granted the affordability and stabilizing service of the Federal Job Guarantee, can there still be enough real public works jobs to make guaranteed employment more than a mirage cloaking fictitious featherbedding "make-work"? Will not the advance of automation remove any possibility of putting all willing and able adult residents to work on meaningful projects serving the common good? Admittedly, mechanization will continue to increase productivity, requiring fewer labor inputs for manufacturing, construction, and some service employments. Nonetheless, there remain vast infrastructure needs that private industry is not fulfilling, which require construction that can neither be out-sourced nor completely provided by automation. For-profit businesses are hardly producing all the conversions to clean energy that should be undertaken, nor are they building affordable high band internet connectivity for all, nor the mass transit facilities so many need. The market has failed to upgrade all the substandard apartments and houses that are already occupied, as well as to build sufficient low cost housing to remedy homelessness. Nor are firms building all the schools, libraries, day care and elder care centers, and other public facilities that we sorely need. Moreover, there remains huge need to provide services requiring a human touch in education, health care, childcare, and eldercare. Finally, artists, musicians, filmmakers, dramatists, actors, and performers of all sorts that the entertainment industry does not employ are available to provide cultural opportunities to the public. In other words, there remains an ample supply of meaningful robot-proof occupation for filling the ranks of guaranteed employment.

Moreover, as Martin Luther King pointed out, human services provide an arena for direct public job creation that government can quickly implement with minimal investment. As King writes, the human service industry "is labor intensive, requiring manpower immediately rather than heavy capital investment as in construction or other fields; it fills great need not met by private enterprise; it involves labor that can be trained and developed on the job" and "less educated people can do many of the tasks" required.[83]

The challenge of organizing these efforts is huge, but the WPA and CCC long ago demonstrated that public works can be run effectively. This need not involve a highly centralized bureaucratic management. State and local municipalities can help design and implement needed projects, with as much citizen input as is possible. Technological developments make it easier and faster than ever to match individuals needing employment with the proposed public works and services for which their occupational aspirations and skills are most suited. A national computerized registry of unemployed individuals, with information on their previous work history, training, aptitudes, and job preferences can provide instant coordination with a similar computerized registry of work projects that federal, state, and local authorities have formulated. Further, we can minimize bureaucratic padding and corruption with such measures as direct wage payments to participants[84] and open records providing transparent access to work performance and overhead expenditures.

All that is required to enforce the right to work is the political will. Now is the time for candidates for public office to make guaranteed employment at a fair wage a cornerstone of their platforms and for voters to put them to work.[85]

Why a Federal Job Guarantee is a Necessary but not Sufficient Condition for the Renewal of American Democracy

A Federal Job Guarantee, combined with a fair national minimum wage and equivalent replacement income for retirees and the disabled, not only wipes out unemployment, but strikes a fundamental blow at poverty. In so doing, these measures provide a necessary anchor of economic independence and security, without which neither health, nor family welfare, nor decent housing, nor educational opportunity, nor legal protection of our rights are universally achievable. Even if proper health services are available to all, no one can be healthy if they are subject to the stresses that unemployment and poverty impose. Even if there are measures to balance work and family and provide free public child and elder care, the absence of employment at a fair wage or equivalent replacement income will still take its toll on household welfare. Even if we fund public education equitably and assure equal access to schooling at every level, anyone lacking a proper livelihood will face obstacles to using these educational opportunities. Even if we furnish an adequate supply of affordable housing and keep rents and mortgage payments within range of a fair minimum income, if people still lack a decently paid job or comparable disability and retirement benefits, they will be at pains to acquire, keep, and maintain decent housing. Finally, even if we liberate the legal process from the influence of money, those without work or fair income will have a harder time making use of the legal resources they need to defend their rights, given all their other difficulties.

In sum, we cannot take full advantage of any of our fundamental social rights unless we securely enjoy a decent livelihood through a Federal Job Guarantee, a fair minimum wage, and comparable replacement income for those who cannot work.

Moreover, unless we eliminate unemployment as well as poverty wages and inadequate replacement income, we cannot remedy the abiding racial disadvantage that continues to shame our nation, despite the triumphs of the Civil Rights movement and affirmative action. Although the three measures fulfilling the right to a decent livelihood have universal application, they disproportionately benefit those who have suffered the most disadvantage. By abolishing unemployment, the Federal Job Guarantee will wipe out the gap in unemployment rates that have subjected people of color to levels of joblessness that far exceed those of other groups.[86] By abolishing poverty wages and poverty benefits, a fair minimum wage and equivalent replacement income will end the depths of destitution that have wracked communities of color to a degree that no other groups have suffered. The Federal Job Guarantee and its two correlative supplements can achieve all this without any means tests or other differentiating measures that stigmatize people because of their poverty, while enflaming resentment.

Furthermore, because rights have no expiration date, their fulfillment provides a perennial annulment of the disproportionate handicaps that past racial inequity has generated. Any policy of reparations exhausts its benefit with some limited compensation for a particular past wrong inflicted on some group and weighing upon its descendants. By contrast, the Federal Job Guarantee and accompanying fair income requirements provide an inexhaustible foundation of economic opportunity. They thereby do not violate the fundamental moral principle that individuals be liable only for that for which they are responsible and compensated only for violations of their own rights, rather than being answerable for and rewarded by the accidents of ancestry. The fulfillment of the rights to employment and fair income escapes this problem by addressing the present opportunity of individuals to exercise their social freedom.

Nonetheless, the abolition of unemployment and poverty wages and benefits is not sufficient to even the playing field between employee and employer, even if the tightest labor market enhances the position of employees in seeking fair treatment. Nor do these measures insure that we all have access to healthcare, to educational opportunity, to decent affordable housing, to equitable legal representation, or to the means we need to balance work and family and secure family welfare without undercutting our social and political opportunities.

We cannot be free without a Federal Job Guarantee, a fair minimum wage, and equivalent replacement income, but we must do more to fulfill our fundamental social rights, allowing us to take care of our families and participate as equal citizens in self-government.

The following chapters lay out the additional policies we need undertake to implement our social rights and enable a renewal of our democracy. We must act before it is too late.

2. Employee Empowerment and the Elimination of Class Advantage

Economic Right and the Polarization of Labor and Capital

Markets allow individuals to satisfy needs as an exercise of right, wielding a freedom that is not a privilege but a common interconnected opportunity. In every market transaction, agents choose what wants to satisfy as well as how to satisfy them under the condition of obtaining what one needs by providing others what they need to satisfy self-selected needs of their own. In this web of mutual need satisfaction, individuals freely advance their particular interest as a right, that is, as a lawful, universal prerogative whose exercise is possible solely by enabling others to exercise that same prerogative. Markets make consumption and production forms of social freedom in which commodity exchange renders the satisfaction of particular wants an opportunity tied to the equal opportunity of others. In participating in the market, individuals fulfill a need for what others have to offer by furnishing in return what their counterparts seek to obtain.

Every commodity exchange depends upon each party meeting two coordinate requirements. Each must want not what each already possesses or can directly obtain from nature, but something that someone else has to offer. At the same time, each must have and offer something that some other party seeks in return. Although this situation involves different needs and commodity ownerships, each participant stands in the same interdependence.

Unsurprisingly, economic thinkers as diverse as Adam Smith and Karl Marx begin their economic masterworks by conceiving of a market consisting of individual producers, who each own means of production enabling them to make different products that they can then exchange to satisfy their corollary needs.[87] This division of labor between independent producers gives the simplest expression to the reciprocity of economic right that markets facilitate.

Commodity exchange, however, cannot remain bound to this simple opposition. Once commodity owners recognize one particular commodity as an exchange equivalent for all other commodities, commodity exchange can operate through money, setting the stage for the further transformation of commodity relations. The money commodity figures as the common measure and standard of exchangeability of all other goods. This overcomes the limitation of barter exchange, where need satisfaction requires each economic agent to offer the particular good that directly satisfies the particular need of someone else, who must serendipitously offer the exact good that satisfies the particular need of the opposing party. With money, commodity owners can *buy* and *sell* goods, exercising their economic freedom to satisfy needs for commodities with much greater ease, since all one needs to obtain a good is sufficient money to meet its price.

Besides extending the transaction options of each market participant, monetary exchange makes possible a new form of economic activity, where commodity owners spend money on other goods, not to satisfy their particular needs, but to obtain more money. This can be done by reselling these goods or the products of their utilization for a greater amount of money than was spent on their purchase. These sequential exchanges of buying and selling give rise to profit-seeking enterprise, which generates a completely new economic dynamic. No commodity owner need be under the compulsion to engage in exchanges to accumulate ever greater and greater amounts of money. Nonetheless, when profit-seeking enterprises emerge, the drive to accumulate wealth becomes imperative due to the dynamic of competition into which they are drawn. Once businesses seek buyers in the same market, the very survival of each enterprise depends upon obtaining sufficient resources to remain competitive. Entrepreneurs must accrue increasing returns in order to invest in improving the efficiency of the production and marketing of goods and services, as well as to develop new offerings with which to prevail in face of competing firms. An inability to accumulate and invest jeopardizes an enterprise's viability. As a result of the imperative to expand, a division of labor between private producers, who exchange what they individually furnish, gives way to a marketplace of competing firms that can only succeed by employing others to carry on their ever enlarging enterprise. Since profit-seeking enterprises must generally grow in size to remain viable, increasing both work force and infrastructure, it is no accident that the market becomes inhabited by far fewer entrepreneurs than employees. Any notion that small business could be the dominant form of economic activity contradicts the reality of how competition drives enterprises to enlarge and engender an economy in which the vast majority of participants are employees of a far smaller number of entrepreneurs.[88]

The current state of the US economy exhibits this polarization of employer and employees. Approximately 85% of all breadwinners are employees of some employer. Although government statistics list 30 million small businesses in contrast to "big" businesses that employ more than 500 employees, 24.8 million of these small businesses actually have no employees whatsoever. These "small entrepreneurs," who make up 82% of small businesses, are actually free-lancers or "contingent" workers such as populate the exploding "gig" economy, where internet connectivity allows employers to replace full time workers and office infrastructure with "contract" employees for any time and at any place. Offering some good or service on a piece-work basis, these "self-employed" individuals net on average little more than a minimum fair wage. These figures expose the falsity of the commonly made claims that small businesses are the driving force of employment in our economy.[89] In reality, more than half of all employees work for "big businesses", employing more than 500 workers, whereas firms employing between 50 and 500 employees employ nearly a third of all employees. Since 24.8 million "small businesses" are actual solitary piece-workers, small business plays a very secondary role in job creation. Those who trumpet the centrality of small business only hide the actual prevalence of the employer-employee polarity and the concentration of wealth in ever larger enterprises.

The same competitive dynamic that fosters the polarity of employer and employees also makes the share-issuing corporation the dominant form of enterprise in an unencumbered, "free" market. Since competitive viability depends upon how much capital an enterprise has to invest, the form of business that has access to the most capital will tend to predominate. An enterprise owned by a single person is limited to the wealth and credit worthiness of that person, whereas a family owned enterprise may access the greater wealth and credit worthiness of the household. A worker cooperative can mobilize the wealth all its members can offer, transcending the limits of family wealth. This cooperative capital is still more limited than what a municipal corporation or state enterprise can muster, since public firms can fund their operations by drawing upon tax revenue of their constituents, as well as deficit spending. Tax revenue and public debt has a geo-political limit, however, as does recourse to issuing money, which cannot indefinitely sustain its value. Share-holding corporations can surmount these restrictions. Unlike tax funded state enterprises, the public limited liability corporation can find investors from anywhere in the world to buy its shares and enlarge its disposable capital, with no need of paying the interest fees of borrowed capital. This advantage is why the dynamic of competition leads to a polarity of employer and employees, where enterprises are predominantly share issuing corporations.[90]

Why No Economic Group can have a Universal Interest

Whenever commodity owners participate in market activity, they engage in a type of earning that places them within the group of individuals pursuing that same mode of livelihood. The options of commodity exchange determine the basic possibilities. First, one can earn income by exchanging one's labor power, one's capability to work for a limited period, for wages or salary. On the other hand, one can earn profit or interest by advancing capital, investing money to earn more money in return. Thirdly, one can earn rent by lending out property for payment in return. These three modes of earning characterize distinct classes of employees, owners of capital, and owners of rentable property, who each earn by marketing a different type of commodity and receive in exchange a different type of revenue.

The defining economic interests distinguishing each economic class are normatively civil in character, in that no class member can fulfill its interest without thereby enabling the member of another class to satisfy its interest in some respect. Employees cannot secure their own livelihood if, in so doing, they undermine the viability of the entrepreneurs who employ them. Similarly, landlords cannot earn their rent if their rates are so high that too few consumers can afford to pay what is due. In each case, the interest satisfaction of one mode of earning is connected to the interest satisfaction of the complementary mode of earning to which it is tied. Despite this universal interdependence of market participation, the interests of each class are particular and this particularity is manifest in how what benefits one economic group may be detrimental to the welfare of another. Employees may gain better incomes by diminishing the profits of their employers, just as landlords may increase their rental income by diminishing the remaining wealth of their tenants. Moreover, what benefits the employees and owners of one enterprise may harm the employees and owners of competing firms, as well as harm consumers and the environment.

Marx in his early days maintained that the interest of employees, that is, of the proletariat, was universal, in contrast to the particular character of the interest of entrepreneurs. Marx based the universality of proletarian interest in the alleged deprivation of wage slavery, according to which employees were devoid of any property. As Marx depicts the employer-employee exchange in his *1844 Manuscripts*, the laborer sells himself to the owner of capital, becoming a genuine wage slave.[91] On these terms, wage-laborers have no positive stake in civil society and their interest represents a pure negation of the status quo, since maintaining their bondage has no value for them. In overthrowing the market economy, workers accordingly have only their chains to loose.[92] What Marx later realized by the time he wrote *Capital* is that wage laborers are not bereft of property but own at least one alienable commodity: their own labor power. In the labor-capital transaction, the laborer exchanges not labor, but labor power, which allows employees to retain self-ownership while relinquishing use of their capacity to work for a limited time. As the mature Marx admits, the wage laborer retains the autonomy of a commodity owner, which is what distinguishes an employee from a genuine slave.[93]

Consequently, workers do have a particular stake in civil society. Like every other class, employees have a particular interest that is not identical to the universal end proper to the state. The common good, at which legitimate politics aims, is no more what is good for General Motors than it is what is good for the United Auto Workers. Although the just state cannot be indifferent to the welfare of its various economic classes, what benefits any one may undercut what the state must do to uphold the political and pre-political freedoms of all.

Those leftists who identify the "people" with workers and peasants ignore the difference between particular social interests and the universal good of the body politic. By limiting the "people" to social groups excluding others, they commit the blunder of treating certain particular classes as if they could substitute for the community as a whole. This conflation of the people with particular groups exhibits the same immediate identification of particular and universal as does the slogan, "the people united can never be defeated," which extols the unanimity of the people's will as if that alone could secure the freedom of its members. Rousseau had similarly regarded the immediate identity of the general and particular will as the only guarantee of political self-determination, rejecting the political plurality of any representative body and demanding unanimity as the only way of insuring that what each individual wills is identical with the will of the state. Like Rousseau before them, these leftists fail to comprehend how political freedom can sustain its universality with political plurality and in distinction from the different particular interests of civil society.[94]

Although no class interest is universal, each class deserves an equal opportunity to promote its welfare. Otherwise, the economy becomes an arena of class domination, where certain classes wield economic privilege at the expense of the welfare of others._

It is commonly presumed that the market, left to its own design, generates an automatic connection between class and different levels of wealth, whereby owners of capital amass the greatest riches, landlords come in second, and employees stand at the bottom of the social pyramid.

Strictly speaking, any direct connection is false. There are, and can always be, employees with salaries far greater than the profits and rental incomes of many, if not most entrepreneurs and landlords. Many professional athletes and entertainment stars not only make astronomical incomes, but belong to trade unions that have helped them secure their riches.

Further complicating any direct correspondence between class identity and ranks of wealth are two other interconnected factors. On the one hand, the ownership of capital can be widely dispersed, especially when share-issuing corporations come to predominate. Large portions of the population may own shares and earn dividends without amassing great individual concentrations of wealth. These owners of capital will hardly be at the apex of income or wealth distribution. On the other hand, individuals may engage in more than one mode of earning and end up belonging to more than one class. Given the dispersion of stock ownership, more and more individuals are able to earn wages or salary, while owning shares from which they draw dividends and capital gains. Moreover, individuals may own rental property, from which they receive rent, while earning both wages and dividends.

Although these options muddle the direct connection between class and wealth, they do not preclude the employer-employee relationship from remaining the principal polarity in the market economy and entailing a disparity in opportunity.

The primacy of the employer-employee relation is rooted in the dynamic of competition. This dynamic reduces the economic importance of the class of owners of rental property on two accounts. First, any rental property that is used to accumulate wealth rather than to provide means of subsistence becomes a form of capital, subsumed under the mode of earning specific to profit-seeking enterprise. Second, whatever rental property does not serve profit maximization becomes a diminishing part of the economy insofar as rental business for profit, as well as all other for profit enterprise, must grow to survive.

Furthermore, even though owners of capital as well as employees may dabble in other forms of earning, the drive to accumulate wealth that competition makes an external imperative causes profit seeking firms to grow. They must increase their means of production and marketing, enlisting more labor, even as automation enhances productivity. Consequently, profit-seeking enterprise becomes a progressively more dominant factor in market activity, together with the employer-employee relation on which it principally depends.

All these tendencies have important implications for the disparate economic opportunity of employers on the one hand and of employees on the other.

The Formality of the Agreement between Employee and Employer

Admittedly, every employer-employee market transaction operates through a mutual agreement. Each party freely enters into the exchange, where the employee sells his labor power for a limited period of time under stipulated conditions in exchange for an agreed upon remuneration. Formally, market exchange allows each employee to seek employment with another employer, just as each employer has the right to seek other employees. This formal equality is not a real equality of opportunity if the market options of employees are significantly more limited than the market options of employers. The options at stake involve not just employment opportunities in general, but the specific terms of employment.

The dynamic of competition generates a very unequal situation because of how the imperative to grow entails the emergence of far fewer employers than there are employees. Since the growth of enterprises requires that they not be limited to a single employee, capital accumulation leads to an imbalance in the respective employment options of employees and employers. Simply put, employers have far more prospective employees to choose among than employees have employers to which to apply. Competition further magnifies this disparity by impelling firms to grow through not only expanding their investments, but merging with and acquiring ownership of other enterprises. The resulting concentration of capital restricts the employment options of employees to a degree only exceeded by the monopolization of all business by centralized state ownership.[95]

Collective Bargaining and the Polarity of Employee and Employer

The disparity in the comparative number of employers and employees puts individual employees in a distinctly weaker position to reach an employment agreement that is to their advantage. Since employers have far more other potential employees to hire than employees have other employment options, the playing field is hardly even. In general, employers can much more easily refuse to reach agreement with an individual than an individual can refuse to reach agreement with a prospective employer.

Accentuating the imbalance in opportunity are two developments that vastly broaden the hiring options of employers: the rise of multinational corporations and the explosion of the "gig" economy. Although these represent separate phenomena, they tend to feed off one another, since the global reach of multinational corporations makes them facile exponents of worldwide contract employment. The challenge to employee opportunity is immense and ever increasing.

With firms growing into international behemoths that can establish production and marketing facilities abroad, prospective employees in nations with higher wage and production costs have little chance to reach agreements that can beat competing offers far afield. Nations may erect tariff barriers to make imports less viable and encourage domestic employment. Multinational corporations may still transfer operations inside of tariff boundaries abroad to produce in and for these markets, leaving domestic employees less clout to sway employers to put them to work instead of investing within other territories.

Compounding these imbalanced options is the growing ability of enterprises to make use of internet connectivity and cell phone ubiquity to supplant full time employees with "contract," "contingent," "free-lance" workers operating anywhere and at any time. Instead of bearing the expense of hiring employees to work in company facilities with fixed hours and benefits, employers can increasingly defray these costs with "gig" economy "zero hour" hires, who use their own spaces and instruments of production for whatever sporadic duration their employers request. Anyone seeking employment must now face competition from not only the foreign operations of multinational corporations, but the scattered piece-work outposts of "gig" free-lancers.

To counter the general imbalance of opportunity between employer and employees, a free civil society permits employees to join together to negotiate remuneration and work conditions from a position of united strength. Instead of facing an employer as an isolated individual, easily replaced by others locally or remotely, employees can band together into a union and seek to rebalance the options facing employer and employee. The private initiative of collective bargaining by voluntary organizations of employees can succeed to some extent in evening the playing field between worker and capital. Historically, virtually all the advances in employee welfare, such as the 40 hour work week, overtime pay, grievance procedures, sick leave, and health and retirement benefits have first been established through union negotiation. Not surprisingly, during those years when union membership in the United States was at its height, wages rose in tandem with productivity increases, allowing the standard of living of most workers to increase while maintaining the share of wages in the national income. Once, however, union membership began declining in the 1970's, wages stagnated, and the share of wages in the national income fell in line with the decrease in union membership.[96]

The growth of multinational corporations and the "gig" economy have both accelerated the decline in unionization. By offering enterprises greater access to workers far afield from local markets, these latest developments of globalization have made it much more difficult for employees to organize and negotiate in common. Employers can now more easily resist the demands of current local employees by transferring operations abroad or by hiring free-lancers for any time at anywhere on the globe.

The resultant decline in unionization has been especially catastrophic in the United States, where the failure of government to provide social guarantees has left individuals dependent upon fixed full-time employment to provide the benefits they and their families need. Currently, union membership has dropped to only 6% of employees in the private sector and 11% over all.[97] This decline has been accompanied by a corresponding drop in the share that wages have in the national income, leading to the greatest wealth inequality in the developed world and a national economic growth rate half of what it had been at the height of unionization.

The legal means for unionizing the unorganized have proven to be incapable of sustaining, let alone growing union membership in face of corporate globalization and "gig" erosion of the full-time fixed job. The legally protected unionization procedures enshrined in the Wagner Act have not been able to stem the collapse in union membership and the growing employee disempowerment this entails. Whereas fifty years ago the largest United States employers were AT&T (the old "Ma Bell"), General Motors, and Ford, all of whom had a unionized work force whose wages kept pace with productivity increases, today, our largest employers are Walmart, McDonald's, and Yum! Brands, whose workforce is completely unorganized and receives close to the minimum wage, with scant benefits.[98]

In face of this predicament, how can we level the playing field between employee and employer? Two radical measures are required, which need to be at the head of our legislative agenda, side by side with a Federal Job Guarantee and a new fair minimum wage.

The Case for Mandatory Collective Bargaining

To remedy the imbalance in opportunity between employee and employer, we should enact legislation requiring all employers of multiple employees to engage in collective bargaining with the elected representatives of their employees over pay and work conditions. This should include employers of multiple part-timers and/or free-lancers. Procedures should be provided to insure that no matter how dispersed employees may be, they have an opportunity to elect representatives to engage in negotiations with management over pay and other aspects of their work situation.

Mandating collective bargaining for all enterprises with multiple employees does not force workers to participate in unions. Rather, it simply provides a framework in which whoever chooses to elect representatives to bargain collectively will have the chance to do so. Whether the chosen representatives are tied to a preexisting union, representing other workplaces, is a matter left for the discretion of those employees who voluntarily participate in the mandated election that establishes the representative employee organization with which employers are legally obliged to negotiate. Employees might choose to affiliate with an existing union or they might decide to keep a purely local organization to represent them in collective bargaining. Since employees will tend to have more bargaining clout the more employees and workplaces they can unite in their negotiations, mandatory collective bargaining may well grow existing unions and not just leave them to stagnate and shrink besides new purely local organizations.

Such a measure is particularly important for participants in the new "gig" economy, whose isolation and geographical dispersion leaves them with little other way to wield any collective power. Mandatory collective bargaining, and the universal unionization it entails, will fundamentally change the balance of power between employer and employee, giving employees a basic social resource with which to diminish the disparity in economic options that the growth and concentration of enterprises fosters. To do so, the elected representatives must be shielded from the manipulations that would render the employee bargaining organization equivalent to a company union, at the beck and call of management. Our government must monitor the elections and negotiations of the new employee representatives to insure that the legitimate interests of employees are respected. Any attempt by management to corrupt or intimidate employee representatives must be countered by due prosecution.

Guaranteed employment and a federal fair minimum wage will enhance the efficacy of mandatory collective bargaining. With government insuring that all who want a job will get one, employees will be able to negotiate in the tightest of labor markets. Instead of facing an army of unemployed, who might threaten to replace them at lower wages and inferior work conditions, employees will be able to negotiate jointly from a position of strength. Furthermore, with a fair minimum wage raising the floor of employee income to a level tied to both inflation and national productivity increases, employees will be in a strong position to improve their standard of living by sharing in any rising tide of prosperity.

Nonetheless, collective bargaining does not directly bear upon a key dimension of economic opportunity. The economic freedom of employees revolves around more than the setting of wage levels and work condition. It also concerns fair participation in the management of enterprises.

The very dignity of work depends upon employees having some legitimate say in how enterprises are run.

The Forms of Ownership of Enterprises and the Relation of Employee and Employer

The issue of employee participation in business management takes on particular importance in respect to the form of ownership that comes to predominate in markets owing to the dynamic of competition. Since enterprises must have access to as much capital as possible to remain viable, it is no accident that share-issuing limited liability corporations have come to dominate business. These enterprises are governed by a board of directors, ostensibly elected by shareholders, which appoints the top management. Under this regime, a chief executive official (CEO), backed by the board of directors, makes the ultimate business decisions with no direct input of employees, let alone consumers. These decisions concern such fateful matters as the outsourcing of jobs, the use of suppliers who may or may not provide fair wages and decent working conditions, the introduction of automation, the buying back of company stock, merges and acquisitions, what new products and services to develop, how production and marketing practices impact upon the environment, and what role the firm should play in the political arena. In the United States, the CEO and the board of directors frequently collude to benefit themselves and their respective stock portfolios. With their hands in the till, they have allowed the compensation of CEO's to become nearly 300 times the remuneration of the average employee and commonly give "golden parachutes" to departing CEO's who leave their corporations in shambles.[99] Much of this parasitic behavior reflects the competing interests of shareholders and those who remain loyal to the prospects of the corporation. The economic interest of shareholders concerns the value of their stock, which may be enhanced by dismembering the corporation and selling off its remnants. Shareholders, like the CEO, may enrich themselves at the expense of the destruction of the competitive integrity of the corporation, with catastrophic consequences for employees and the communities they inhabit. The lack of any participation by employees in corporate boards accentuates the disparity in opportunity that the expansion and concentration of firms entails and that globalization and the "gig" economy intensify. With no say in corporate governance, employees have a very restricted power to balance the playing field between corporate and employee interests by relying solely on collective bargaining.

The Remedy of Employee Co-Determination

If social right were reducible to property right, there would be little justification for restricting the managerial control of shareholders. The owners of corporations would have exclusive right to determine how this, their property, is used. In a just, civil society, however, all market participants deserve to have their economic right recognized and treated on a par with that of others. Moreover, as family members, they are entitled to have their household welfare respected as much as the household welfare of any other family. The workings of corporations do not just affect the private domains of shareholders. Corporate governance has an obvious impact upon the economic welfare of employees and their families, as well as upon consumers and the environment on whose livability all exercise of freedom depends.

Mandatory collective bargaining over remuneration and working conditions cannot alone reliably balance the economic opportunities of employers and employees. Of equal importance are measures enabling employees to have a fair say in the management of the enterprise for whom they work.

The providing of employees with stock options or limited share holdings cannot ensure that they will have an equitable say in the running of their enterprise.[100] Company founders may retain special classes of shares that keep managerial control in their hands. Moreover, as firms grow and increase their stock offerings, employee shares will get continually diluted.

Only with due representation on the governing boards of corporations can employees equitably assert their interests with respect to vital managerial decisions regarding outsourcing, free-lance hiring, supply chain accountability,[101] automation, and mergers and acquisition that bear upon job security and the continued integrity of the enterprise.

Several European countries have implemented this approach for providing fair employee empowerment. Germany was a pioneer,[102] first introducing work councils representing employees in mining companies employing more than 100 workers (1905) and then more extensively in war production enterprises employing more than 50 workers (1916). The 1920 Works Council Act (*Betreibsrätegesezt*) introduced consultative organs for workers in all enterprises employing more than 20 workers. Although the Nazi regime abolished all works councils in 1934, the postwar German Federal Republic enacted in 1951 the Coal, Steel and Mining Codetermination Law (*Montan-Mitbestimmungsgesezt*), which required supervisory boards of firms employing more than 1,000 workers to have employee representatives fill half of the seats on company supervisory boards. In 1955 the *Bundespersonalvertertungsgesetz* granted similar employee codetermination to civil service workers and the 1976 Codetermination Law (*Mitbestimmungsgesetz*) extended it further to all enterprises employing more than 2,000 workers. Several other northern European democracies have followed suit and given workers seats on corporate boards. The share of seats varies from country to country, as does the responsibility of the board on which employee co-determination operates. In some corporations, multiple boards have different functions and employees have been allotted seats on boards with very restricted control over company governance.

Employee Codetermination Versus Economic Democratization

Whatever its magnitude, employee participation in corporate boards should not be confused with either the democratization of the economy or the extension of democracy beyond the alleged confines of parliamentary representation.[103]

Employee participation in company management is concerned with the governance of a particular market entity, whose aims are economic interests that may be interconnected with those of other market agents, but are themselves never universal in character. For this fundamental reason, employee codetermination is neither a direct participatory extension of political self-determination nor a training for representative self-government. Normative politics is always concerned with universal ends, consisting in the ordering of the entire body politic so as to realize the totality of rights in face of changing domestic and international conditions. The problem of insuring that the will of every citizen has an equal opportunity to determine the workings of government is never equivalent to insuring that particular economic interests have direct political representation. If any particular social interests are allowed to take control of state action, then the reflexivity of self-rule is annulled. Instead of the citizenry acting upon itself as a whole, a particular social group usurps political power, enforcing its interest upon everyone else. Self-government then gives way to the domination of one economic force upon the rest of the citizenry.

Similarly, the experience of participating in the management of an enterprise is not a tutelage for self-government because it does not at all concern the universal aims of normative politics.[104] Hegel made the mistake of thinking that incorporating social interest groups into government through a "corporate" legislative assembly could directly unite the particular strivings of the members of civil society with the common good of politics. Like the Italian Fascists, who made corporatism a political reality, Hegel fails to understand that social interests are not equivalent to the individual *political* will of the citizen. What legitimately distinguishes the different political strivings of citizens are distinct political programs, not distinct social interests. Political programs all concern themselves with the universal aim of politics, which consists in ordering the totality of the body politic. Legitimately *political* programs differ in promoting distinct plans for best fulfilling the common good of the entire citizenry, not for best advancing a particular social interest.[105]

Consequently, worker participation in corporate management is not an exercise in participatory democracy, overcoming the limits of representative government. What is at stake in worker co-determination is participation in the management of a particular economic interest, not participation in self-government, where the citizenry acts upon itself as a whole.

Democracy already presides over the economy by regulating economic activity to uphold the household, social, and political freedoms of all citizens. In so doing, self-government does not directly determine production and consumption. If government did so, collectively mandating the occupations and need satisfactions of every individual, political freedom would absorb all economic activity, canceling any space for the exercise of specifically *economic* self-determination. Since the supreme value of freedom applies to all its spheres, a democratic collectivization of the household and society would commit the wrong of constricting the range of self-determination without enhancing self-government.

The legitimate basis for employee participation in corporate boards is not to advance democratization, but to contribute to balancing the playing field of the respective economic interests of employees and employers. Just as mandatory collective bargaining helps overcome the disparity in contractual options facing employees on the one hand and employers on the other, so giving employees seats on corporate boards helps mitigate the disparity in economic power that is institutionalized in company management.

Achieving equity in employee codetermination depends upon both what share employee representatives have on corporate boards and how much company control corporate boards wield. If employees are allotted half the seats of corporate boards, then the interests of employees and employers will balance one another, without either having unilateral control. Under that apportionment, consensus will be required to achieve anything. Otherwise, one side will dominate and the representation of the minority will have negligible effect.

Equal representation, however, will only signify equal managerial control if the corporate board has the final say over all company decisions. This does not require that the board micromanage every executive decision, but rather that the board has the power to appoint and replace the chief executive/s at will.

If both of these conditions are met, the interests of employer and employee will have equal sway. This does not mean that the citizenry no longer needs to oversee civil society's play of social interests. The balance between employer and employee in particular enterprises does not guarantee that their conciliated interests conform to the common good with which self-government is concerned. An employee-codetermined corporation may still harm the economic welfare of competing firms, consumers, the environment, and equal political opportunity. Social right does require giving all economic agents equal opportunity, but the state must regulate the economy to insure that the workings of economic freedom in collective bargaining and employee codetermination do not undermine family and political wellbeing.

For these reasons, the task of a new social bill of rights is not exhausted by guaranteed employment, a fair minimum wage, and employee empowerment through mandatory collective bargaining and co-determination.

3. Enforcing the Right to Healthcare and a Healthy Biosphere

Why Access to a Healthy Biosphere and Healthcare is a Right

Every exercise of right rests upon two natural preconditions, one more encompassing than the other.

The more encompassing natural precondition is a biosphere in which intelligent life can satisfy its biological needs with sufficient ease to allow individuals to determine themselves as owners, moral subjects, spouses and parents, members of civil society, and self-governing citizens. Since human conduct can alter our biosphere, we are obliged to safeguard our environment so that we can continue to exercise our freedoms and future generations can exercise theirs. Action to this end can be undertaken in each sphere of right, for environmental health can be affected by how one uses one's property, acts morally, behaves as a spouse and parent, leads one's economic affairs, and participates in democracy. Nonetheless, the severity of human alteration of our biosphere, so evident in environmental degradation and accelerating global warming, calls for national and international initiatives that go beyond what private endeavors can accomplish. Securing clean water, clean air, and unpolluted oceans is impossible without state action and international cooperation. Capping and reducing world net carbon emissions requires political measures that limit fossil fuel production and consumption while mobilizing public and private investment in safe green energy on a domestic and international scale.

Given the gravity of our situation, repeatedly acknowledged by overwhelming international scientific consensus, we cannot afford to hesitate. First, to curtail expansion of fossil fuel production, we must put a halt to fossil fuel exploration here and abroad. Second, we must take measures to prohibit adding any new fossil fuel usage, in either energy production or powering machinery, vehicles, and appliances that does not substitute for current consumption that generates equal or greater carbon emissions. In the near term, this can involve substituting more carbon efficient fossil fuels, such as natural gas for coal. Market incentives, such as a fossil fuel carbon tax,[106] can also be used to help make green energy more economically attractive. Ultimately, however, the capping and reduction of fossil fuel production and consumption will depend upon legislative prohibitions and supplementing private ventures with massive public investment in power generation and machinery that uses bio-fuels, solar radiation, wind, geothermal emissions, hydropower and other non-fossil energy sources. Due to the inability of solar and wind power to provide reliably continuous energy, these efforts should include greatly expanded research into developing better batteries and other technologies for storing power. In addition, we cannot ignore undertaking to make atomic fission power production safer and useless for nuclear weapons proliferation, to securely store atomic reactor radioactive wastes, and to develop practical fusion power. Although countries such as China and India are making huge investments in renewable energy sources, they and other developing nations cannot meet their growing power needs on this basis alone. We, and other affluent nations, must assist them to keep their fossil fuel production within diminishing levels by providing both capital and expertise for increasing green energy development.

In all these endeavors, the Federal Job Guarantee can play a crucial role by putting millions to work building a new green energy infrastructure, including more energy efficient public transportation and affordable housing that both consume as little fossil fuels as possible. With guaranteed jobs at fair wages, a Green New Deal can avert environmental catastrophe without undermining the livelihood of anyone employed in the fossil fuel industries, whose day of replacement must come as soon as possible. The achievement of a full employment transition from fossil fuel power to green power will then demonstrate how the economic expansion fostered by market competition need not wreck the biosphere on which all our freedoms depend.[107]

If we, as well as more and more other nations, fulfill our social rights, and in particular, our right to employment at fair wages, we can have just economic growth on a global scale that keeps our planet hospitable for intelligent life.

Maintaining the environmental health of our planet is, however, not enough to enjoy our freedoms. We must attend to the second principal natural enabling condition of any exercise of autonomy: the health of individuals. No mode of self-determination can be undertaken unless agents have sufficient physical and psychological well-being to act autonomously. Although sickness may be innocent, failure to provide possible treatment is not blameless. Because ill health robs agents of the full capacity to be free, rights stand in jeopardy unless all individuals have equal access to the physical and mental healthcare they need to exercise their entitled opportunities. If healthcare is instead a privilege that only the advantaged can enjoy, the universality of rights is undermined, leaving a community in which equal opportunity is absent.

RICHARD DIEN WINFIELD

Healthcare in Civil Society

In a civil society, virtually all factors critical to the maintenance of health take the form of commodities, whose production and marketing become subject to the dynamic of competition. Medicines, medical supplies, clinics, hospitals, nurses, doctors, health aids, health insurance, and every other sort of healthcare service and infrastructure are furnished in and through the economy. Consequently, the fulfillment of the right to healthcare must contend with the workings of the market as they bear upon each element that contributes to our physiological and psychological well-being.

It is imperative for justice to organize research to deepen understanding of physiology and psychology, as well as to develop treatments and drugs that can cope with disease, injury, and congenital disabilities. In order for research and development to be economically feasible for enterprises, they must be able to reap sufficient revenues and profits from its fruits to bear the costs and remain solvent in face of competitors. This requirement does not stop enterprises from engaging in massive medical research and development investment, for remaining competitive requires coming up with new treatments and remedies to keep and increase market shares. Nonetheless, the pressures of competition equally block research and development with respect to diseases that afflict either too few people or too impoverished a populace to promise profitable returns.

A similar market dynamic applies to the growth and distribution of health services. Medical practitioners, whose practice depends upon being able to earn sufficient profits to remain competitive, may expand and concentrate their operations in line with the requirements of market survival. These provisos may limit the distribution of medical services to those regions where market demand is sufficient to bring the revenues needed to exceed their costs of marketing and production. Rural areas and inner cities may find themselves deprived of sufficient health care practitioners because they lack enough buying power to support medical services that must be profitable to remain viable.

Parallel economic considerations affect how much investment is made in training medical personnel, in constructing medical facilities, and in manufacturing the medical instruments and supplies they require. Although every individual may have an equal claim to the use of medical practitioners and healthcare infrastructure, the variations of market demand may foster an inequitable distribution and shortage of caretakers, facilities, and supplies.

The development of a health insurance industry may capitalize upon the social imperative to spread risk in order to widen access to healthcare, but competition compromises this imperative in fundamental ways. To remain competitive, private health insurance companies must reduce their costs and increase their revenues, which may involve such maneuvers as mandating high copay and deductible fees, refusing to insure individuals with pre-existing conditions, charging women and the elderly higher premiums, and restricting which health providers and what medications their insurance policies cover. Although one might imagine that all these efforts would tend to lower costs of health insurance, medical treatments, and medicines, contrary tendencies drive competition to increase, rather than lower health care expenditures.

First, the very proliferation of private insurance companies adds huge administrative costs to health care practitioners, who must deal with the complexity of filing insurance claims to multiple insurers. Competitive pressures exacerbate this complexity by driving insurance companies to develop new and "improved" coverage plans that may target different parts of the market. Moreover, competition impels insurance companies to spend significant sums on advertising and other marketing devices, adding to the cost of their products. Since insurance companies will be able to raise the most capital to remain competitive by becoming shareholding corporations, they will also incur the costs of colluding CEO's and corporate boards. The more these get away with padding their own compensations, the more health care costs balloon.

The same added expenses apply to the corporate organization of health care providers, including hospitals, clinics, and medical practices. Advertising and marketing costs, managerial costs, and costs of market capitalization all add to the bill of healthcare.

Similar explosions in costs apply to the pharmaceutical industry, where competition hardly guarantees that drugs will be affordable to all. Drug companies will be able to invest in research and development to come up with new medicines only insofar as they have sufficient patent protection to be able to recoup their costs soon enough to stay solvent. Accordingly, drug prices will reflect not just their costs of development and production, but the monopoly advantage patent protection provides, as well as the additional marketing and advertising costs that competition makes imperative. Rather than make medicines more and more inexpensive, competition in the pharmaceutical industry is likely to drive up prices.

The manufacturers of medical equipment and supplies will contend with analogous pressures. To develop new medical instruments, companies will need patent protection to be able to afford their research and development investments, but this monopoly will allow them to raise their prices well above their costs, which include the marketing expenses on which success depends. The growth and concentration of these manufacturers and their organization as share issuing corporations only exacerbates price elevation, particularly when top management and corporate boards enrich themselves.

In face of these tendencies, the enforcement of healthcare as a right cannot rely upon the invisible hand of the market. Nor can equitable access to healthcare rely upon the efforts of social interest groups, such as trade unions, which may negotiate contracts with health benefits for their employees. Such groups can never be sure of success in obtaining affordable healthcare for their own members, especially in face of the challenges presented by the growth and concentration of multinational corporations and the explosion of the gig economy. Even when social interest groups do succeed in using their collective bargaining strength to obtain health benefits for their members, that success does not extend healthcare to anyone else in civil society.

Consequently, to recognize and enforce healthcare as a right, the state must intervene to insure what neither the market nor social interests groups can guarantee themselves. The tasks of public intervention are manifold.

What Public Intervention Must Do to Enforce the Right to Healthcare

To begin with, government must overcome the shortfalls of private investment in research and development for medical treatments, medicines, and medical devices. Public funding should be mobilized to support the basic and applied research that serves healthcare but that the market is not able or willing to underwrite. This can involve tax supported research grants to universities, both public and private, as well as contracts to private enterprises. When no private firms will produce needed medicines and medical equipment, government may have to produce them itself on an emergency or ongoing basis, depending upon the circumstances.

Similarly, if the market does not provide an adequate supply of health providers and medical facilities, government must step in to insure that patients are not left in the lurch. This may require government initiatives to increase the number and enrollments of medical, nursing, and technical schools. To achieve such growth, government may need to establish new public medical training schools as well as offer grants and scholarship aid to private institutions. When these efforts are inadequate, government can modify immigration regulations to attract medical personnel that the domestic market cannot supply.

When needed personnel are available but unwilling to work in areas short of health providers, government must provide sufficient incentives to effect the needed distribution to serve neglected populations. Various options are possible. Government scholarships for medical training can be contingent upon beneficiaries working for several years upon graduation in areas in need of medical staffing. Wherever enough doctors, nurses, and attendants are lacking, government can supplement salaries to attract health practitioners. Public clinics and hospitals can be set up in regions where private initiatives are inadequate.

The public fulfillment of all these tasks does not guarantee that everyone can afford to pay for the services in adequate supply. This is true even if everyone benefits from guaranteed jobs, a fair minimum wage, equivalent income replacement for the disabled and retired, and employee empowerment to level the playing field between employee and employer. The cost of ordinary medical services may still be financially challenging and emergencies requiring extended treatments will confront all too many individuals with expenses they can never meet themselves.

Modern nations with civil societies have made use of three basic alternatives to solve this problem of healthcare affordability: a national health service, a single payer public health insurance system, and a system of non-governmental health insurance options.

The first alternative consists of enacting a government health service that owns medical facilities and employs medical personnel, providing medical services and medicines to all residents at no charge, supporting the entire effort by tax revenues. The prime example of this option is the National Health Service in the United Kingdom, which has succeeded in providing necessary medical care to all residents with an annual cost per person of $4,192, just two fifths of the annual per person health care expenditure in the United States.[108]

The second alternative consists of a single payer health insurance system, where government provides a unitary health insurance policy to all residents, without owning medical facilities or employing medical care providers. Instead, residents are free to go to any health care provider they choose, with all costs covered by the unitary health insurance policy that is paid for by taxation. Only two nations have adopted this option, Canada and Taiwan, both of which cover all their residents at a cost per person half of what health care costs individuals in the United States.[109]

The third and most widely adopted alternative is a system of government regulated insurance plans, operated by independent organizations. All residents are required to obtain coverage by one of these plans, which government regulates to provide sufficient coverage at affordable rates. In most cases, these independent insurance plans are non-profit undertakings and any individuals who cannot afford their rates receive government subsidies to support their coverage. Because the insurance providers are non-profit organizations, their rates need not be inflated by the extra costs incurred by for-profit insurers, who spend on marketing and advertising, proliferating "new and improved" plans, and paying out dividends and extravagant compensations to top management, board of directors, and investors. Generally, the nations that have adopted this third option spend half per person of what individuals pay for healthcare in the United States.[110]

All other affluent nations have managed to provide their residents with the healthcare they need by adequately funding one of these three options and insuring that coverage extends to everyone. In doing so, they have managed to spend no more than half of what the United States pays per person for healthcare, even though a significant number of United States residents are not receiving the healthcare they require.

RICHARD DIEN WINFIELD

The Limitations of the Affordable Care Act

The Affordable Care Act, signed into law in 2010 by President Barack Obama, attempted to better fulfill our right to healthcare, but undertook to do so while retaining the for-profit private health insurance industry. Following a plan drawn up by the conservative think tank, the Heritage Foundation, which Governor Mitt Romney had implemented statewide in Massachusetts in 2006, the Affordable Care Act (ACA) has basic features that have thwarted its purported aim to treat healthcare as a right, not a privilege. To its credit, the ACA has prohibited private health insurers from refusing clients with pre-existing conditions, from charging women higher rates than men, and from capping annual and lifetime benefits on essential care. Further, the ACA has required private health insurance policies to offer a basic standard of coverage including mental health care expenses and it has provided subsidies to lower income groups to make their insurance plans more affordable. Although the ACA does oblige health insurers to cover preventive care with no deductibles or copays, it has not eliminated the copays and deductibles for all other care that leave many people unable to afford to use their coverage. Despite providing health insurance coverage to a wider population than before, the ACA does not guarantee health insurance coverage to all residents of the United States. Moreover, by retaining the market place of private health insurance plans, the ACA has failed to eliminate the inefficiencies of proliferating competing offerings, as well as the overhead costs of corporate dividends and huge executive compensations. As a result, health expenditures in the United States continue to far exceed those of other developed nations, while millions, both insured and uninsured, cannot afford the physical and mental health care they need.

How to enforce the Right to Healthcare in the United States

At the end of 2016, twenty eight million Americans had no health insurance.[111] Many others who have insurance could not afford to get healthcare because their insurance copays and deductibles were beyond their means. Nonetheless, most Americans participated in health care systems that resemble to some degree one of the three options that other developed nations have successfully employed to provide universal affordable coverage.

Veterans Administration Hospitals, which serve United States military veterans, follow the model of a national health service within their restricted reach. Like the United Kingdom's public healthcare system, where the state owns medical facilities and employs their medical personnel, Veterans Administration clinics, hospitals, nursing homes, and pharmacies belong to our Government, which hires their staff. Whereas the British National Health Service covers healthcare with no copays and deductibles, the Veterans Administration healthcare system charges both, while limiting its coverage to veterans, leaving their family members as well as the rest of the public ineligible to receive its care. Moreover, Veterans Hospitals and clinics do not cover all types of illness. Consequently, even if those not entitled for Veteran Health Services received affordable medical care, the Veterans Health Services would need to expand their coverage to insure that veterans had all their health needs met, without copays and deductibles. Only then could the services of Veterans Hospitals be a model for providing healthcare to all residents, following the lead of the British National Health Service.

Two organs of America health care, Medicare and Medicaid, follow, in a limited sphere, the second major path that developed nations have chosen to secure healthcare as a right. Medicare and Medicaid offer government medical insurance coverage to older residents and the poor, respectively. Eligible individuals can go to any health provider of their choice and, in principle, have their government insurance pay for much of their care. In this manner, Medicare and Medicaid resemble the approach taken by the single payer national insurance system adopted by Canada and Taiwan. There are, however, fundamental differences concerning both range and affordability. Unlike a single payer national insurance that covers the medical needs of all residents affordably, Medicare and Medicaid target only part of the population and fail to cover all medical costs. Medicare and Medicaid both have copays and deductibles, which all too often fall beyond the means of many recipients. Moreover, Medicare and Medicaid do not cover all necessary, non-cosmetic medical treatments, nor the entire cost of medications and medical equipment. Medicare does not cover dental care, annual physical exams and other preventive care, or long term in-home or nursing home care. Nonetheless, both Medicare and Medicaid benefit from lower administrative costs than private insurers, thanks to the absence of competitive pressures to spend on marketing and paying out dividends to investors.[112] Further, because Medicare has a unitary national scheme, health care providers expend fewer clerical expenses on handling filings and reimbursements than in dealing with the proliferation of private insurance plans. The same is true to a lesser degree for Medicaid, since while Medicaid benefits are determined and administered by each individual state, within each state they comprise a single scheme. Nonetheless, the limited coverage offered to recipients of either Medicare or Medicaid leaves them with a truncated single payer plan that fails to enforce their right to healthcare. The old and poor will only enjoy health care as a right if we modify Medicare and Medicaid to eliminate unaffordable copays and deductibles and extend their coverage to all necessary health needs, including not just physical, but mental and dental care as well.

The third option of coverage by independent health insurers is exhibited in our private health insurance industry, which covers much of the population, largely through insurance plans related to employment and partially funded by employer contributions. Despite the alleged cost-saving benefits of competition, the private insurance industry has saddled the public with increasingly unreliable and expensive coverage. The costs of private insurance plans are padded with the expenses of ballooning executive pay packages and marketing, as well as the expenses of health care providers to service the cornucopia of competing offerings. Meanwhile customers must cope with rising copays and deductibles, restrictions on health care providers, attempts to resist covering pre-existing conditions, other failures to distribute the costs evenly among all participants, and the insecurity of having health insurance tied to employment. To remedy these difficulties, we would need to modify the private insurance industry in line with how many other countries have provided affordable health care to all while relying upon independent health insurers. These nations have succeeded by requiring everyone to purchase coverage, mandating that coverage extend to all essential healthcare, minimizing marketing costs, making independent insurers non-profit enterprises, and guaranteeing everyone the means to pay for health insurance.

One can imagine various ways of achieving affordable healthcare for all in the United States, either combining modified versions of our Veterans Health Administration, Medicare and Medicaid, and private health insurance programs, or opting for just one of the three alternatives and making its coverage exclusive and universal.

With proper adjustment, each of the three principal options can fulfill the right to healthcare, either in combination or as exclusive policy. History has demonstrated this through the manifold ways in which virtually every affluent nation other than the United States has provided affordable medical treatment to all its residents.

Does the current context of United States healthcare favor one option over the others? In addressing this issue it is important to keep in mind the two most vexing obstacles to enforcing the right to healthcare in the

United States: the failure of each existing option to provide universal coverage and the explosion of expenses that leaves the United States paying twice as much per person on healthcare than any other nation.

Of all three options, the most expensive to erect in the American context would be a national health service. A huge expenditure of public capital would have to be made to expand government ownership of health care facilities and government employment of health care workers beyond the confines of the Veterans Administration. All the private hospitals, clinics, and medical practices would have to be bought or replaced with new public facilities, and all private medical personnel would have to be hired for the new public monopoly. The centralization under one ultimate ownership and management might involve certain economies of scale, but it risks undermining the accountability, attention to local conditions, and nimble flexibility that a more decentralized remedy could afford. Not only might abuses abound, but costs could end up increasing due to the absence of competitive providers.

Some of these liabilities of centralization would be absent from enlisting the third option of independent non-profit insurers, with universal coverage and public subsidies. In large degree, we could implement such a system by reforming the existing private insurance industry, setting employers free of having to contribute to its costs, mandating health insurance purchases for all, reducing the marketing costs of independent insurers, and requiring all insurance plans to cover necessary physical, mental, and dental care, with no copays or deductibles. Moreover, opting for independent non-profit insurers could leave in place private health care providers, with all the choice and competitive accountability their plurality might provide. This would involve a far smaller initial public investment than erecting a national health service.

Nonetheless, depending upon independent non-profit insurers would retain the clerical costs incurred by health care providers of having to process a multiplicity of insurance plans. In addition, the plurality of insurers would limit their ability to negotiate effectively with pharmaceutical companies and health care providers to lower prices of drugs and care.

If instead, we implement nationally the second option of a single payer health insurance system, these limitations can be overcome without incurring the huge initial costs and potential inefficiencies of a national health service. We can enlist the existing infrastructure of Medicare and Medicaid to help administer a new public health insurance program that covers all residents and all necessary physical, dental, and mental care under a single unitary plan. That plan can offer beneficiaries complete freedom to choose whatever health care provider they want and thereby leave in place the existing array of private as well as public hospitals, clinics, pharmacies, and all their employees. To insure that no one is unable to pay for medical services, the single payer public insurance plan should have no copays and no deductibles and cover all costs of medicines, physical therapy, and home care.

This universal, but simplified coverage can be affordable to the community at large due to two factors that enable reducing the costs per person of health care in the United States to the level of other developed nations, which currently spend little more than half of what we spend per person on populations that enjoy better health outcomes.

The first cost-saving factor is the simplicity of a single payer system. Since all health care providers will have only one insurance plan to deal with, there will be none of the extra administrative costs of handling a proliferation of health plans with different coverage and different reimbursements for each service. Moreover, with just one public insurance plan, there will be none of the expenses of marketing competing plans, let alone of paying the extravagant remuneration of the executive brass at every competing private health insurance firm.

Secondly, a single payer system will provide the public health insurance administration with the strongest position to negotiate affordable prices for drugs, for hospital and clinic services, and for the care of doctors, nurses, and other health practitioners. Unlike individual private insurers, who compete with others in a limited share of the health care market, the single payer government insurer will wield a monopoly power that can serve to keep medical expenses affordable for society at large. Such a single payer system can escape the predicament of Medicare and Medicaid, which only cover the aged and the poor. That limited coverage enables health care practitioners to refuse to treat patients on Medicare and Medicaid and earn a more profligate living treating patients on private insurance plans that pay higher reimbursements for services. No such opportunity would be available under a single payer system, since medical practitioners offering necessary health care services would have no other option than to accept patients covered by the one and only insurance plan.

Admittedly, a single payer system could coexist with supplementary insurance plans that cover inessential medical services, such as cosmetic surgery. Then certain health care providers could escape subordination to the public health insurance plan and devote their practices to "elective" care. Nonetheless, every other type of health care would fall under the scope of the single payer system and benefit from the cost reductions its monopoly can enforce.

Would, however, the monopoly of a single payer system over necessary health care engender the type of inefficiencies that may occur in a national health service with a relatively compromised accountability? Medicare has lower overhead costs than any private insurer. If the single payer system that arises as an improved "Medicare for all" can keep its overhead under control while negotiating lower prices for pharmaceuticals, hospitalization, and other medical care, the health insurance monopoly need not undermine the quality of its service or its expense reduction.

On the other hand, the single payer system leaves in place all the public and private health care providers that currently operate. It can mobilize and tailor their competition to increase their productivity and efficiency without the distortions that an unregulated market produces. This would be possible thanks to the unified negotiations over prices in which all health care providers would participate with the single payer system administration on which they depend for reimbursements. There is no reason why the United States could not lower its health care expenditures in line with those of other affluent nations once the health insurance payer occupies the strongest position to bargain over costs. Unlike a national health service, the single payer system need not purchase existing health provider infrastructure nor hire medical staff. The establishment of its bargaining monopoly requires little investment beyond the expansion of the bureaucracy already administering Medicare and Medicaid. That expansion will not face a shortage of trained personnel, for it can draw upon the staff of private insurance plans, much of whose business will contract. On all these counts, the single payer system can be expected to provide the most efficient and affordable solution to our health care crisis, while leaving individuals with maximum choice of health care providers.

How should we fund the single payer system? Today, the total bill of United States health care is 3.4 trillion dollars. If our health care costs decreased to the level of all other affluent nations, we would still face the challenge of an expenditure approaching 1.7 trillion dollars. Instead of spending more than $10,000 per person on health care, we would need to pay $5,000 per person, which remains a sizeable chunk of our national income.[113] If, however, one takes into account that the national income exceeds 18 trillion dollars, the 1.7 trillion dollar health care bill would by less than one tenth of that total, appreciable certainly, but not so large as to overwhelm annual earnings.

Currently, spending on health care falls heavily on not just private individuals, but employers, both private and public, who contribute to work-based insurance plans. Whereas other countries use general taxation to fund their health coverage, many of our businesses find themselves at a competitive disadvantage by having to pay for health insurance contributions that do not encumber their foreign competitors. In addition, when health care coverage is tied to employment, beneficiaries are at risk whenever they lose or change their job.

These difficulties disappear when we fund the single payer health insurance system by general taxation, rather than by employer and employee contributions. Then businesses no longer bear higher costs due to health insurance contributions, while individuals carry their coverage with them, whatever happens in their employment history.

Although income taxes could pay the health care bill, wealth taxation provides an untapped alternative with definite advantages. Our national income is dwarfed by the national wealth in private hands. The total private wealth in the United States is the greatest accumulation of national riches in human history, surpassing more than 94 trillion dollars. This wealth is much more unevenly distributed than income. The richest 1% possess almost 40% of our total private wealth. A 5% wealth tax on the richest 1% would likely pay for the total bill of national health expenditures. Such a wealth tax payment would hardly affect the 1%'s personal livelihoods, while putting part of their hoarded wealth back into productive circulation, helping to foster economic growth. In this way, both corporations and 99% of United States residents would be relieved of any health expenditure burden at the same time that wealth taxation would combat economic stagnation.

For all these reasons, the embrace of a public single payer health insurance system offers a compelling and affordable solution to our health care crisis. By following this option, we can enforce the right to health care, on which all engagements in freedom depend.

4. Balancing Work and Family

Families and Livelihood in Civil Society

The demarcation of family, civil society, and state is a precondition for the realization of freedom in all these domains. If kinship relations determine social and political roles, as they do in pre-modern communities where birthright shackles personal destiny, no one can escape the bonds of legacy and freely participate in society and state. Similarly, if social position conditions political participation, no citizens can engage in self-government, wielding political power on an equal footing with their fellow members of the body politic. Instead, government operates as an instrument of social domination, where social privilege directly wields political power.

On the other hand, the separation of household, society, and state is not enough to realize freedom unless each of these spheres provides its adult members an equal opportunity to participate in family, social, and political self-determination.

If equal economic opportunity is absent in society, the social disadvantage of the economically underprivileged will adversely affect household welfare and political opportunity. Family rights will be imperiled, as the economically disadvantaged struggle to keep their households together, while democracy will give way to oligarchy, where wealth wields undue political influence.

Conversely, individuals will be unable to exercise fully their social and political rights if the family has not emancipated itself. Unless marriage has become a co-determined union, overcoming all hierarchy based on natural differences such as gender and sexual orientation, the unequal roles of adult family members will obstruct their equal engagement in social and political activity.

If, for example, husbands rule over wives within the household, their patriarchal management of household property and welfare will rob wives, sisters, daughters, and any other female household members of full autonomy to participate in society and state. Without the unilateral authorization of their male overlords, females in the family will be unable to pursue careers in the economy and politics. Moreover, with the male household master retaining the patriarchal privilege of representing the family in society and state, domestic toil will disproportionately fall on the shoulders of daughters, wives, and other female relatives, further impeding their activities outside the household.

Similarly, if marriage is limited to heterosexual unions, those excluded from matrimony will be disadvantaged in their social and political involvements from all the benefits that marriage can offer. These include the care and shared resources that spouses can provide, as well as whatever pension benefits and tax advantages that marriage may afford.

So too, the right of every child to become an autonomous member of a family, society, and the state will be impeded if parents deprive their children of the upbringing enabling them to exercise their freedom as adults. If parents limit the education of their children to rob them of the knowledge and skills they need to navigate the world and take their place as independent citizens, their children will be comparatively unprepared to wield the rights to which they are entitled. Similarly, if parents impose attitudes, training, and expectations that restrict their children by gender and sexual orientation, they will hinder the equal progress of their children as independent members of society and state.

The achievement of equal family prerogatives for spouses and of parental respect for the autonomous development of their children do not, however, ensure that social and political relations allow members of an emancipated household to participate in society and politics without conflicting with the demands of their family life.

This problem is particularly acute due to the demarcation of household, economy, and state on which freedom depends. Pre-modern traditions may bar equal social or political opportunity by letting kinship bonds condition what occupations individuals can pursue and what role they can play in the state. Nonetheless, these same bonds provide a certain security by giving individuals a specific relation to wealth and governance offering some level of livelihood and protection. The liberation from the bonds of birthright that governs caste and feudal societies removes these traditional guarantees.

The resulting predicament is familiar to all members of modern civil society. Once kinship relations no longer determine individuals' occupation and relation to rule, family members must look outside the household and independently enter the economy to earn a livelihood that will allow them to support their household and participate in politics. It is uncertain, however, whether the market will provide the opportunities on which individuals must now depend to sustain themselves and their families. The "invisible hand" of the market provides no guarantee that other commodity owners will sufficiently need what any individual has to offer in exchange to furnish enough income to prosper. Public intervention to provide guaranteed jobs at fair wages, equivalent support for the disabled and retired, and employee empowerment may alleviate much of the insecurity that the "children of civil society" confront in the social necessity of earning a living in the market. Nonetheless, the welfare of the emancipated family presents a challenge of its own, since the conditions of gaining a livelihood in the economy are not in any automatic harmony with the fulfillment of family rights and duties.

The market offers a variety of fundamental ways of earning a living. Individuals can provide for themselves and their families by becoming entrepreneurs, if they have access to enough capital or credit to do business and live off profits and dividends. Alternately, those who own sufficient rentable property can earn a living off rent. Finally, those who have neither enough capital or rentable property to make do with profits, dividends, or rent, can seek a livelihood by working for others as employees. Further, individuals can participate in more than one type of earning if they have enough resources to do so. It bears repeating, however, that the nature of competition fosters a situation where the vast majority of economic agents must earn a living as employees. To stay in business, enterprises must grow and accumulate capital to have sufficient funds to invest in more efficient production and marketing infrastructures, develop new products and services, and have expanding access to credit. This leads to both an expansion and concentration of capital in enterprises that must employ multiple workers to sustain their growing operations.[114] In every developed nation with market interdependence, the results are the same: employees far outnumber entrepreneurs and landlords, and ever larger enterprises dominate the economy.

We should not forget that the idea that everyone can be a viable entrepreneur is a fantasy that conflicts with the dynamic of competition that market activity unleashes. So too is the oft repeated idea that small businesses are the anchor of economic growth and employment. Both of these notions are refuted by the concentration and consolidation of enterprises that competition continually engenders. As we have seen, recent government figures state that the United States has about thirty million small businesses employing less than 500 individuals. Of these, twenty four million or more than eighty per cent employ no one.[115] Instead, these alleged "small businesses" are actually independent contract employees, so-called "contingent" workers, many in the expanding "gig" economy, who provide goods and services on a piecework basis, with net earnings on average less than a fair minimum wage.

If one includes these small "entrepreneurs" among employees, the ranks of employees among breadwinners in the United States, amount to well over 95%. Consequently, the problem of resolving family welfare with the conditions of earning a living primarily revolves around the relation of employers and employees.

Markets give both employers and employees the formal freedom to come to agreements that meet their respective needs. This formal freedom, however, operates under the pressure of what competition requires for maintaining economic viability. Employers may want to adjust work schedules to give employees time to cope with family emergencies and pregnancies, as well as care for children, spouses, and elders. If doing so involves extra expenses, such as paid leave, those employers will be at a competitive disadvantage in face of others who ignore these accommodations. Competition will then foster working conditions that confront employees with the problematic choice of keeping a job at odds with fulfilling family duties or giving up work to care for a family whose economic sustenance depends upon employment.

Moreover, family members may find child- and elder-care expenses so steep that taking an available job becomes a self-defeating prospect. Wages may be so comparatively low that employment provides too little income to cover the costs of leaving children and elders under the paid care of others. Competition is indifferent to these problems so long as enterprises can find employees who accept employment at odds with family welfare and bear the consequences for their households. These may involve putting off having children or having fewer than one may desire. The result may be a general decline in population such as currently jeopardizes the future well-being of nations such as Japan and Italy, where diminishing birth rates are making the number of retirees dangerously outstrip the number of breadwinners. This problem will reach epic proportions when China reaps the consequences of its one-child policy and faces the challenge of supporting the world's largest population of retirees with a precipitously diminished workforce.[116]

Tensions like those between family involvement and economic engagement apply to participation in politics. Family responsibilities can very easily hinder a citizen's ability to assist political campaigns or to run for office. How can citizens take time for politics if household duties need attention and enough funds are not available to hire others to attend to family members in need of care? This problem applies to supporting political campaigns and social movements as well as to running for political office and for leadership positions in political parties and social activist organizations. Whoever must contend with family responsibilities will have a harder time marshalling the time and resources to engage in public life as an active member of civil society and the body politic.

If we leave the market to its own devices and government neglects taking measures to accommodate our family involvement with our public engagements, free enterprise will threaten household wellbeing and our other freedoms in civil society and the state. Those who have spouses, children, or elders and must contribute to their welfare will suffer a disadvantage in exercising their social and political freedoms.

This is especially true of women, who disproportionately shoulder the burdens of childcare and eldercare, as well as of general household affairs. In the United States, more than 83% of single parents are women, as are nearly three quarters of those who care for family elders.[117] Consequently, the economic and political prospects of women suffer, even if they receive equal pay for equal work and protection against workplace sexual harassment and gender discrimination. Women cannot advance equally in work and political life if they must take time off for childbirth, childcare, and elder care without receiving adequate paid compensation (including pension adjustments) and guarantees of resuming their economic and political positions with no loss of seniority and associated benefits. The failure to provide these compensations and career guarantees is a key reason for why women still lag in pay, pension benefits, and positions of economic and political leadership despite fifty years of equal pay for equal work legislation and legal reforms combatting gender discrimination.

The persistence of childhood poverty and the impoverishment of single-parent households is also in large part due to a failure to accommodate family responsibilities with the conditions of work and political involvement. So long as childrearing takes a toll on the economic and political opportunity of parents, children will grow up in families with comparatively less wealth than families with fewer or no dependents. The disadvantage will tend to be greatest in single parent households, since they will have only one breadwinner to contend with all the added expenses and career impediments imposed by childcare responsibilities. So long as women remain disproportionately head of single parent households, they will disproportionately suffer the impoverishment such families undergo.

One of our greatest shames as a nation is our toleration of a degree of childhood poverty and family neglect that is unequaled among developed nations. It is high time that we consider the scope of our negligence and address how we can remedy our contempt for the true value of the family.

Social Rights and Family Freedom

To understand the full depth of the difficulties facing families in our insufficiently civil society, we must consider how the tensions between our roles as family members, economic agents, and citizens impair our fundamental social rights. Every family responsibility that can hamper economic and political opportunity poses specific challenges to fulfilling these crucial entitlements to healthcare, nourishment, clothes, decent housing, education, and legal representation.

Individuals who support spouses, children, and other relatives must provide for the health, food, clothing, housing, education, and legal expenses of not just themselves, but also their dependents. Guaranteed employment at a fair wage as well as equivalent disability and retirement benefits may secure individual security. These foundations of economic independence, however, do not suffice to cover the extra costs of dependents, even with the addition of mandatory collective bargaining and employee seats on corporate boards. So long as a fair minimum wage and negotiated incomes apply to wage earners individually, other measures are necessary to meet the added expenses of family responsibilities.

The most crushing family expenses commonly consist of medical expenses, which are the number one source of personal bankruptcies in the United States.[118] A single payer national health insurance can largely alleviate these costs, provided it covers all physical, dental, and mental health care with no copays or deductibles. So long as this coverage extends to every individual, it will relieve family members of funding the necessary health care expenses of their dependents. What a national health insurance program will not eliminate are the time and effort that individuals must expend to take children, spouses, and elder relatives to health care providers, as well as to fill prescriptions and provide whatever lay homecare is required. These tasks can conflict with work and political involvement and impose hardships on patients and family caregivers alike if no adjustments are made.

Enforcing the right to nourishment and clothing confronts family members with a twofold challenge. On the one hand, each family income provider must bear the additional expense of feeding and clothing dependents, both to protect their health and to give them a basic respectability that does not disadvantage them in their social interactions.

When spouses have no other dependents and enjoy guaranteed jobs at fair wages or comparable disability and retirement benefits, they incur no such expenditure. When, however, adult providers have dependents, they bear extra food and clothing expenses, which individuals without such family responsibilities can escape. On the other hand, when individuals have family dependents to feed and clothe, they must devote time to shop for their dependents' food and clothing, as well as spend extra time in food preparation. These chores can conflict with work and political involvement unless the latter are adjusted to accommodate these family responsibilities.

Family burdens also impinge upon securing decent housing and its effect upon economic and political opportunity. Family members are likely to incur more housing expenses the more dependents they have. To accommodate spouses and children, income providers must pay for the added cost of larger apartments and houses. These costs involve not just larger rent and mortgage payments, but larger utility, repair, and upkeep bills, as well as greater furnishing expenditures. In addition, income providers may have to spend more time on household chores in function of larger living quarters and more dependents. Once again, these additional tasks can weigh upon work schedules and diminish opportunities for career advancement and political involvement.

Fulfilling the right to education also has its added challenges when individuals belong to families with more dependents. Costs, of course, multiply when children attend private schools at any level. Current average annual tuition at private elementary and secondary schools in the United States amounts to $10,413,[119] which is unaffordable for many families, especially single parent households. The public option is not without family expenditures, even when the educational environment is satisfactory. Although United States' public schools are tuition free, parents must meet extra costs for school supplies, gym uniforms and equipment, and certain fees, such as rentals for school music ensemble instruments.

Higher education, whether at public or private institutions, presents formidable costs for tuition, student fees, books, and room and board. Although post-secondary technical schools may be cheaper than liberal arts colleges, they still have significant tuition and educational supply charges, not to mention living expenses for full time students. The more dependents parents have who are doing post-secondary studies, the more education costs weigh upon family budgets. This difficulty is reflected in the mushrooming of student debt, which now has become the largest form of personal debt in the United States.[120] The larger the family, the more likely and the more will students be forced to borrow to fund their higher education, other things being equal.

Money is not the only cost higher education imposes upon family members. The more children parents have, the more time must parents spend attending school conferences and events, all of which may impact upon work and political engagements. These commitments are most important during elementary and secondary school, and if parents cannot find the time and afford to be fully engaged in the education of their children, the latter will suffer. Without accommodating adjustments, parents face a choice between neglecting their part in the education of their children and jeopardizing their careers.

Finally, the last mainstay against the deprivation of rights becomes a special challenge for families. No right is secure if individuals cannot obtain legal representation to defend their freedoms. To defend family welfare and right, access to adequate legal care is imperative for the civil and criminal cases that involve spouses, children, and other dependent relatives. Legal expenses can strain individual budgets, but when the legal protection of spouses, children, and other relatives is at stake, the costs can far outstrip family resources. Although the U.S. Constitution guarantees legal representation in criminal cases, there is no guarantee of legal representation for civil cases, which address many crucial family issues. The widespread difficulty of affording civil legal care is reflected in how more than 85% of all participants in civil cases in the United States go to court with no legal representation.[121] Moreover, family members may have to spend significant amounts of time tending to the legal affairs of dependents, be it in meetings with lawyers, court proceedings, or visits to penal institutions. All these expenditures of money and time can easily conflict with the demands of work and politics and put in jeopardy the legal protection of family members.

Adjusting Work to Accommodate Family Right

Employment is the basis of livelihood of the overwhelming majority of breadwinners in a civil society upholding market freedom. Consequently, a key remedy to resolving the tension between household and economic right lies in adjusting the conditions of employment to balance work and family.

These adjustments require legal mandate and enforcement. This is because any voluntary or local initiatives will invite economic ruin when competing enterprises keep their costs of business lower by refraining from making these accommodations. If a municipality enacts legislation to impose family friendly adjustments that cut into the profit margins of enterprises, business may simply relocate to other localities where they can be more competitive. Statewide legislation may be more viable, since it governs all localities within state boundaries, but even state regulations may be ineffective if companies shift business to states with less costly standards in order to remain viable. National legislation and enforcement has far greater resilience, since it presides over the entire nation. Still, a nation must contend with the global market and the international pressures on businesses to move their operations to regions where wage, price, and regulatory conditions favor higher profit margins. International treaties that extend the reach of family friendly work regulations can reduce these pressures, as can the power of any sovereign nation to regulate its foreign trade with tariffs and import quotas. Moreover, the larger the economy and the more powerful the military of a nation, the easier will it be able to resist the pressures of international competition while making domestic business family friendly.

No nation can rival the advantages that the United States possesses as human history's largest economy and most militarily powerful country. We are in the strongest position to use our domestic market to stand up to international economic influence, to take advantage of our geopolitical position and military and scientific prowess to avoid foreign domination, and to negotiate international agreements that secure our freedoms and those of humanity in general. We can enact the legal framework enabling our enterprises to respect household, social, and political rights without forsaking economic viability. We can save the souls of our entrepreneurs and make it possible for them to do the right thing and remain competitive. Here are basic policies that can successfully balance work and family.

We all know that the schedule of work can conflict with the demands of caring for children, spouses, and family elders. These care demands involve time and resources to address their health needs, the provision of food and clothing, the upkeep of adequate housing, the facilitation of their education, and legal defense.

Time is of the essence and the United States is notoriously lax in permitting employers to avoid providing paid leave for family emergencies, for childbirth and infant care, for school meetings and events, for attending to family legal affairs, and for family vacations. Other nations have recognized that paid leave for these commitments is crucial to uphold family welfare without economic deprivation. By contrast, the United States has offered either no allowance for taking off from work to address family needs or has limited leave to unpaid breaks, putting family finances in peril. Moreover, unlike most other developed nations, the United States has not prohibited employers from requiring employees to work overtime. This creates havoc with family life, undermines the sleep and general health of workers, and increases the frequency of workplace accidents, which takes an additional toll on family welfare. Today, employees in the United States work longer hours than in any other developed nation and have no universal guarantees of paid leave or paid vacations.

We can change this.

Paid Family Emergency Leave

First, we need federal legislation requiring all employers, whether private or public, to give their employees paid leave for illness and family emergencies. These emergencies include instances requiring an employee's leave from work to assist family members in securing medical care, in managing their legal affairs, in dealing with housing emergencies, and in dealing with their education. Such paid leave should apply to part time and contract employees as well as full-time employees, since all face the same challenge in balancing work and family. Without leave, they must keep working and neglect their family or risk termination by taking off without authorization. Without *paid* leave, they risk financial loss that can jeopardize their family welfare. Although the Family and Medical Leave Act of 1993 provided unpaid leave to United States workers, many cannot take advantage of it because they cannot afford to forego the income they would lose. This lost income varies according to wage levels and hours employed. Since the amount of paid leave is a replacement income, it should vary according to employee compensation. The need for replacement income is, after all, invariably common to part-time, contingent, and full-time employees alike.

Moreover, in every case, paid family emergency leave should not affect the seniority or promotion of employees. Otherwise, the recipients suffer career handicaps that undercut their equal economic opportunity, as well as those of their family dependents.

When possible, employees should give employers reasonable notice so that others can fill in to do the work. So long as paid emergency leave is mandatory for all employers, its added expense becomes a general cost of doing business to which competition can adjust. Nonetheless, the burden of paid emergency leave can weigh very differently on enterprises depending upon both how much of their labor force is affected and how the cost influences their financial health. To ease any economic difficulties that may result, a common paid leave insurance fund can spread the cost among all enterprises. The support of this insurance fund can eliminate most of the incentive for enterprises to avoid hiring individuals with family dependents. Then, mandatory paid emergency family leave can be absorbed in the general costs of production with minimal impact upon the career opportunities of individuals, commodity prices, or profits.

Paid Parental Leave

Equally crucial to balancing work and family is the legal enactment of paid parental leave for all employees. If parents are to bring children into the world and give them the infant care they need without jeopardizing family well-being, paid leave should cover the period of childbirth and early infancy. Otherwise parents cannot navigate the challenges of childbirth without compromising their economic, as well as political, prospects.

Every nation except the United States, Surinam, Papua New Guinea, and several Pacific Ocean island countries has made paid parental leave mandatory.[122] Among developed nations, we remain the great exception, compounding our singular failure to cover all the costs of prenatal care, delivery, and post-natal care. A proper single payer health insurance system with no copays or deductibles can overcome the latter failure, but we must add paid parental leave to ensure that families can sustain their economic welfare while bringing the newborn into the world.

The beneficiaries of paid parental leave, like those of any family friendly work adjustment, should suffer no negative repercussions to their seniority or promotion. Only then will parents and women in particular be able to engage in childbirth without hampering their economic and political opportunities. Although the woman who undergoes pregnancy and childbirth will most directly warrant paid leave at least during and immediately after delivery, it is up to co-determining parents to decide how to manage the shared responsibilities of infant care. Accordingly, paid parental leave should extend to parents, whatever their gender, who do not give birth but will be caring for their newborn children. This applies to parents who adopt young children for whose care time off from work is initially important. Either partner should be entitled to take paid parental leave for its entire duration or alternate as desired.

Affluent nations differ in how long they guarantee paid parental leave. The United States, being the richest nation in human history, should lead in facilitating parental care for its newest additions. Among the more family-friendly nations are Bulgaria and Sweden. Bulgaria offers 58 weeks of maternity leave at 90% of pay and 52 weeks of parental leave at 90% of pay.[123] Sweden offers twelve weeks of maternity leave at 80% of pay and fifty-six total weeks of parental leave at up to 80% pay.[124] Although the burdens of childbirth and breastfeeding fall directly on mothers, general infant care can quickly become a challenge for other parents, for whom paid leave can be imperative, especially if a mother wants to enjoy equal opportunity to return to work or political activity. Consequently, it makes sense to have a general allowance for parental leave that any parent can utilize. Moreover, since only full replacement income removes all economic hardship, paid parental leave should be equal the pay of whomever takes off from work. A full year of 100% paid parental leave is therefore a reasonable goal for a country that disposes of history's greatest national wealth.

Since paid parental leave will usually be significantly longer than paid emergency family leave, employers can here face far greater difficulty in finding and paying for replacements. Without any relief, enterprises will have good reason to avoid hiring employees who are likely to have children, especially when measures balancing work and family make it more feasible for families to have as many children as they desire. To remove the disincentive to employ people planning to rear children, we need to provide a public insurance policy that will compensate enterprises for parental leave expenses, as well as for paid family emergency leave. If all employers are required to pay into such a public family leave insurance fund, the costs can be equitably distributed among enterprises and minimize the impact on prices and profits.

On that basis, all enterprises will benefit from the increased demand generated by the additional income that parents on leave receive. Enterprises will also likely enjoy far less employee turnover, with all its associated costs. Moreover, more adults will be able to participate in the labor force without detriment to their career advancement, contributing to increased growth in the production of wealth in aggregate and per capita, as well as to greater purchasing power.

Furthermore, we all will eventually reap the rewards of a new generation of human capital whose upbringing begins on the best possible footing. Studies have confirmed that paid parental leave increases breastfeeding, decreases low birth weight, and reduces infant mortality.[125] Our failure to provide paid parental leave is one reason why, as of 2014, the United States ranks 56th in the world in infant mortality rates.[126] Paid parental leave also contributes to strengthening the psychological bonds that enhance child development and strengthen the mental health of parents. Not surprisingly, the opportunity to receive replacement income and return to work has been associated with a significant reduction in depression among mothers in particular.[127]

Balancing the Schedule of Work with Family: The Case for Limiting the Working Day and Working Week, Prohibiting Mandatory Overtime, and Requiring Paid Vacations

Paid emergency family leave and paid parental leave tackle particular circumstances that challenge the balance between employment and family welfare. They do not remedy perennial problems with which the general work schedule afflicts family members.

The length and schedule of work always affects the health of employees, workplace safety, and the opportunity of individuals to enjoy their family life and to participate in self-government. The history of capitalism vividly displays how unconstrained competition can drive enterprises to extract hazardously long and uninterrupted workdays that endanger the life and family welfare of employees. For several centuries, workers have fought to retrieve a humane part of their time from the daily grind of work. The struggle to limit the working day to eight hours and to limit the working week to forty hours came to an early head in the nineteenth century with the Haymarket rally and bombing in Chicago, which made May Day an annual international workers holiday. Yet, in the United States, it was not until the 1938 Fair Labor Standards Act when legislation recognized forty hours to be the "normal" duration of the working week, with overtime pay required for additional hours for some, but not all, categories of employees. This measure has not kept in check the duration of work for neither the Fair Labor Standards Act nor any subsequent federal legislation restricts the working week to any number of hours, nor provides employees with any guarantee of paid holidays.

Although we tend to think of the eight hour workday and the forty hour workweek as the norm, United States workers are working more hours than those of any developed nation, increasingly laboring overtime, as well as taking on second or third jobs. Recent statistics confirm that the overwhelming majority of Americans work more than forty hours per week.[128] As the ILO reports, "Americans work 137 more hours per year than Japanese workers, 260 more hours per year than British workers, and 499 more hours per year than French workers."[129]

Whereas all the nations of the European Union guarantee four weeks of paid vacation to their workers and prohibit mandatory overtime, the United States mandates no paid vacations and allows employers to require employees to accept overtime assignments and "comp time" arrangements, where extended hours are worked without overtime payments in exchange for shorter hours on other days. Moreover, the Fair Labor Standards Act exempts many workers from overtime pay, including outside sales personnel, farm laborers, domestic live-in workers, and certain transportation workers. In addition, many employers avoid paying overtime by classifying employees as "independent contractors."

Lengthy overtime hours take a toll on the health of employees, lessening sleep and increasing stress, which accentuates many of the physical problems that undermine the quality of life and longevity of United States workers. In addition, the longer the working day, the higher the rate of workplace accidents. The threat to health and safety that overtime represents is equally a threat to family well-being. Not only does the detrimental impact upon the health of employees jeopardize the livelihood they provide for their families, but it also diminishes their ability to care for spouses, children, and other dependents.

Lastly, the extension of work hours conflicts with the very basic need to spend time with family members. A Sabbath may set one day of the week free from work, but a two-day weekend and a month paid vacation offer employees a much better chance to enjoy and contribute to their family life. Further, the eight-hour workday and forty-hour workweek need hardly be set in stone, especially with increases in productivity and automation.[130]

The practice of mandatory overtime is particularly disruptive to family involvement. We allow our employers to lengthen the working day with little notice and threaten employees with dismissal if they refuse the overtime. Mandatory overtime plays havoc with any plans employees may have to eat dinner and spend evenings with their family. This is particularly destructive to the family welfare of single parents, who have the greatest difficulty arranging for the care of their dependents when employers spring overtime upon them.

There is a simple remedy that most other developed nations have adopted: the strict prohibition of mandatory overtime. We should follow suit and require all employers to offer overtime, with increased pay, only as a voluntary option for employees, no matter what their category. Employees should have the right to refuse overtime with no negative repercussions to their pay or career advancement.

Of course, the optional character of voluntary overtime is largely formal when employees earn poverty wages, cannot collectively bargain, and find the costs of health care, food, clothing, housing, education, and legal representation overwhelming. Under these conditions, the freedom to refuse overtime gives way to the necessity of working longer hours to meet basic social needs. If, however, everyone benefits from guaranteed jobs at fair wages with employee empowerment, as well as from the enforcement of our other fundamental social rights, voluntary overtime becomes a much more authentic choice.

Limitations upon the working day and working week are crucial to upholding our family and political freedoms, but they fail to provide the sufficiently uninterrupted time on which life, liberty, and the pursuit of happiness also depend. A mandatory paid vacation serves our freedom in multiple ways. The respite from work offers relief from the stress that takes a physical and psychological toll. A decent paid vacation offers families a chance to spend uninterrupted time together, which can uniquely strengthen household bonds and welfare. It allows families to take advantage of school holidays, instead of facing added childcare challenges. Paid vacations also permit individuals to have special time to devote to social and political involvements that cannot be so fully attended to when work calls.

The increase of part time jobs and of "contingent", "contract", "zero-hour", "gig" economy employment may obscure the need for paid vacations, but the same benefits apply to part-timers and those who supply goods and services on a piece-work basis. They too deserve a comparable paid vacation. Since what needs replacement is the income lost in taking off from work, their paid vacations deserve support with whatever equals their ordinary earnings over a comparable period.

Most other developed nations have seen fit to assure every employee at least one month of paid vacation annually. The United States is the only advanced economy that fails to guarantee paid vacations or holidays for its workers.[131] U.S. private sector employees enjoy on average merely fifteen days of paid vacation and holidays, whereas one quarter of U.S. workers have no paid vacation whatsoever.[132]

Although one might worry that a one month paid vacation will drive up labor costs by one twelfth and diminish productivity by a comparable amount, the benefits more than compensate for any possible drawbacks. If a one month paid vacation becomes a universal requirement of all employers, whether private or public, none will suffer any competitive disadvantage in complying with this measure. All will likely enjoy greater employee retention and a more healthy, energized, and satisfied work force. Moreover, since labor costs are only a fraction of costs of production, there is no need for prices to rise as much as the period of work decreases. Paid vacations may well increase the productivity of employees and more than compensate for the shortened work year. Moreover, paid vacations will contribute to the wellbeing of our families and reduce the costs of the household dysfunction to which family-unfriendly work schedules contribute.

For all these reasons, we, the nation with the largest economy and most productive work force in human history, have no excuse for not matching the rest of the developed world by guaranteeing all American employees at least a month's paid vacation every year.

The Need for Free Public Child and Elder Care

The benefits of paid family emergency leave, paid parental leave, paid vacations, and the prohibition of mandatory overtime are life changing, but they still are not enough to overcome the challenges that family members face in providing childcare and elder care for their dependents. As more parents work and more single parent households proliferate, the need for child and elder care has become more pressing. For many, however, the costs of childcare and of eldercare are prohibitive. Increasingly, breadwinners confront a situation where they cannot earn enough to pay for the care of children and elders during the working day, but where giving up work to tend for dependents forfeits the income needed to support themselves and their families.

The need for childcare is ordinarily a more long-lasting challenge. School may diminish the need for childcare, but only for a limited time. The pre-school period may last from birth until five or six years old, but unless public schools extend free pre-school care to younger ages, parents must deal with caring for their youngest children round the clock. Even when children attend school, parents must cover any interval between the end of school and the end of work. Moreover, when school is in recess, parents must contend with finding childcare to fill the gap. Consequently, the need for childcare can extend for every child from birth through early adolescence, until children become independent enough to be on their own.

By contrast, the need for elder care is usually more short-lived, but more intense. As our population ages, more and more families face a predicament where elders need round the clock care during their final years. This becomes a 24/7 responsibility that imposes forbidding expenditures of time and money that weigh heavily upon all other family, career, and political involvements. The problem remains daunting even if elders receive a fair retirement or disability replacement income that is equivalent to the fair minimum wage. When elders require round the clock assistance, hiring caretakers at a fair wage will amount to paying for three eight-hour shifts. The resulting expense will be at least three times the retirement or disability income that an elder receives. Family breadwinners then face a daunting Hobson's choice. If they take on caretaking responsibilities themselves, they must largely abandon career, politics, and other household duties to devote themselves to the continual assistance of dependent elders, putting the welfare of the entire family at risk. Alternately, if they remain at work and involved in other family and political affairs, they must assume a financial burden equivalent to hiring two eight hour shift employees (assuming that the elder's replacement income covers one eight hour shift). Some elders may have enough savings to cover some or all of this cost, but to do so, the average individual must keep in reserve two years of wages for every year of elder care. In a land with the greatest wealth and income inequality of any developed nation, all too many families are unable to bear the cost of needed elder care.

Currently, full time childcare in the United States costs on average $180 per week, which amounts to 16% of the 2016 median household income of $57,827.[133] The expense for just one child can strain family budgets, especially in single parent households. When two or more children need care, many more families face difficulty.

The costs of elder care are far greater. In the United States today, weekday adult day care comes to $17,750 annually, whereas weekday home elder care amounts to $40,000 annually. Assisted living costs on average $45,000 per year, whereas skilled nursing home care comes to $82,855 per year.[134]

These expenditures go beyond the means of all too many United States residents and guaranteed jobs at fair wages with employee empowerment are not enough to make up the difference. If we are to ensure that breadwinners can pursue their careers and political involvements without neglecting their family affairs, public action is necessary to defray the costs of both childcare and eldercare.

When the United States committed itself to provide public education to all its people, it did not use means tests to subsidize the school expenses of the poor while letting the rest pay their way. Instead of stigmatizing the disadvantaged by dividing the nation into haves and have nots, we aspired to treat public education as a fundamental right to which all were entitled, irrespective of their private wealth.

We should follow the same approach to childcare and eldercare and provide a public system with strictly regulated standards, for which we levy no fees. In doing so, we properly acknowledge that all family providers have a right to the resources to care for their children and elders and need not jeopardize their other freedoms in return. We will hardly be the first nation to recognize this fundamental family right. France has already established a public childcare system and it is high time that we develop public childcare and eldercare programs that parallel what our public school system should achieve in securing the right to education. In one key respect, however, we must depart from the practice of our public school system. If we are to finance public childcare and eldercare equitably, we must not base funding on local property values, which privilege richer neighborhoods and under-privilege their poorer counterparts. Instead, we should evenly allocate public support so that we meet all care needs adequately, irrespective of the wealth of different neighborhoods.

The Need for Child Allowances

The expenses of childcare and eldercare are only part of the extra burden that breadwinners must shoulder if they are to provide for their family members. Household providers must feed, clothe, house, and entertain each dependent and neither guaranteed jobs at fair wages, employee empowerment, single payer health insurance, or public childcare and eldercare cover the costs of these additional provisions.

The more dependents a breadwinner has, the more resources he or she will need to nourish, shelter, and divert them. Since a fair minimum wage and collectively negotiated pay and benefits abstract from the number of dependents an employee has, family welfare hinges upon some allowance for the added expenditures for children and other dependents who do not earn a full income of their own or do not receive a full replacement income due to disability or retirement. If retirees and the disabled receive benefits equivalent to a fair minimum wage, this due replacement income should suffice to cover their living expenses. Accordingly, allowance for dependent expenditures addresses primarily the costs of rearing children.

Obviously, the more family members there are, the more food and drink gets consumed, the more clothing is worn, the more furnishings are needed, and the larger the residence must be, which entails not only higher rent or mortgage payments, but higher utility bills and greater maintenance costs. Further, if family life is to partake of culture, high and low, and diversions that enrich the home, we must pay for these adornments of life, which will be more costly the more family members are involved. Moreover, the natural processes of growth and maturation will accentuate the expense, as clothes, furnishings, and entertainments will rapidly be outgrown and discarded.

The amount of money paid by families for raising children in the United States varies according to their household income, family size, and region. The most recent data compiled by the United States Department of Agriculture in its "Consumer Expenditures Survey" (also called "The Cost of Raising a Child Report)[135] shows that a middle-income ($59,200-$107,400), two-child, married couple family spends $12,980 per child each year. Housing accounts for the largest share of child raising costs, amounting to 29% of the total. Food comes second, at 18%, with childcare and education expenses (not including higher education) following in third place. Expenses increase as children grow, with expenditures peaking at $900 more for teenagers. On the other hand, the more children a family has, the less need be spent per child, since rooms can be shared, clothing and toys can be passed down, and food can be purchased at cheaper bulk rates. Child rearing expenses are lower in rural areas than in urban areas, with costs ascending from the urban Midwest to the urban South to the Urban West and finally reaching a peak in the urban Northeast, where families pay a premium of 27%, due primarily to higher costs for housing and childcare and education.

If we implement free public childcare and sufficiently support our public schools so that no family need resort to private education at the elementary or secondary level, child rearing costs can, on average, be reduced by 16%. The child rearing expenses of a "middle-class", two child, two parent family, can be taken as a benchmark of what every American family should be able to provide. Subtracting 16% from the average total of $12,980 per child per year, we have an average child rearing expense of $10,903, or $909 per month.

How can we guarantee that every family has the resources to raise its children at a socially equitable level? Tax deductions for dependents will do relatively little for lower income groups, who pay smaller income taxes, while favoring the rich, whose tax breaks will be the largest. To the extent that income inequalities reflect historical racial and gender inequities, the unequal results of tax deductions will only exacerbate these inequities. Allowances that are need based will openly divide our society into haves and have-nots, stigmatize the disadvantaged, and foster political resentment on the part of those who receive no allowances.

A better solution is to take the social rights approach and recognize child allowances as a fundamental anchor of family welfare and social and political freedom. Every breadwinner with children should benefit from this allowance so that no family lacks enough resources to feed, clothe, shelter, and acculturate its children. Then, we can guarantee all our children the material foundation of an upbringing enabling them to take full advantage of the opportunities that should await autonomous individuals upon maturity. Anything less is a crime against our families and our future.

Today there are about seventy-four million children in the United States.[136] If every family receives approximately $900 per month per child, the total cost comes to $799,200,000,000. From this total can be subtracted all the family support welfare expenses that currently aid disadvantaged families, as well as all tax credits for child dependents. The expense of equitable child rearing is easily affordable for an economy the size of our own. The proof will become evident when we address how we can fairly fund our complete social rights agenda.

5. Enforcing the Right to Decent Housing

The Right to Decent Housing

Whether one wanders as a nomad or lives rooted in one place, some abode is necessary to exercise any of one's freedoms. Although one may carry with one the inalienable property of one's body, together with the clothing one wears and whatever can be stuffed in it, homelessness puts in jeopardy the possession and use of all one's property. Without a dwelling to shelter one's mind and body from the elements, as well as to store and protect one's food, clothes, tools, documents, and other possessions, one can hardly sustain and exercise one's property rights, let alone the other rights that depend on property. Without a home within which individuals can carry on conjugal and parental activities shielded from the intrusions of the world, the family's joint private domain lacks a space in which to operate. With no lodging in which property and family can be secure, individuals face huge disadvantages in participating in the economy or any other social dealings. When work ends they have no place to rest and conduct their private affairs, whereas while work proceeds they must worry about their property and family. Nor can citizens properly engage in self-government if they lack a home with which to maintain their domestic and social life. Homelessness puts strains upon family and livelihood that impede political involvement, leaving citizens without the basic anchor of domestic and economic independence from which they can share in self-government. On every front, homelessness robs individuals of the secure footing on which all their freedoms depend.

Access to housing, however, is not enough for freedom if that housing is too small, unhealthy, or unequipped to enable its inhabitants to exercise their equal opportunities in the family, society, and the state. We have a right not just to housing, but also to *decent* housing in the specific sense of having dwellings fit for wielding our freedoms on a par with others. In today's world, decent housing should be spacious enough to meet family needs. It should be sufficiently heated and air-conditioned to meet climactic conditions. It should be equipped with the plumbing, electricity, and adequate kitchen and laundry facilities together with the utilities they depend upon. It should be accessible to and useable by the disabled. In addition, decent housing should have adequate furnishings, including the cybernetic devices and broadband connection on which so much social and political activity now depends.

Access to decent housing is a fundamental social right because on it depend family welfare, economic well-being, and political engagement. The Universal Declaration of Human Rights, which the United States ratified in 1948, recognizes this right in Article 25. It declares, "Everyone has the right to a standard of living adequate for the health and well-being of himself and his family, including food, clothing, housing and medical care and necessary social service." Nonetheless, the right to decent housing is still not enshrined in the Constitution of the United States, any more than is the right to earn a fair living, the right to healthcare, or the right to balance work and family.[137] One only has to walk the streets of any city in this, the richest nation in human history, to encounter the shameful spectacle of homelessness, giving its daily tawdry witness to our Constitution's neglect.[138]

During 2017, more than 1.5 million Americans experienced the trauma of homelessness, reaching levels not seen since the Great Depression.[139] According to the latest Department of Housing and Urban

Development's "Annual Homeless Assessment Report" (December 2017), every night in the United States more than half a million people straggle into homeless shelters or sleep out on our streets, under bridges, in cars, or on neglected scraps of land.[140] Many more inhabit substandard housing that impairs their health and welfare,[141] while they and further millions find housing costs too high to meet their other basic needs. With jobs insecure, wages stagnating, mortgage balances outpacing home values, and rents rising faster than income and inflation, more and more Americans face the specter of foreclosure or eviction. Among these, a disproportionate number are African American.[142] What should we do to halt deepening disadvantage and fulfill our fundamental social right to decent housing?

Housing in Civil Society

In a civil society, in which property rights are universally recognized, families are emancipated from hierarchies of gender and sexual orientation, and privileged birthright has been superseded by the self-seeking enterprise of market interdependence, housing has become a commodity. No longer can we simply camp out in virgin nature, scavenge the landscape for the materials to build shelter, and derive sustenance directly from the wild. Nor are homes and land subject to traditional restrictions that prohibit their sale and purchase. Instead, all inhabitable places and building materials are already under public or private ownership, making dwelling obtainable in the first instance only through market transaction. Whether a dwelling be a fixed apartment or house, or an itinerant houseboat or camper, it is accessible only by purchase or rent. In order for a member of civil society to obtain a dwelling, there must be a sufficient supply brought to market and that member must have wealth sufficient to pay for what its owner is willing to accept.

The owner of housing may be an individual, a family, a cooperative, a share issuing corporation, or a public authority, such as a municipality, a state, or the federal government. No matter who the owner may be, the housing can be on offer for sale or on loan for rent.

If it is for sale, the housing unit may be purchased with cash or credit, and if by credit, with a mortgage that charges a monthly interest over an extended period until the principal is repaid. Moreover, if the unit is an apartment or a free-standing house in a development, it may be sold as a cooperative, where the other cooperative members levy some control over the sale and common maintenance costs of units. Alternately, if the apartment or house is for rent, the rental charge may or may not include utility and maintenance expenses.

To have access to decent housing, individuals must be able to afford what the market has to offer. This depends on two factors: on the one hand, the price of housing, the interest rate of mortgages, or the level of rent, and, on the other hand, the available income, wealth, and/or access to credit of the purchaser or tenant.

The housing needs of individuals depend upon the size of their household and geographical preferences related to job opportunities, schooling, healthcare, and ties to friends and families. There is no guarantee that the housing market has available units meeting those needs, nor that any available units are affordable. Since affordability depends on both the financial resources of individuals and house prices, rent levels, and mortgage interest rates, any guarantee of decent housing must address both sides of the matter, as well as the supply of housing in general.

Today in the United States millions of Americans lack funds sufficient to obtain decent housing because they are jobless or earn poverty wages. Others who have jobs at a fair wage still cannot afford decent housing due to increases in house prices and rents that are outstripping income and inflation.[143] Many simply cannot buy homes or afford available rentals due to the burden of other expenses, such as those for healthcare, child and elder care, child rearing, education, and legal representation.

We can alleviate much of these difficulties by fulfilling the social rights agenda. A Federal Job Guarantee at fair wages with employee empowerment can eliminate unemployment and poverty wages. A single payer public healthcare insurance system with no copays or deductibles can remove the drain of medical expenses. A free public child and elder care system and child allowances can diminish the toll of dependent expenses and compensate for the added cost of larger dwellings. Measures to lessen the burden of educational and legal expenses can eliminate these as factors sapping the ability to pay for decent housing.

With all these measures in place, many will still not be able to exercise their right to decent housing due to mounting costs and insufficient supply. The challenge of guaranteeing decent housing revolves around more than income and wealth. It also concerns the availability of decent housing as well as the levels of prices, rents, and mortgage interest.

Housing Policy and the Fabric of Life in a Democracy

Public measures to ensure the supply and affordability of housing should not ignore the impact that the design of urban, suburban, and rural communities has upon the ability of individuals to exercise their household, social, and political freedoms. In the United States, cities, suburbs, and rural areas have developed in ways that accentuate poverty, reinforce racial disadvantage and residential segregation, diminish opportunities for family togetherness, reduce occasions for social and political community, and accelerate production and consumption of fossil fuels that endanger our environment.

Urban renewal policies have produced islands of huge apartment complexes, civic centers, and commercial malls, dividing our cities into single-use areas, where residential neighborhoods are divorced from business, industrial, and cultural districts. Despite the high density of urban settlement, our city planning has separated more and more housing from a vibrant, walkable cityscape in which shopping, schools, cultural venues, parks, and employment opportunities are nearby. The widespread gentrification of city neighborhoods has further geographically segregated our urban population by race and wealth, while intensifying the isolation of poorer districts from all the social amenities that relocate to the privileged quarters.

The growth of suburbs, where now most Americans live, has left our cities increasingly polarized between rich and poor, while proliferating a surrounding sprawl that magnifies the dislocation that former city dwellers leave behind. By following policies that favor low density, single use neighborhoods and disfavor walkability and public transportation, we have facilitated an explosion of suburban subdivisions with single family dwellings. This has created an environment whose inhabitants must use private automobiles to go anywhere, where parking lots far outnumber public spaces, where energy consumption is maximized, where contact between different social strata is minimized, where old and young rarely meet, and where busy commuting between home and work or school eats into the time for any other activities. Moreover, the low density of suburban development entails a less efficient, more expensive infrastructure due to longer utility connections and roads.

The even greater dispersion of rural homes accentuates these costs as a price for country living. Our rural settlement scatters households across the landscape, instead of concentrating them in hamlets, in which services, amenities, and employment could be much more easily in reach. Those unable to drive or too poor to maintain automobiles are stranded, with little opportunity to get to stores, schools, training, work, medical care, friends, religious institutions, or meetings of social and political groups. Meanwhile, the march of mechanization in agriculture and mining, the decline in rural manufacturing, and the lack of public investment in rural development has left the remaining small towns struggling for survival, with well paid jobs few and far between and housing costs rising faster than incomes and inflation.

In addressing the challenge of providing affordable decent housing to all, we can do more than make the available stock of housing widely accessible. Since we cannot fulfill the right to housing unless there is an adequate supply of homes, we, as democratic citizens, have an opportunity to mobilize private and public resources to create new housing that provides a more freedom-friendly, environmentally sound design for our communities. If we follow principles of intelligent and just habitat planning, we can fulfill the right to decent housing in ways that remedy the pitfalls of our past development. We can promote a healthy ecological balance, constructing an efficient infrastructure that reduces energy consumption. We can enhance existing cultural endowments and utilize technology and construction techniques that are contextually appropriate. We can provide accessible public spaces that are conducive to friendship, family togetherness, neighborhood community, and social and political gatherings. In sum, we can strive to guarantee decent housing by erecting and refurbishing communities whose design facilitates equal access to all the opportunities to which residents are entitled.[144]

Home Rental versus Home Ownership

In light of these considerations, should we promote apartment instead of single-family housing? Should we foster home ownership as opposed to rentals? These are separate questions since individuals can rent or own both apartments and single-family houses.

Home ownership, whether of apartments or single-family houses, is often touted as a superior option since homeowners acquire home equity, whereas renters having nothing to show for their years of rental payments. Home equity is supposedly a crucial anchor of economic security, providing capital and credit worthiness, especially for times when income is lacking.

Admittedly, for many Americans, personal wealth predominantly consists in home equity. This is least true for the most affluent, whose wealth resides in financial investments whose value far outstrips that of their multiple homes. Nonetheless, the value of home equity is rarely enough to provide enough dividends to make up for deficits in retirement or disability replacement income. This is especially true in a time of low interest rates. Moreover, for most homeowners in the United States, the route to home equity traverses years saving for a loan deposit followed by decades of mortgage payments and home maintenance expenditures. As the 2008 Great Recession demonstrated, the quest for home equity can turn into a financial trap where mortgage debt exceeds housing values. During that crisis nearly ten million residences were foreclosed and a decade later an additional four million United States homes remain financially underwater, with their market price sunk below their mortgage balance.[145] The worth of home equity as a foundation of economic welfare depends upon interest rates, inflation, income levels, retirement and disability benefits, and how much savings individuals can otherwise accumulate. The advantages of home ownership are questionable given the variability of all these factors and the economic independence provided by implementing the social rights agenda.

By contrast, rental housing escapes the financial perils of fluctuating home values and interest rates, each of which can make home equity more of a financial liability than a bonus. Nonetheless, rents can outstrip the income and savings of many, purging neighborhoods of the less affluent, compounding racial inequity and residential segregation, while leaving our streets haunted with the weary homeless.

Whether housing costs consist of payments towards home ownership or rent, their affordability depends on our preventing these payments from overwhelming the financial resources of individuals. Since the Great Recession of 2008, United States home ownership has declined, with more households turning to rentals, whose vacancy rates are nearing historic lows.[146] As home rental prices outpace incomes,[147] the fulfillment of our right to decent housing depends increasingly upon making rent affordable.

Rent Regulation

Public regulation of rents historically arose in many countries in response to housing shortages and skyrocketing costs brought on by the demobilization of armies after the two world wars, the destruction of housing stocks, and the diversion of funds from civilian to military investment.[148]

A so-called first generation of rent regulation was implemented in the United States and elsewhere that consisted in a rent control that froze rents at fixed levels, while establishing procedures for eviction that protected both tenants and landlords. This first generation rent control only had an effect so long as the level at which rents were frozen fell below that to which market competition drove rentals. Otherwise the level of rents would not reach the ceiling of rent control, leaving rent regulation devoid of any benefit.

On the other hand, rent control would defeat its own purpose if the level at which it froze rents was too low. The fixed ceiling has to provide landlords with sufficient revenues to be able to maintain adequately their properties, since otherwise apartments will cease to be decent living environments.[149] Moreover, rent control must be high enough to give landlords sufficient incentive to keep their properties for rent at the publicly established rate, instead of either demanding extra payments under the table or withdrawing them from the rental market,[150] reducing the stock of available rental housing. In those cases, the ceiling of rent control becomes a fiction, increasing rather than freezing the housing costs of renters.

Furthermore, if rent regulation is to serve its purpose of providing affordable decent housing, the procedures it imposes to govern evictions must sufficiently respect the interests of landlords as well as tenants. If landlords cannot evict tenants when they damage or destroy their property or when landlords need an apartment for their own personal use, landlords may be reluctant to put their units up for rent. The resulting shortage of rental units will likely drive up rents, once more defeating the aim of rent regulation.

History has confirmed that too meager fixed rents and too rigid eviction policies lead to widespread deterioration in the upkeep and condition of rental apartments and houses, the proliferation of black money payments that drive up the real cost of rent, and a decrease in rental units as many get transformed into condominiums for sale.

Rent control accentuates all these problems when it imposes a fixed ceiling on rents. Under such an unyielding rent regime, landlords cannot recoup rising expenses due to increases in property taxes, maintenance costs, and utility prices.

In response to these problems, a second generation of rent regulation has arisen that allows for a rent stabilization, where, instead of freezing rents, rent increases are permitted in line with the cost increases that landlords face. These publicly regulated rent increases make it feasible for landlords to maintain both the quality and the quantity of their properties. Tenants will be able to bear these rent increases if their earnings or replacement incomes are adjusted for inflation and productivity gains. The social rights policies of guaranteed jobs at fair wages and equivalent disability and retirement benefits are crucial for enabling incomes to match flexible rent stabilization.

Finally, second generation rent regulation has adjusted eviction procedures to permit tenants to be evicted when they damage apartments and when owners need their unit for personal use. These reforms provide added incentive to landlords to keep units for rent.

Together, these measures go a long way to enabling rent regulation to serve the end of fulfilling the fundamental social right of individuals to decent housing.

The question remains as to how rent stabilization levels should be determined. The right to *decent* housing demands that apartments and houses for rent meet basic standards for size and utilities, including adequate plumbing, electricity, heat and air-conditioning as needed, and broadband connection. The level of stabilized rent must reflect the costs of these provisions and the return that makes such rental property investment a viable business opportunity.

Currently, the situation of landlords and renters presents a stark challenge as well as great opportunity. On the one hand, the revenues of landlords are larger than ever before, with rental income reaching in 2017 an all-time high as a share of gross domestic product.[151] On the other hand, while levels of home ownership decline, the national rent vacancy rate is nearing an historic low, with rents rising faster than income or inflation.[152] According to the U. S. Department of Housing and Urban Development (HUD), "a family with one full-time worker earning the minimum wage cannot afford the local fair-market rent for a two-bedroom apartment anywhere in the United States."[153] Nationally, one must now earn $17.90 an hour to rent a basic one bedroom residence and $22.10 an hour to rent basic two-bedroom housing.[154] As a result, the median U.S. rental has risen to nearly 30% of income, which means that half of all American renters are spending at least 30% of their income on rent.[155] HUD considers families to be "cost burdened" and facing difficulty "affording necessities such as food, clothing, transportation, and medical care" if they "pay more than 30 percent of their income for housing".[156] When families spend more than 50 percent of their annual incomes on housing they are "severely burdened" and HUD reports that this is the plight of 12 million U.S. households.[157]

Although the percentage of all renter households that are rent burdened and severely rent burdened has increased, the increase has been greatest among African-American renter households and among renter households headed by seniors. In 2015, 34% of white renter households were rent burdened, compared with 46% of African-American renter households and 50% of renter households headed by seniors.[158] The share of African-American households suffering severe rent burdens compared to those of White households grew by 66% between 2001 and 2015, while a fifth of senior headed households became severely rent burdened.[159] These disproportionate developments have compounded racial disadvantage and the hardship of families depending on fixed retirement benefits.

To evaluate rent burdens properly, we must consider not just the share of income taken up by housing costs, but the amount of income left over to spend on all other living expenses. Whatever proportion of income families spend on housing, more affluent households will always have more funds left over to meet their other expenses. The burden of residential costs thus depends not simply on their share in family expenses, but on the residual income remaining after we deduct housing payments.

According to a recent Brookings Institute study using data from 2015, American families falling within the lowest fifth of income spend more than half their income on rent and have less than $500 per month left over for all other expenses.[160] The United States Census Bureau's Supplemental Poverty Measure (SPM) calculates that a family of average size will need nearly $1,400 per month for non-housing expenses to stay on the brink of poverty.[161] So long as we allow one fifth of our families to have $900 less monthly than this minimum residual income, we condemn these households to severe deprivation that not only impairs their current family welfare, social opportunity, and political engagement, but scars the development of their children for decades to come.

The second lowest income quintile has an average residual income after rent payments of $1,933, almost $500 greater than the poverty threshold.[162] This represents a modest buffer to impoverishment, which will be erased in high rent localities.

The third, fourth, and fifth household income quintiles do progressively better, with residual monthly incomes after rent of $3,691, $6,127, and $11,191 respectively. Moreover, the fraction of households who rent, rather than own housing, diminishes as household income increases, starting at 58% for the lowest fifth, and falling to 46%, 35%, 24%, and 13% with each increasing income quintile.[163]

These figures have important implications for rent regulation. First, rent costs pose a severe burden primarily for the lowest income quintile, no matter where they reside. Although their rent-to-income ratios are greatest within cities and suburbs and lowest in rural areas, everywhere the ratio is higher than the 30% threshold of HUD's cost burden standard while everywhere their residual incomes fall below the SPM threshold for impoverishment.[164] Households in the second lowest income quintile face rent burdens that keep them poised modestly above poverty, but their residual income provides little buffer against financial emergencies or higher rent conditions. By contrast, all the higher income groups escape significant rent burdens and have sufficient residual income, provided they maintain their economic position.

Secondly, the great variance in rent burden reflects not just significant differences in income, which usually follow even greater differences in household wealth. It also reflects how rents do not rise in proportion to income levels. Whereas the lowest quintile of renters have only a tenth the income of the highest income renters, the former pay nearly half the median rent of the latter.[165] Accordingly, the discrepancies in rent burden have only accelerated as the share of income spent on rent has risen. Although all income groups are spending higher proportions of income on rent, the toll falls greatest upon the bottom quintile. As of 2015, rent payments of our poorest fifth of households take up 11% more of their meager income than they did in 2000.[166]

Thirdly, a significant factor in the increasing burden of housing costs on our poorest families is the decline in real incomes that has accompanied the rise in rents. Whereas since 2000 their median monthly rent has risen by $60, their median monthly income has declined by slightly more than $100, eroding their paltry residual income.[167]

Under prevailing conditions, where the social rights agenda remains unfulfilled, rent regulation is absolutely necessary to provide to members of the bottom quintile of household income access to decent housing without jeopardizing satisfaction of their other basic needs. Rent regulation is also necessary to guarantee decent affordable rentals to members of the next lowest income quintile in face of higher rent localities and the variability of non-housing expenses. It is not enough to keep low cost rentals below the rent burden limit of 30% of household income. Rent regulation must ensure that those rents are kept low enough to leave a residual income sufficient to meet other expenses, which may be calculated in terms of the SPM monthly minimum of $1,400 per household.

As we have seen, households in the higher income quintiles can cope with prevailing rental rates in most localities, due to both more disposable income and how rents lag behind income levels. Consequently, rent regulation need not apply to the rental market that caters to the more affluent residents.

The resulting policy mandate presents significant challenges. Rent regulation must address a segmented rental market, in which it is possible to control separately low cost rentals, while leaving higher cost rentals largely free to fluctuate as market conditions allow. If landlords can receive significantly greater returns from higher than lower cost rentals, the limited jurisdiction of rent regulation may lead to a decrease in available low cost rentals and an increase in more expensive residences. This result seems all the more likely given how low rents must be kept to enable low income residents to pay for housing costs and retain sufficient residual income. If we accept HUD's 30% rent/income ratio standard, the lowest household quintile will require a monthly rent ceiling of $310. This rent falls under the prevailing operating costs for modest apartments almost everywhere in the U.S., while still not providing the minimum residual income according to the SPM standard.[168] Imposing the requisite rent ceiling risks undermining the supply and upkeep of the low cost rentals needed to fulfill the right to decent housing under our prevailing conditions of unemployment, poverty wages, and severe income and wealth inequality, not to mention unaffordable health care, child and elder care, and education costs.

A significant, but incomplete solution to these conundrums is provided by fulfilling those measures of the social rights agenda that guarantee and increase income and support the costs of non-housing expenses. If we guarantee jobs and fair wages, provide equivalent income replacement for the disabled and retirees, make healthcare affordable with a public single payer health insurance system, provide public child and elder care, as well as child allowances, then we can have an adjustable rent ceiling for lower cost residences that will fall near prevailing market rates. A fair minimum wage that is adjusted to increases in inflation and productivity gains now approaches the monthly rental of an average basic two-bedroom residence, which is affordable for anyone earning at least $22/hr. This monthly rental, periodically adjusted for duly substantiated landlord cost increases, can then serve as a rent ceiling for that portion of the rental market serving those income groups making close to the fair minimum wage.

Moreover, with guaranteed jobs at fair wages combined with

equivalent income replacement, we can protect tenants from eviction for failure to pay rent by means of mandatory payment rescheduling. Since tenants will have a reliable stream of income, that stream can be tapped for reasonably rescheduled payments, protecting the interests of landlords and tenants alike.

In addition, rent regulations should provide fair procedures for landlords to retain rentals for personal use and to evict and receive compensation from tenants who damage or destroy rental property.

With all these measures in place, landlords can afford to maintain these rent regulated rentals, resist pressure to demand under the table rent supplements, and avert reducing their supply by converting low cost residences into higher cost rentals or condominiums for sale.

What such rent regulation cannot guarantee is that the supply of affordable rentals is adequate or that home ownership is an affordable option that can help fulfill our right to decent housing. Even if guaranteed jobs, fair minimum wages, and equivalent income replacement allow a corresponding adjustable rent ceiling to preserve the *given* supply of low cost rental housing, this supply may fall short of what all individuals in every locality need to shelter properly themselves and their families.

We therefore should supplement rent regulation in two ways. On the one hand, we can extend affordable housing options by widening access to existing non-rental housing. On the other hand, we should mobilize private and public investment to provide additional affordable housing, while improving the freedom fostering, environmentally sound design of our communities.

Home Ownership and the Fulfillment of the Right to Decent Housing

The fulfillment of the right to decent housing does not require home ownership. Rental housing may suffice provided rents are affordable and the stock of rental housing is adequate in number and quality. Moreover, the lure of home equity may turn into a financial disaster, if, as befell millions during the 2008 Great Recession, house values fall below mortgage balances and foreclosure looms due to unemployment, the lag of incomes behind interest rates, the burdens of education loans and health care expenses, and the costs of home maintenance and real estate taxes. The risk is all the greater for low-income and minority households, for whom home equity makes up a disproportionately large part of family wealth.[169]

Nonetheless, home ownership may make up for shortfalls in decent affordable rental housing and, under favorable conditions, provide a financial anchor for those who can acquire stable home equity. In these circumstances, access to affordable decent home ownership becomes a key element in securing the right to housing.

The possibility of purchasing housing depends upon, on the one hand, the financial assets, disposable income, and availability of credit of prospective purchasers, and, on the other hand, the supply and price of decent housing. Although some purchasers may have enough wealth to pay for housing without borrowing, most households need financing to buy a home. This financing ordinarily involves both a down payment and periodic outlays that pay back the remaining principal and interest over a specified time. The affordability of home loans depends upon both the size of the down payment and how high the periodic payments are, which depends on both the loan interest rate and the length of the mortgage. If the down payment is a high proportion of the purchase price and the mortgage is relatively short, the resulting "balloon mortgage" will be affordable to far fewer households than when the down payment is smaller in relation to home price and the length of the mortgage is longer. Alternately, whatever the finances of prospective buyers, the opportunity for housing ownership will be greater the larger the supply of reasonable, so-called "starter" homes that households without previous home equity can afford.

Today in the United States many homes lay vacant due to foreclosure and millions more have dropped below their mortgage balance in value. In addition, since World War II, the equity of homeowners has continuously fallen on average to less than half the value of their homes.[170] Nonetheless, homeowners generally have more financial assets, as well as higher incomes, than non-homeowners. Currently, the net worth of the average homeowner is $195,400, whereas the net worth of the average renter is a paltry $5,400, 36 times smaller.[171]

The economic advantage of homeowners reinforces racial inequity owing to the gap in home ownership rates between white households on the one hand and Hispanic and African American households on the other. As of 2017, 72% of white households owned their housing, whereas only 47% of Hispanic and 43% of African American households did the same.[172] This racial discrepancy reflects two factors diminishing the opportunity for home ownership.

One is the persisting lag in income and wealth of Hispanics and African Americans behind white Americans, reflecting our failure to overcome the economic consequences of past oppression. According to 2016 figures, the earnings of Hispanics and African Americans are, respectively, 61% and 64% those of white Americans,[173] whereas the median wealth of black households ($17,100) and of Hispanic households ($20,600) are, respectively, ten and eight times smaller than that of white households ($171,000).[174]

The other factor hindering home ownership by minorities is the persistence of discrimination in housing and home loans. Federal housing policies dating back to the New Deal expressly deprived people of color of publicly subsidized mortgage credit and mortgage insurance, as well as denied them access to public housing whose reduced rent facilitates savings for future home down payments. Compounding this public discrimination has been the "redlining" practices of private lenders that have starved minority neighborhoods of housing loans as well as the persisting bias of homeowners who have refused to sell to people of color.

Today, with rents rising faster than incomes and inflation, with rental vacancies approaching historic lows, and with affordable rental options dwindling for too many Americans, the need for more and more equitable home ownership opportunity is crucial. The possibilities of affordable home ownership, however, are themselves diminishing for larger and larger parts of our population. Between 2012 and 2017, while national median household income inched up 1.6%, home prices rose 26% in our thirty largest metropolitan areas. As a result, during this span, the share of affordable home listings declined by 12% to only 32% for families of median income. Compounding this problem is the 6% decline in the number of houses for sale and the failure of construction of reasonable starter homes to keep up with demand.[175]

Not surprisingly, the opportunity for affordable home ownership opportunity is still worse for people of color. In 2016 in our 30 largest metropolitan regions, the percentage of homes that were affordable dropped to only 18% for median income Hispanic households and only 14% for median income African American households.[176] In such fast-growing metro areas as Denver, Phoenix, San Diego, Los Angeles, San Francisco, and Portland, less than 5% of the homes for sale are affordable to median income Hispanic and African American families, expanding residential segregation and the barriers to opportunity it entails.[177]

Across our most economically dynamic regions, homeownership is becoming an idle dream for more and more moderate and lower income Americans, consigning them to rental living.[178] Yet as rent skyrockets in these same communities, it is becoming too expensive for many to remain in or move to the areas in which good jobs are on offer. With far off suburbs the only option, many face the prospect of long commutes that strain our environment and leave less time for our family and political engagements.

The crises in affordability of rental and residential ownership housing are intertwined. The lack of home ownership opportunity for lower income households fuels the high rate of rental occupancy, which contributes to higher rent. The growing toll that rent puts upon the residual income of renters makes it harder to save for house down payments and to maintain credit ratings that qualify for home mortgages.

Compounding the hindrance of rising rents is the meteoric rise of student loan debt, which has fast become the largest type of personal debt in the United States. With more and more monthly income going to principal and interest payments on student loans, prospective first time buyers are facing increasing difficulty saving for mortgage down payments, let alone meeting monthly mortgage payments. This predicament applies particularly to the Millennial Generation, whose 80 million members will soon include most first-time home buyers.[179]

Further exacerbating the lack of affordable home listings are zoning regulations that maintain homogeneous single-use residential neighborhoods with low density, large, expensive homes. These regulations bar inclusionary zoning, which encourages construction of more reasonable, compact, and walkable residences near schools, stores, factories, and civic facilities.

Similarly, tax policies, such as our Mortgage Interest Deduction, benefit most the high income owners of the highest value homes. This adds further incentives for housing markets to tilt to high end residences and reduce the supply of affordable homes and rental units.

Home ownership opportunity has also continued to suffer from the consequences of the 2008 Great Recession, when banks flooded the market with predatory home loans targeting low-income, disproportionately minority, households. Not only have millions of these households suffered losses of wealth that make any return to home ownership impossible, but banks have tightened access to mortgage credit, despite historically low interest rates. More than 6.3 million mortgages have been lost between 2009 and 2015.[180] These developments have intensified the general trend since 1990, as the United States homeownership rate has lost pace with that of most other developed nations. Whereas a majority of these nations increased homeownership rates, ours has edged lower.[181]

In light of all these circumstances, what can we do to provide enough opportunity for affordable home ownership to fulfill our right to decent housing?

Obviously, guaranteed jobs at fair wages, equivalent replacement income for the disabled and retired, employee empowerment, single payer health insurance with no copays and deductibles, paid family leave, public child and elder care, child allowances, and affordable education at all levels can remove much of the shortfall in income and savings that blocks homeownership for many. Still, with the prices of the given stock of homes steadily rising, access to credit remains a crucial challenge. Moreover, many homeowners face the risk of foreclosure due to the burden of mortgage payments, home maintenance, and real estate taxes.

These are national problems and they call for national remedies. With respect to the given stock of non-rental housing, we should act federally on two fronts. On the one hand, our federal government should extend the opportunity for obtaining home loans in ways that respect the interests of both prospective homeowners and credit institutions. On the other hand, our national government should provide foreclosure protection that allows homeowners to escape the trauma of eviction without jeopardizing the financial solvency of lenders.

Past government policy has sought to broaden access to home loans through such measures as mortgage interest deductions, Veterans Administration (VA) subsidized mortgages for veterans,[182] and Federal Housing Authority (FHA) loans and mortgage insurance, which expands access to sustainable housing credit by protecting lenders from loss. Our government has also sponsored independent home credit agencies, such as Freddie Mac, Fannie Mae, and Federal Home Loan Banks, which have provided $6.5 trillion to facilitate wider homeownership.[183]

Our Mortgage Interest Deduction (MID) subtracts annual mortgage interest payments from annual taxable income, which amounted to a $77 billion dollar subsidy in 2016.[184] The MID subsidy is of greatest benefit to those least in need, namely, homeowners with larger mortgage payments, which may apply to multiple residences. Homeowners with modest incomes and small home loans receive less benefit. Renters, of course, receive no such equivalent subsidy, and so long as homeowners retain greater wealth than renters, a mortgage interest subsidy ends up reinforcing the wealth inequality between these two groups. A mortgage interest deduction would better serve its purpose if it only applied to the primary residence of homeowners and if it had a low enough ceiling so that those with enough wealth to afford higher mortgage payments would receive no tax subsidy.[185]

Public home loan and mortgage insurance assistance programs may not have disproportionately benefited most affluent Americans, but originally, they did follow discriminatory policies that specifically excluded African Americans and other people of color. FHA and VA home loan programs both denied access to minority communities with flagrantly unconstitutional redlining, which appraised their neighborhoods as ineligible for housing credit.[186] As a result, minorities largely lost out on the vast post-war expansion of home ownership where government credit guarantees and mortgage interest deductions helped underwrite sprawling suburban developments with single-family housing.[187] Whereas VA mortgages made up more than 40% of home loans in the immediate post war years, in 1950, FHA and VA loans funded more than half of the 1.35 million home starts.[188] In just four years between 1953 and 1957, these federal programs loaned $3.6 billion to construct 2.4 million homes, dwarfing all other public infrastructure spending.[189] As the beneficiaries of these subsidies abandoned rental apartments for the new suburbs, they left people of color behind, who continued paying rent in inner cities that became centers of poverty and urban decay. Removing discriminatory policies is crucial, but it is not enough when large numbers of residents remain unable to purchase housing that meets their needs.

The aim of intervention in the home credit market should be to enable homeownership for as wide a spectrum as possible of individuals who cannot find satisfactory rental opportunities and otherwise cannot obtain the mortgages they need to buy decent housing. Regulation of mortgages can contribute to this aim by ensuring that private lenders offer enough home loans with reasonable down payments and monthly charges so that no buyers lack enough residual income to meet their other essential expenses. The affordable ceiling for monthly mortgage payments should be similar to that of monthly rentals, unless the rental market completely covers the need for affordable decent housing, without financially disadvantaging renters. Residents whose income and wealth are sufficient to afford housing with higher mortgage expenses need not fall under such regulation, just as rent regulation need not apply to the high end of the rental market. So long as guaranteed jobs at fair wages and fair income replacements are adjusted for inflation and productivity gains, mortgage regulation, like rent regulation, can maintain high enough ceilings to not jeopardize the solvency of lenders and landlords in face of rising interest rates.

Two further measures can protect lenders, as well as home loan recipients, against non-payment of home loan installments: mortgage insurance and eviction protection.

Mortgage insurance helps lenders and buyers maintain loan payments when facing financial strains by drawing upon privately or publicly underwritten funding that spreads the cost of keeping loans afloat so that no particular lender faces ruin. In the event that privately underwritten mortgage insurance plans are insufficient to ensure affordable home credit, public underwriting should step in to meet the need. However it be underwritten, mortgage insurance, like rent insurance covering non-payment of rent, should be mandatory, drawing contributions from all lenders as an affordable cost of doing business. The cost should fall on lenders so that mortgage insurance does not become a further obstacle to homeownership. Lenders, in their aggregate, will get back what they contribute, while avoiding the added costs of foreclosures and subsequent vacancies. Homeowners, for their part, will escape the trauma of foreclosure and loss of home equity, without, however, foregoing all liability. Since guaranteed jobs at fair wages and comparable income replacement provide a steady stream of earnings to virtually all homeowners, lenders will be able to tap that stream and eventually make up any shortfalls.

This ability makes it feasible to enact foreclosure protection for all homeowners. We can and should legally prohibit foreclosures in conjunction with mandatory mortgage payment rescheduling whenever households are unable to meet their home loan bills. Public authority can enable lenders to draw rescheduled payments directly from income and benefit streams at levels maintaining household welfare. Doing so will eliminate one of the major sources of homelessness as well as end the blight of vacant neighborhoods full of foreclosed homes.

Social and Public Housing

All the above policies concerning affordable rent and home ownership apply to the existing stock of housing. Even if we implement them all, together with the rest of the social rights agenda, shortages of reasonable rentals and homes for sale can continue to block fulfillment of the right to decent housing. The for-profit housing market may still fail to provide an adequate supply of offerings, leaving individuals unable to find affordable dwelling without which their freedoms remain in jeopardy. In face of this predicament, we have two remaining options to which we can turn: non-profit "social" housing and public housing.

The private sector can help remedy market failure to supply affordable housing by voluntarily mobilizing private wealth to fund non-profit housing developments that offer reasonable rentals and/or "starter" homes for sale. Such so-called "social" housing has a long history, dating back at least to the Fuggerei, the walled enclave in Augsburg that Jakob Fugger the Younger founded with a charitable trust in 1516 to house indigent citizens. The Fuggerei remains in operation today, still charging the same annual rent of one Gulden (worth less than a Euro today), while requiring tenants to pray three times a day. The qualifications to occupy a Fuggerei apartment are unchanged: tenants must have resided in Augsburg for at least two years, must be Catholic, and must be indigent, but without debt.[190] These conditions exhibit the limits of private non-profit initiative. The residency and debt-free indigence requirements reflect how particular private endowments lack enough resources to meet the needs of residents at large. The restriction to members of one faith is indicative of how private initiative not always addresses all inhabitants, as secular democratic public measures should.

Despite such limitations, non-profit social housing can put charitable funds to work to help house the homeless and extend the supply of affordable housing, both rental and for sale. It is our responsibility to ensure that social housing does not discriminate by creed, race, ethnicity, gender, sexual orientation, or any other factor irrelevant to exercising due rights. We should also impose guidelines that require social housing to be decent and properly furnished, as well as environmentally friendly and conducive to neighborhood design that fosters family welfare, social opportunity, and political involvement. On these terms, social housing can extend opportunity for decent housing and diminish the remaining need for public intervention.

Today, in the United States, two examples of social housing stand out: the Habitat for Humanity home building and home restoration program and the Community Land Trust movement.

Habitat for Humanity builds and restores homes for low income families, who receive affordable low cost mortgages in conjunction with contributing a certain amount of labor in constructing their future homes. Through this "sweat equity," families who otherwise could not afford to purchase a home obtain ownership of decent housing. In 2017, Habit for Humanity provided new and rehab construction homes for 16,832 families, while repairing the homes of 13,804 more.[191]

The non-profit Community Land Trust Movement, by contrast, offers low income families home ownership under two defining conditions intended to serve the cause of preserving the supply of its contribution to affordable housing. First, the Community Land Trust offers families a reasonable mortgage with which they can buy a decent house, but they do not take ownership of the land on which it stands, which remains the property of the Community Land Trust. Second, if families ever sell that house, they can only do so under a contractual requirement to follow a resale formula designed to give them a reasonable equity return while keeping the home price affordable to other low income families. In this way, low income homeowners build home equity, while new prospective home buyers retain affordable housing options and the Community Land Trust grows its own equity. According to a 2018 report of the Grounded Solutions Network, Community Land Trusts in the United States provided homeownership to 18,946 families.[192]

Although these numbers are sizeable, they fall far short of what can fulfill the right to decent housing. As admirable as the Habitat for Humanity and the Community Land Trust Movement undertakings may be, we can never count on social housing to guarantee access to housing for all. To honor the right to decent housing, we must supplement private initiative with public housing for anyone left out in the cold (or the ever more stifling heat) by market failure and the contingency of charity.

Public housing, unlike social housing, can draw upon the full national resources of the state. Whereas private non-profits cannot be counted on to relieve all the shortfalls in affordable housing that the for-profit sector may bequeath us, our federal government has the financial reserves and national jurisdiction to transcend the limitations of social housing.

This is especially true when our government fulfills the social rights agenda, which greatly extends the ability to afford rentals or home ownership, while putting in place measures that reduce the lack of supply of proper housing. On the one hand, with guaranteed jobs at fair wages, equivalent income replacement for retirees and the disabled, single payer health care with no copays or deductibles, public child and elder care, child allowances, and the removal of student debt, we can overcome poverty and provide far more individuals with the income and wealth they need to afford decent housing. On the other hand, the Federal Job Guarantee can put millions to work constructing housing, both for rent and sale, which can overcome much of any shortfall in decent affordable housing.

Under these conditions, where we eliminate unemployment and poverty, the abiding task of public housing is very different from what public housing programs have heretofore accomplished. In face of mass poverty, our government housing programs have replaced financially disadvantaged, but vibrant mixed use neighborhoods with isolated blocks of dwellings. Whether low-rise or high-rise developments, the results are the same. During construction, which begins with slum clearance, former residents are at pains to find affordable interim housing, while suffering all the dislocations of leaving their neighborhood behind. Upon completion, the new public housing projects may supersede dilapidated tenements, but they still warehouse the poor in subsidized residences that become magnets of urban decay. Instead of renewing urban areas, such measures have intensified racial and economic residential divisions, which mortgage subsidy policies for private single-family homes have compounded by leaving public housing communities more deprived of resources and amenities than before. Converting public rental housing to residential ownership is no solution if residents still lack the economic security to maintain their dwellings and forestall foreclosure. The privatization of public housing then only renews the problems that called for public initiative in the first place. Alternately, tearing down failed public housing projects is only a capitulation to despair if we continue to ignore the conditions for successful public housing.

The key lies in putting the social rights agenda to work. Once we begin to do that, we transform the prospects for public investment in housing. No longer does public housing shelter a population suffering all the ills of unemployment, poverty wages, unaffordable child and elder care, inadequate health care, failed schools, and lack of legal representation. Instead, public housing addresses lower and middle income groups that are already removed from poverty and other social disadvantage, but still face difficulty finding reasonable dwellings. If we can build public housing at rents and mortgage levels they can afford, we will foster neighborhoods whose inhabitants have enough social resources to prosper.

Whether public housing be for rent or for sale, the conditions need be no different than those that apply to rent and mortgage regulation of private sector housing. The same ceilings apply since affordability is relative to the levels of guaranteed fair income and income replacements, as well as of child allowances. Since these levels fluctuate with inflation and productivity, public housing ought to incorporate the same flexibility that should apply to private sector housing regulation. In both cases, there is no need to impose income limits upon the beneficiaries. What matters is that a sufficient supply of decent housing be available to all inhabitants. In that way, public housing can avoid segregating residents by wealth. Sweden has followed the path of never imposing income limits on public housing residents,[193] which enhances the vitality of their neighborhoods while forestalling gentrification.

If we can construct and maintain public housing at levels of expense that regulated rent and mortgage payments can match, public housing can break even. If any deficit arises, we can close the gap through the various funding options available to any sovereign government.

Habitat Renewal and the Architecture of Freedom

We have not fully implemented the right to decent housing so long as people reside in homes that are unhealthy and unsafe. Rent and mortgage regulation may extend affordability to the existing stock of housing, while social and public housing may supplement the supply to overcome market shortages. None of these measures, however, directly remedies the problem of substandard housing, whose conditions impair the health, safety, and opportunities of its residents.

Today in the United States, hazardous housing conditions jeopardize millions of people. As of 2016, 30 million dwellings suffer from grave health and safety dangers, including leaking gas, seeping plumbing, failing heating, and rampant mold and vermin. Of these residences, six million have serious structural issues,[194] while lead paint threatens residents in 24 million homes.[195] The families who are affected are disproportionately African American and Hispanic.[196]

These deficiencies are in part due to the negligence of property owners, which government should combat by providing enough resources for proper inspection and compliance enforcement. The prevalence of hazardous substandard housing is also due to a lack of financial resources leaving many homeowners and landlords unable to make necessary repairs and maintain housing properly. Eliminating unemployment and poverty through implementation of the social rights agenda can remove some of this shortfall in private resources. Many of the necessary renovations and maintenance expenses will still fall beyond the means of all too many individuals unless private and public initiatives come to their assistance.

"Social", charitable interventions can provide some help to upgrade substandard housing. These voluntary private initiatives, however, can no more guarantee the elimination of unsafe and unhealthy housing than social housing can guarantee a sufficient supply of decent affordable dwellings. Charitable upgrades can reduce the problem, but only public intervention can secure our right to live in housing that is neither unhealthy nor unsafe.

The Federal Job Guarantee can tackle some of the abiding problem by putting people to work at fair wages renovating substandard housing. Our national government can also supply grants to homeowners and landlords to carry through the necessary repairs and renewals that make current housing healthy and safe.

These private and public efforts at habitat renewal provide an opportunity to do much more than make housing healthy and safe. They also allow us to upgrade housing in ways that make it much more environmentally sound and conducive to the freedom of its inhabitants. Whenever housing renovations take place, we should take the opportunity to improve energy efficiency, curtail consumption of fossil fuels, and increase generation and use of renewable energy. At the same time, we should improve resource conservation and diminish the vulnerability to climate change. No longer should we rebuild substandard and damaged housing in ways that perpetuate or expand our exposure to the growing costs of global warming. Moreover, when we upgrade substandard housing, we should provide the broadband access and other utilities on which opportunity in a cybernetic age depends.

All these considerations apply to the construction of new social and public housing. The need to make housing more energy efficient, unreliant on fossil fuels, more environmentally friendly, and more cybernetically connected should be mandatory for all new construction. In addition, social housing and public housing can lead the way in forging new designs of living that promote household, social, and political community, while diminishing de facto racial, ethnic, and economic residential segregation.

Instead of reinforcing the energy and infrastructure inefficiency of single-use neighborhoods and suburban and ex-urban sprawl, we can use public housing to foster an architecture of freedom for our communities. Our public investment can construct new walkable and bikeable neighborhoods that put residences closer to work, schools, shops, health providers, entertainment, civic facilities, parks, and public spaces, while tying them in to public mass transportation. We can thereby build communities with a more energy conserving and infrastructure efficient density, while providing open spaces for recreation and environmental preservation. All these design imperatives should be implemented with democratic local participation and as much architectural and artistic creativity as possible.

Although nations differ in their level of wealth production and financial strength, all can enforce the right to decent housing, as well as every other social right, by providing general accessibility to the opportunities that national prosperity can support. Given the unparalleled wealth and military security of the United States, we can extend equal housing opportunity at a level second to none. In our concluding chapter, we will address how we can fairly tap our national wealth to fund the full social rights agenda without which our democracy cannot flourish. The only obstacle is our political will. Otherwise, we need have no doubts about our ability to eliminate homelessness and provide a decent home to all our residents.

6. Fulfilling the Right to Education

The Right to Education

Every right involves a dual recognition. One cannot exercise one's rights if one does not know what they are and how to wield them. On the other hand, one cannot exercise one's prerogatives as *rights* rather than *privileges* unless one recognizes one's specific duties to respect the entitled freedoms of one's fellow right holders. Right and duty always go together and both depend upon the knowledge and appropriate conduct in which the rectitude of recognition consists.

Ideally, a nation's constitution should authoritatively proclaim and protect all the rights to which its inhabitants are due. A constitution also contains positive stipulations, such as the number of representatives and length of terms, which reason cannot dictate, but which we must know in order to participate in self-government. Consequently, a nation's inhabitants must obtain knowledge of the constitution under which they live to be able to enjoy their freedoms and respect those of one another. Knowledgeable recognition of the constitution is ultimately that on which national identity should rest. A nation devoted to realizing freedom should not exclude individuals from participation on the basis of race, ethnicity, religion, gender, sexual orientation, or any other factor unrelated to recognizing and respecting the rights on whose realization its authority depends.

One is not born with knowledge of rights nor does one's natural maturation suffice to supply that knowledge. Reason may be able to conceive the different forms of freedom in which consist property relations, moral accountability, household freedom, civil society, and self-government. We all are not, however, in a position to reinvent the wheel of the philosophy of right and independently conceive the institutions of freedom. Moreover, the actual exercise of rights always requires knowledge of the natural and historical reality in which our freedom operates, together with exposure to all the conventional positive provisions that reason alone cannot determine. In order to employ any of our liberties, we must thus be educated about the content of our rights and duties and provided with the general knowledge we need to wield our due freedoms.

This requirement provides the basis for our fundamental right to an education sufficient to be free. We should all have the opportunity to learn enough about our constitution and our positive laws to participate and respect one another as free property owners, moral subjects, co-determining spouses and responsible parents, interdependent members of a civil society, and self-governing citizens. We should all have adequate education about the natural world on which our existence depends, in the psychology that provides the mental bases of our free agency, and about the wealth of history on which the full understanding of our institutions and those of other nations rests. In addition, we need to obtain sufficient spoken and written knowledge of languages appropriate to communicate with our fellow right holders and participate without disadvantage in every sphere of our freedom. Lastly, we should all have enough philosophical training to be able to think about justice and the legitimate boundaries of our freedom, especially when our constitution fails to recognize all rights that deserve constitutional protection. These opportunities apply to all individuals who grow up in our body politic, as well as to adults who join our nation later in life.

Several millennia ago, Plato and Aristotle focused attention on the importance of education in enabling the rulers of the best state to achieve justice. Music, physical training, the proper literature, mathematics, astronomy, and finally philosophy all were enlisted to prepare the guardians of the body politic to lead. Once we recognize the good to reside in self-determination, however, education can no longer be restricted to a privileged ruling class, but must become the common facilitator and uniting bond of all members of a free community.

These general considerations prescribe a common education to which we are all entitled insofar as we have any rights whatsoever. As such, this common education does not provide the specialized training upon which opportunity depends in a civil society. There the market's proliferation of different goods and services continually engenders new varied occupational qualifications. These conditions of social freedom make it imperative that individuals have equal opportunity to obtain the specialized training that particular occupations require. Otherwise, those who lack access to such training will remain economically disadvantaged, undermining their household welfare and political opportunity. Admittedly, technical occupational education cannot be common to all, given its inherent specialization. Nonetheless, we should all be able to obtain whatever specific training we need to earn a decent living of our choosing if we are to enjoy real equal economic opportunity. Accordingly, access to both common education for democratic freedom and particular occupational education is a fundamental right, which deserves constitutional protection.

The responsibility for fulfilling the right to education is a public matter. Parents are obliged to bring up their children so that they can achieve independent autonomy. Families cannot alone provide the education to which we are all entitled, however, due to two factors. First, parents have limited time, owing to the demands of household duties, earning a living, and participating in politics. Second, parents do not have the training or resources sufficient to provide either the common education for freedom or the technical training on which economic opportunity depends. Our common democratic education requires mastering manifold subjects and providing manifold learning materials, both of which challenge the capabilities of parents and recourse to "home-schooling." The specialization of technical education further heightens these difficulties. Private institutions may be able to organize instruction with better endowed facilities and more and better trained educators than a family can provide. Nonetheless, the limited scope and access of private initiative still leaves the right to education unfulfilled. Private schools may serve some, but just some individuals. Only public schooling open to all levels from pre-K to post-secondary levels can guarantee the common and particular technical education on which our freedoms depend.

International versus Our National Recognition of the Right to Education

The fundamental right to education has received international recognition in the *Universal Declaration of Human Rights*, adopted by the United Nations in 1948 after submission by a committee headed by Eleanor Roosevelt. Article 26 proclaims:

> "1. Everyone has the right to education. Education shall be free, at least in the elementary and fundamental stages. Elementary education shall be compulsory. Technical and professional education shall be made generally available and higher education shall be equally accessible to all on the basis of merit.
>
> 2. Education shall be directed to the full development of the human personality and to the strengthening of respect for human rights and fundamental freedoms. It shall promote

understanding, tolerance and friendship among all nations, racial or religious groups, and shall further the activities of the United Nations for the maintenance of peace.

3. Parents have a prior right to choose the kind of education that shall be given to their children."

All three sections of Article 26 raise issues concerning how the right to education should be fulfilled, issues that we citizens need to address. Before doing so, we must confront the ramifications of a fundamental omission in the United States Constitution. Although many nations have followed the *Universal Declaration of Human Rights* and given constitutional protection to the right to education, the United States has not. The United States may have voted in the United Nations General Assembly to adopt the *Universal Declaration of Human Rights*, but our Constitution still makes no mention of the right to education.

In the absence of any Federal constitutional protection for the right to education, we face a situation where fulfillment of that right depends upon other measures. Until we adopt a constitutional amendment guaranteeing the right to education, we have two avenues for recognizing and enforcing our access to the education we need to exercise our rights. On the one hand, our national congress can make laws towards fulfilling our right to education. On the other hand, our state governments can and have adopted both state constitution statutes and state legislature laws that support education.

Complicating the option of national legislation is the 10th Amendment, which mandates that "The powers not delegated to the United States by the Constitution, nor prohibited by it to the States, are reserved to the States respectively, or to the people." On various occasions, the Supreme Court has treated this Amendment as if it prohibited the Federal Government from fulfilling any of the fundamental social rights not specifically protected under the United States Constitution. Such was the case when the Supreme Court ruled unconstitutional many New Deal initiatives until the Court changed its tune, due to retirements and the specter of "packing" the court with additional appointees favoring Franklin Delano Roosevelt's social rights agenda. More recently, the Supreme Court invoked this alleged prohibition to prevent Federal intervention in behalf of equitable funding of education. In its 5-4, 1973 decision in *San Antonio Independent School District v. Rodriguez*, the Supreme Court denied any Federal Constitutional right to equal funding of education, leaving responsibility for education to the states.[197]

The abdication of national fulfillment of the right to education is reflected in the historical development of public education in the United States, as well as in the current state of public funding for education. From colonial times onward, the institution of public education has varied from region to region, with different policies holding sway under different state jurisdictions. Despite growing recognition of the importance of public education in a democracy, federal initiatives have been limited in scope, leaving states chiefly in charge of educational policy.

The primacy of state responsibility was pointedly in play immediately after the Civil War, when, in every Southern state, the newly freed slaves demanded two measures that they regarded as essential to any real emancipation. It was not enough to benefit from the Thirteenth, Fourteenth, and Fifteenth Amendments, which granted the former slaves the formal status of free persons, equal legal standing in the courts, and the right to vote if they were men. The former slaves knew that their life, liberty, and pursuit of happiness remained hobbled without two further measures: first, government had to distribute land and livestock to the former slaves to provide them economic independence and, second, government needed to establish free public schools to provide the former slaves with the opportunity to be educated, which the slave states had legally prohibited. Although the former slaves never received and retained the "forty acres and a mule" they needed, they did achieve some fulfillment of their right to education. With the political empowerment of former slaves in Reconstruction state governments, they launched public education in the South, establishing, for the first time anywhere in the United States, free public schooling supported by general state taxation.[198] Admittedly, the public schools ended up being racially separate and unequal, but the right to education received a belated, if limited, recognition.

In the continued absence of a constitutional guarantee of the right to education, United States public schooling has since expanded on a state by state level, with control and responsibility for funding primarily vested in state and local authorities. Today, the Federal Government supplies less than a tenth of the financial support for public education, leaving more than 90% raised through state and local taxation.[199] This situation has had fateful consequences for public education in the United States. Although some state constitutions protect the right to education, others do not. Educational funding varies between states, as do regulations concerning the length of mandatory schooling, curriculum, teaching qualifications, and disciplinary procedures. Some of these differences reflect a concern for decentralization and local control, but others represent a license to obstruct educational equal opportunity. Despite the fact that the United States has been a pioneer in the institution of public education, how we have organized the governance and support of our schools has fostered inequities that jeopardize fulfillment of the right to education and the democratic freedom that depends upon it.

Why Education for a Democracy is not itself Democratic

A democracy cannot function unless its residents have an equal opportunity to receive a common education for freedom, affording them the knowledge they need to exercise all their rights on a par with others. The educational process itself is not, however, democratic in character. The two constitutive parties to education, students and teachers, do not face one another as equals. In order for education to proceed, teachers must have knowledge to transmit and the ability to convey it to students, who must recognize that they lack that knowledge and that that knowledge is worth obtaining. This inequality applies to the educational situation of both child and adult students. If instead there is no such inequality between teacher and student, nor any recognition of its existence, teachers are impostors and students are wasting their time.

By contrast, citizens of a democracy face one another as political equals, entitled to participate on a par in determining the destiny of their body politic within the constitutional limits that protect the rights of all residents. Insofar as self-governing citizens engage in deciding what ends should be pursued, they do not need any special expertise. Expertise becomes a requirement only once the goals of the state have been determined, at which point specialized knowledge and skill are needed to provide the proper means to achieve those goals. For this reason, the state bureaucracy, which is concerned with implementing the law that citizens co-determine through their legislative representatives, should be filled by experts. Unlike legislators, bureaucrats of the executive properly qualify for holding their positions not on the basis of an election, but by passing tests, drawn up and graded by those who have the expertise in question. It is just as much a mistake to treat all public positions as subject to election, as to treat them all as subject to qualification by expertise.

The greatest thinkers of Western Classical philosophy, Plato and Aristotle, tend to treat politics, as well as fine art and philosophy, as crafts, in which experts impose given ends upon some given material thanks to their specialized understanding and skill of how to do so. Fine artists may need some knowledge of technique to produce their works of art in a particular medium, but if they are to achieve aesthetic worth, they must be creative and provide something more than technical excellence. Similarly, philosophy cannot be reduced to a craft, in which some given knowledge and skill is put to work in seeking the proper means to fulfill given ends. Philosophy cannot begin with any given content and method, since doing so would render all its results relative to those assumptions. Instead, philosophers must call into question all given dogma concerning what they should address and how they should do so, and take responsibility for establishing what the proper topics of philosophical investigation are and what philosophical method should be.

Teaching is different from both democratic political engagement, creative artistry, and philosophizing because it does have a given array of knowledge to convey and must engage the expertise that can fulfill the teaching of this knowledge. One can and should teach about democratic politics, but this does not involve an activity of democratic participation, where the parties to the process relate as equals. One can and should teach about the fine arts. Studio classes in fine art, however, can only teach technique. As for philosophy instruction, it too is not equivalent to engagement in philosophizing, whose genuine starting point is exemplified by Socrates' recognition of his own ignorance. To teach about philosophy, one must instead already have knowledge of the subject matter and be in a position to determine what texts and topics deserve study, as well as how to think through this material in a way that engages the student to participate in the thought experiments that build the history of philosophy.

I myself have been teaching philosophy for nearly four decades and never have I, nor should I have, asked my students to vote on what the class syllabus would be, what assignments would be required, nor what grades they should receive. Instead, I have benefitted from academic freedom to use my professorial prerogative to decide all these matters based on my expertise, whose reality my teaching better have substantiated.

I have experienced, however, as a student the folly of the all too prevalent misconception that education in a democracy is a democratic process. While doing a Masters in Philosophy at the University of Heidelberg, I attended a graduate course led by a preeminent professor, Dieter Henrich, in which students, claiming democratic student empowerment, demanded that he step down and allow a student moderator to lead the class. The result was a succession of class meetings in which discussion wandered to too little avail, until the students sheepishly relented and allowed Herr Professor to wield his expertise.

Years before I had experienced what is commonplace in much elementary and secondary school education in the United States, namely, studying under teachers who had been trained in schools of education. Instead of being required to have advanced study in the specific subject matter of their teaching, they had had to obtain teaching certificates based on completion of education school programs that taught a general technique of teaching. Such training has a suspect formality, for it presumes that the ability to teach rests on a skill that is independent of mastery of the subject matter. This approach brings a democratic deformation to the education of teachers, for it downplays the element of expert knowledge on which teaching qualification properly rests. By accepting this approach, our schools of education have turned out a generation of teachers who have less expertise in their fields than their counterparts in other nations, which require public school teachers to obtain advanced degrees in their area of instruction.

Tellingly, we who teach at the college and university level are not required to undergo any formal "general teacher training". Instead, we qualify to instruct higher education in virtue of our mastery of our subject area, attested by completion of doctoral studies in our specific academic area.

Another trend in our "democratized" education compounds the neglect of advanced subject area study in teacher preparation at the elementary and secondary level: the acceptance of play and student self-direction as principles of schooling.[200] Here we have "student power" set free at any early stage, where learning is supposed to flourish when students are left to their own devices. Although teachers supply students with educational materials with which to cavort, students are supposed to wield their autonomy as best they can, as if they could play their way through the crucible of learning.[201] Admittedly, play and self-direction certainly have their place in developing resourcefulness and creativity,[202] but central to education is an other-directed element of instruction that depends on the subject matter mastery of teachers and the respect for that authority on the part of students.[203]

These considerations bear upon the governance of schools. Although we as citizens preside over what aims public education should achieve, when it comes to administering schooling, teachers deserve a preeminent say due to their educational qualification. Community control should respect the expertise of teachers and make their voices count in determining the content and methods of public education.

The centrality of expert teachers is manifest in both the allotment of resources in public education and assessments of what investments most improve the learning of students.

Among public in-school expenditures, teacher salaries are the largest component, comprising nearly half of operating costs. This is true despite the fact that teachers' pay lags behind that of similarly qualified workers. Today public school teachers are suffering a record pay penalty of 18.7%, earning that much less than employees of comparable training and experience. Significantly, the teacher pay penalty is 15.6% for female public school teachers and 26.8% for their male counterparts.[204] This reflects the historical situation of the teaching profession in the United States, where for many decades school teaching was one of the few careers open to women. Even today, more than three fourths of U. S. public school teachers are women.[205] School teaching, like other professions with predominantly women workers, has pay rates that are generally lower than professions dominated by men, whose greater career options put them in better position to command higher compensation. The larger teacher pay penalty for men indicates how men still have more opportunities than women for better paid work.[206]

Investment in teachers has proven to be the most important school expenditure in improving instruction and educational outcomes. The only other factor that has been shown to have any unequivocal impact in enhancing school education is class size, which has an effect no more than half that of comparable expenditures for teachers. Significantly, class size has proven to have a noticeable effect only in the early grades of elementary school, whereas investment in teachers maintains its efficacy throughout schooling.[207]

Of course, under conditions of extreme social inequality, the impediments afflicting disadvantaged students hold hostage their educational achievement. Academic performance is bound to suffer when students are malnourished, lack adequate physical and mental health care, are deprived of decent housing, have no broadband connectivity, and are brought up by parents or other relatives who themselves suffered educational deprivation and have little time or resources to enrich and assist the education of their dependents. Moreover, whereas the less advantaged have nothing to supplement what schools can provide, more affluent students can benefit from all the learning, literature, and cultural resources of which their families dispose, as well as from private lessons in music, art, dance, and sports.

In a nation like the United States, which tolerates massive income and wealth inequality and violates fundamental social rights such as the entitlements to healthcare and decent housing, investment in public schools cannot alone guarantee that every student receives a viable education for democracy. If we fail to enable disadvantaged students to learn to read, write, and reckon by the early years of elementary school, they are condemned to continual humiliation and discouragement as they pass on to higher grades without the literacy needed to tackle advancing subject matter. We leave them a fundamentally handicapped underclass.

Fulfilling the social rights agenda may eliminate unemployment and poverty, while securing proper nourishment, decent housing, healthcare, and legal representation, all of which can remove much of the barriers to educational success that injustice outside of school imposes. What cannot be alleviated for the present generation, however, are the developmental deficits that students have already suffered due to past deprivations, as well as the handicap of being raised by family members who lack enough education themselves to assist learning at home.

In face of these challenges, how can we in the United States fulfill the right to education as it applies to elementary and secondary schooling?

Private and Public Schooling

Parents have a right to choose appropriate schooling for their children, in fulfillment of their parental duty to provide children with an upbringing that will enable them to exercise all their freedoms upon maturity. Section 3 of Article 26 of the Universal Declaration of Human Rights explicitly acknowledges this entitlement, declaring, "Parents have a prior right to choose the kind of education that shall be given to their children." This right is limited since parents are not entitled to choose an education for their children that neglects the common learning and skills, as well as specialized training, on which unimpeded opportunity in any democracy depends.

Parents can fulfill their parental duty by choosing to send their children to private, rather than public schools, provided those schools offer an education that meets those requirements. Depending on the level of public funding, private schools may be better endowed and offer higher educational standards than their public school counterparts. Insofar as private schools require tuition payments that not every family can afford, the choice of private education may turn into a privilege, fostering a social and political hierarchy in which the privately schooled children of more affluent parents go on to command greater wealth and power thanks to their educational advantage. In a nation like ours, which tolerates severe social inequality compounding racial inequity, private schools readily become vehicles of de facto educational segregation, where public schools warehouse poor and historically disadvantaged minority children. Fulfilling the social rights agenda can make private school tuition affordable for more, but not necessarily all families. So long as private schooling is not available for everyone, public schooling remains the foundation for fulfilling the right to education.

The first and foremost task of public intervention in education is to ensure that public schools offer an education for freedom with a standard of excellence that all students have an opportunity to share. Private schools must also meet standards regarding curriculum and teaching quality so that no child is disadvantaged when parents choose a private option. Nonetheless, so long as adequate public education is available for all students, focusing public assistance upon public schools does not infringe the right to education. Although not every family may afford private schooling, the children of families who cannot will not be disadvantaged if the public option is properly supported.

Parental choice might seem to be impaired so long as private schooling lies beyond the means of many who would prefer to remove their children from public schools. To address this "impairment", one could divert government funding to voucher programs subsidizing enrollment at private schools, instead of concentrating public resources upon public schools open to all. This diversion might be benign if it did not detract from support for public schools and further de facto school segregation. In practice, voucher programs and their analogues sap public schools of both funding and enrollment, leaving them in a weakened condition, putting their remaining students at risk. Moreover, subsidies for private tuition are insufficient to finance the expansion that private schools would have to undergo in short order to accommodate any significant inflow of students from public schools.

For all these reasons, our commitment to fulfill the right to education must concentrate first and foremost on public schooling from pre-K through the secondary level.

The Inequities of Public School Support in the United States

Due to the absence of any national enactment of the right to education in the United States Constitution, the fulfillment of that right has primarily rested upon state and local initiative. This decentralization of public education control and support may serve the cause of wider citizen involvement, but so long as it is detached from any guarantee of educational opportunity, it fuels inequity. It does so by permitting substantial state disparities in the adequacy of school curriculum, teaching compensation and preparation, school facilities, and general educational funding. Moreover, of the ninety-two percent of school funding that state or local governments provide, localities supply close to half, relying on property taxes.[208] The variance in local property values and property tax rates thus compounds the unequal levels of school funding between states.

The differences in funding levels of public education between states are themselves large enough to jeopardize equal educational opportunity. Average annual 2016 teacher salaries, adjusted for cost of living, vary from $71,773 in Michigan to $40,246 in Hawaii.[209] To the extent that salary differences impact upon the ability of schools to recruit and retain the best teachers, the variation in state teacher salaries cannot be benign for the quality of public school education in the lower paying states. Similarly, the average spending per student in public elementary and secondary schools diverges tremendously between states. According to the U. S. Census Bureau's 2016 Annual Survey of School System Finances, extreme disparities exist between the states with the highest and lowest per student expenditures. Whereas New York State tops the list, spending an average $22,366 per student, Utah figures at the opposite extreme, spending only $6,953 per student.[210]

If the disparities in public education support between states were not problematic enough, the funding inequities within states bring matters to an extreme from which generations to come will suffer unless we remedy the situation. A prime source of intrastate funding inequity is the prevalent reliance of local educational funding upon property taxes. This reliance upon property taxation goes back to the earliest colonial times, starting in 1646 with the Puritans in Massachusetts, who used property tax receipts to fund town schools to teach reading and writing.[211] Although the early colonies may have had relatively restricted variations in property values, those day are long gone.

With the rise of neighborhoods distinguished by large disparities in wealth, local school funding based on property taxes inevitably leaves different localities disposing of school resources mirroring the divergent value of their real estate. The children of poorer neighborhoods are at a distinct disadvantage so long as half the funding of their schools depends on local property taxes. Although impoverished students need extra support to counteract the handicaps of household poverty and past educational deprivation, our local property tax school funding regime has left these pupils doubly disadvantaged. Connecticut, which spends the third highest amount per student in the United States,[212] offers a glaring example, providing public schools in relatively impoverished Bridgeport $6,000 less per pupil than their counterparts in affluent Greenwich and Darien.[213] According to the U. S. Department of Education, the pattern of inequity extends nationwide, with high poverty school districts receiving 15.6 percent less funding than low poverty ones.[214]

These inequalities in local school support only compound the economic disadvantage that poorer areas already suffer. They condemn the new generation to a second-class education, fostering inferior opportunity.[215] In addition, these inequities reinforce racial injustice to the extent that our heritage of legal discrimination, generational poverty, and redlining all concentrate minorities in neighborhoods with the lowest property values and least public school resources, undermining any educational ladder to social mobility.

Admittedly, certain states, such as Vermont and California,[216] have enacted "Robin Hood" laws to equalize educational funding between localities. Nonetheless, differences within school districts have persisted that exceed the disparities between them. Some of these funding disparities between schools in the same district reflect differences in the relative experience of teaching staff, with schools having larger cohorts of new teachers having smaller salary outlays. Similarly, differences in student body account for some variances, where special needs students (eligible for lunch subsidies, bilingual education, disability services, gifted programs, or vocational training) draw extra funding. Despite these factors, per student "non-categorical" funding, applying to students with no exceptional spending requirements, has still varied between schools in the same district more than between school districts.[217]

Funding Equity and Student Weighted Formulas

Equal educational opportunity in elementary and secondary schools depends upon equitable funding of public schools, so that every student has access to teachers of relatively equivalent preparation and experience with comparable resources, similarly rich curriculum, and beneficial class size. This entails special provisions for physically and mentally handicapped students. It also requires that children from economically and educationally disadvantaged households receive whatever extra attention and resources are necessary to ensure that they can do as well as children from more advantaged circumstances.

In light of these concerns, state governments should hold localities responsible to overcome the inequities in funding between schools within the same school districts. States, for their part, should do the same in respect to the disparities in local funding between different school districts. To do so, states should use state taxes and redistributed local property tax revenues to even the educational playing field for all state pupils, whatever neighborhood they inhabit. States, however, lack the resources or jurisdiction to overcome the inequities in educational funding between different states. Moreover, states may fail to provide adequate funding for public schools in general. Such was the case in California after the 1978 passage of Proposition 13, which capped property taxes and led to a precipitous decline in state support of public education at all levels.[218] Only the Federal Government is in a position to remedy the disparities in state funding, guarantee adequate levels of support nationwide, and insure that students have equal educational opportunity no matter where they reside.

How then should our national government guarantee sufficient and equitable funding for public elementary and secondary schools?

The achievement of educational parity in elementary and secondary schools is not equivalent to equalizing funding per student. Vermont took this approach in 1997, passing *Act 60*, which mandated that towns spend per public school pupil the same amount of tax revenue.[219] An equal per student allocation ignores the extra needs of disadvantaged students, even if it improves upon the underfunding of poorer neighborhoods in general. It also can violate the educational opportunity of all, if the level of equal funding is too small to support quality public education. What we need is not rigidly equal per student allocations, but a weighted allocation formula that provides an adequate common baseline of support, while channeling extra funds to the disadvantaged students most in need of more educational resources.

The 1990 New Jersey Supreme Court ruling in *Abbott v. Burke* pointed in this direction by requiring the state to spend not just equal, but more money per student in poorer school districts.[220] Holland has extended the student weighted policy nationwide by mandating equal per student funding for all, with additional funding for students with special needs, including overcoming economic disadvantage and the relative educational deprivation of their families. Our own government did take a small step in this direction with the 1965 *Elementary and Secondary Education Act (ESEA)*, which allocated extra federal funding to poorer school districts across the nation.[221] What ESEA did not do is remove the overarching disparities in public school funding within and between states. As a result, we remain one of the few developed nations in which access to quality public education remains hostage to the real estate values of different neighborhoods.

The most effective way to overcome inter- and intra-state disparities of funding of public education is to transfer all support of elementary and secondary schools to the federal budget and then apply a nuanced student weighted formula to insure that every pupil receives sufficient resources to thrive.

Above all, this requires addressing the most important in-school factor in education: teachers. To recruit and retain high quality teachers we need to insure that salaries are high enough to remove any teacher pay gap. Moreover, teacher compensation must be sufficient to attract teachers who meet higher standards of preparation, including advanced degrees in their area of specialty. We can institute nationwide the requirement that all new teachers have a masters in the area of their instruction and that all department heads have a corresponding doctorate. Moreover, by enacting the social rights agenda with a fair minimum wage and employee empowerment, teachers, like all other employees, will be able to support themselves and their families with only one full time job. This will not only diminish the debilitating fast turnover of teaching staffs, but enable teachers to concentrate their energies on education.

Secondly, federal funding can enable schools to improve that next most important in-school factor for educational improvement, class size. We can mandate a national standard for academic class size and supply the funds to build enough classrooms and hire enough teachers to make this feasible.

Curriculum improvement comes next. To prepare our children to be responsible self-determining citizens, we must provide nationwide a suitable common course of study. Our mandatory public education should include much more than just reading and writing as well as mathematical and scientific literacy. Our common curriculum should also provide sufficient national and world history to orient students in our global context, training in a second language to communicate with fellow citizens and fellow inhabitants of our planet, study of our constitution and laws to prepare students to exercise all their rights and duties, and an introduction to philosophy to explore truth and justice. Moreover, we should not deprive public school students of equal opportunity to play sports and study art, music, dance, film, and theater, which too often remain the privilege of affluent pupils. Instead, elementary and secondary public schools should be required to offer every pupil daily classes in sports and the fine arts. We should guarantee at a federal level that all of these studies are generally available as essential elements of a common democratic education.

National funding and national curriculum standards need not eliminate an important role for local school administration in which community parents, teachers, and school staff participate. Federal support should insure that decentralized control never jeopardizes equal educational opportunity.

Post-Secondary Schooling and the Right to Education

The common public education that the United States provides without cost has come to extend from pre-K through the twelfth grade of secondary school. In most states, children are required to attend school through the age of 16, but some states have higher age limits for mandatory schooling.[222]

This common schooling cannot exhaustively fulfill the right to education, providing pupils with the knowledge and skills to exercise their freedom as members of our democracy. What pre-K through secondary school does not offer is the specialized vocational training that individuals need in order to enjoy equal economic opportunity in our civil society. Due to its inherent specialization, this technical schooling cannot be part of any common curriculum. Nonetheless, if individuals are unable to access the technical training they desire and need in order to earn a decent living, their right to education is fundamentally impaired.

There is no reason why we should not organize this post-secondary technical training in the manner of public schools, with free tuition and materials. What alone would need adding are cost of living stipends to enable the post-secondary adult students, who no longer are dependents of their family, to make ends meet while they pursue full time technical studies. So long as public technical schools receive equitable funding between and within states, they can insure that individuals receive the vocational training they need to participate in the economy on a par with others.

Unique among nations, the United States has established a vast system of post-secondary schools that combine the common education for democracy with an element of vocational specialization. This mixed higher education operates in the thousands of colleges, both public and private, that add a concentration in a field of specialty to a "liberal arts" training. Ordinarily, college students must spend no more than a quarter of their coursework on a self-selected "major," while three quarters of their courses are selected from a general curriculum for which distribution requirements insure that students receive a "well-rounded," non-vocational higher education. If this higher liberal arts education seeks to provide a common foundation for responsible participation in the institutions of freedom, it should be available to all. We can readily guarantee this availability by organizing such college education, as well as post-secondary technical schooling, on the tuition-free basis of public schooling, to which we add living stipends to allow adults to afford full time study. Moreover, the mandatory period of schooling would warrant extension beyond secondary school if secondary schools fail to deliver essential aspects of a democratic education that liberal arts college education offers.

In most other countries, higher education is specialized from the outset. Whereas in the United States, students go to law school, medical school, and business school after completing the undergraduate degree, elsewhere these vocational trainings all begin directly after the completion of secondary school. Partly responsible for this difference is that secondary education in many other nations reaches an academic standard comparable to the level of studies in American colleges. The British "A" level secondary school, the French *Lycée*, and the German *Gymnasium* all teach subjects at a more advanced level than their American counterparts. I experienced this difference myself when I enrolled at the Sorbonne in Paris and found that my two years of undergraduate studies at Yale would only count as the equivalent of a French high school diploma. Admittedly, the first year curriculum in philosophy at the Sorbonne was too regimented to be very challenging. Fortunately, I had the chance to switch to the university campus at Vincennes, where I could enroll in any class I wanted thanks to the agreement ending the May 1968 upheaval, which established Vincennes as a center where the masses could be educated and prerequisites were waived.

The equivalence of the first years of American college with secondary school general education in other nations is indicative of how the "liberal arts" component of United States higher education may really be part of the common education to which all residents should have access. To the extent that college education plays a significant role in securing equal opportunity for its recipients, the right to education cannot exclude it as part of the post-secondary schooling to which all residents should have the chance to undertake if they are able and willing.

In the United States today, the costs of college education have reached levels that jeopardize the opportunity for higher education of large sectors of our population. Student debt has climbed to gigantic dimensions, dwarfing all other credit besides home loans.[223] The increase in college costs reflects the difficulty of applying to higher education the cost-saving technologies of automation that have dramatically reduced the cost of many manufactured commodities. Some colleges have attempted to use massive on-line courses as a way of reducing costs, but their "virtual" instruction has proven to be no substitute for real student-teacher interaction. Colleges have also sought to reduce costs by increasingly employing graduate students to teach courses of their own and to hire legions of underemployed academics on an adjunct basis to teach classes at meager wages without benefits.

We can curtail the erosion of educational standards at colleges and universities by supporting and expanding the proportion of full-time tenure track positions. The costs, however, of maintaining a properly trained academy cannot be allowed to undermine educational opportunity. The

United States should follow the lead of most other affluent nations by making higher education at state institutions tuition free and by offering full time students a stipend sufficient to support them during their studies. Moreover, we must end the three-decade long decline in public funding of higher education[224] so that state colleges and universities do not become impoverished second-rate counterparts of private institutions. Private colleges, for their part, should be required to provide scholarship aid as needed. Otherwise, private higher education may become a bastion of privilege and de facto segregation.

The right to education requires taking a similar approach to technical higher education. Public technical schools should be accessible to all qualified students. We can guarantee accessibility by having tuition free programs, supplemented by living stipends to support full time students. Then we can fulfill our right to both a common education for democracy and a specialized training for economic opportunity.

These measures come too late for those already burdened by crushing student loans. The educational debt burden has trapped all too many former students in a financial vise, blocking the path to home ownership, viable retirement, and the very possibility of supporting a family. Today more than 44 million Americans struggle with an aggregate 1.4 trillion dollar outstanding student loan debt.[225] We can eliminate their chains of student debt by requiring lending institutions, including government, to absorb that debt at a pace that insures their financial stability. Certainly the too big to fail financial institutions can write off student debt in exchange for some of the vast public funds they consumed in weathering the Great Recession of 2008, for which they are largely responsible. If private lenders cannot survive student debt forgiveness, the federal government can take over their student loans and write them off with little impact on our deficit to GDP ratio.[226] Freed of student debt, millions will be able to build their families, advance their careers, and contribute to the economic vitality of the nation. According to a

2018 report of the Levy Economics Institute, student debt cancellation will increase the net worth and disposable income of millions, fostering additional consumption and investment. Student debt cancellation will thereby lift the U.S. GDP by between $86 to $108 billion annually over the next 10 years, reducing unemployment from 0.2 to 0.3% and adding from 1.2 to 1.5 million jobs annually, with little effect on inflation and interest rates.[227]

Most importantly, student debt cancellation will remove the curse that higher education has meant for those least able to afford its steepening cost. The fulfillment of the right to education must redress past inequities as well as secure future opportunities.

7. Legal Care for All

The Right to Legal Representation

The natural capacity to choose is a merely subjective liberty, whose decisions have no power or authority to escape obstruction from the opposing choices of others. Rights, by contrast, make freedom objective because they grant every right holder a sphere of choice that others are obliged to respect. Since rights are not privileges that only some enjoy, but entitlements shared by all individuals, rights are universal freedoms, whose exercise always consists in a general prerogative that is thereby lawful in form. Whether one wields property, moral, family, social, or political rights, one is always abiding by rules circumscribing choice that apply to all other right holders. The objective freedoms of rights are thus susceptible of legalization.

The legalization of rights is imperative. If we are to have our rights respected, we must give them an authoritative public specification in law and a legal process must authoritatively adjudicate any violation of rights and provide due compensation and punishment, as the case may warrant. Without legalization, public adjudication, and public enforcement, our rights remain in jeopardy, since we as individuals have no authority to determine the objective boundaries of our entitled freedoms or identify and remedy violations of them.

Law should be accessible and made intelligible to legal subjects so that they can know their legal obligations and the legal procedures they need to follow to protect their rights. Otherwise, we fall into the predicament of those subjects of old whose tyrant posted the laws on top of a pole too high for anyone to read, so that he could rule with arbitrary impunity. The publication of law is not enough, however, to ensure that legal subjects can comprehend their legal rights and duties. The complexity and ever growing enormity of legislation makes it impossible for ordinary individuals to know all the laws to which they are beholden or how to navigate the legal system to uphold their rights. It is not enough to organize the entire body of law into a searchable code that is made generally available through such measures as free online access and placement in public libraries. Individuals with no special legal training will still face forbidding obstacles in locating and comprehending the laws with which they must contend. For this reason, it is crucial that we all have access to legal expertise to obtain proper advice about the law and proper representation in court. Otherwise, we cannot duly exercise and defend any of our rights.

Legal affairs fall into two broad categories: criminal and civil. Criminal cases involve malicious infringements of law, where a perpetrator violates the law with knowledge and intent to do so. Criminals will on purpose against what the law specifies to be right, with an understanding that they are acting illegally. A criminal act may or may not succeed in actually harming victims. Attempted crimes, for example, may completely fail to cause any infringement of the legal rights of others. Similarly, so-called victimless crimes may cause no harm to any other individual. In every case of crime, however, the perpetrator commits the wrong of intentionally willing against the law. The criminal deserves punishment in recognition that legal right should not be violated with impunity. Since punishment properly addresses the intentional and knowing willing against right, the retribution against crime should not consist in attacking the body of the criminal, through such physical measures as torture, branding, or maiming. Nor should punishment be considered a vehicle of rehabilitation, as if the criminal were not fully responsible for willing against right and needed to be transformed so as to be able to act with rectitude. A criminal can only be held guilty if he or she is recognized to be capable of distinguishing between right and wrong and capable of freely choosing between respecting or violating the rights of others. Consequently, punishment properly consists in a retribution that lies in imprisonment, which specifically curtails the willing against right of the criminal.

Punishment thereby entails recognition of the rights of the criminal, who can only be liable for punishment by being judged responsible to respect the rights of others, which, as rights, are shared by the criminal. The length of imprisonment should fit the crime, but confinement should never involve any further deprivation of right. Prisoners should retain whatever exercise of their property, family, economic, and political rights is possible under the conditions of imprisonment. We should never deprive imprisoned individuals of their right to vote. Our current policy of taking away voting rights from the 2.4 million people we incarcerate and nearly 4 million more former felons is an inexcusable voter suppression that strikes disproportionately at the poor and people of color.[228]

Civil cases, in contrast to criminal cases, do not involve righting wrongs that are committed with malicious intent. Instead, civil violations infringe upon legal rights either inadvertently or with non-malicious intent. They include cases of accidental harm for which someone is responsible and disputes where parties disagree over property agreements, family arrangements, economic transactions, or some other arena in which legal rights are at stake. Since malice is absent, crime is not at issue and punishment is not warranted. Instead, victims deserve compensation for the wrong they have suffered, which may involve monetary payment, transfers of property, divorce settlements, child custody decisions, contract fulfillments, and other remedies that resolve infringements of legal right.

Criminal cases may differ from civil cases by warranting punishment, which may drastically affect the lives of the convicted felon. Nonetheless, civil cases are no less important to the rights of individuals. Harms deserving compensation may equal or far exceed those inflicted in crimes, which may cause none. Moreover, civil disputes can concern the most crucial issues of property and contract, marriage and child custody, housing, economic livelihood, sexual harassment, and discrimination. If one cannot obtain legal representation in *both* criminal and civil cases, one's rights are in peril.

The Imperfect Right to Legal Representation in the United States

Amendment VI of the United States Constitution assures that, "In all criminal prosecutions, the accused shall enjoy the right to a speedy and public trail, by an impartial jury of the State and district wherein the crime shall have been committed, which district shall have been previously ascertained by law, and to be informed of the nature and cause of the accusation; to be confronted with the witnesses against him; to have compulsory process for obtaining witnesses in his favor, and to have the Assistance of Counsel for his defense." Amendment VII of the United States Constitution does mandate that, "In Suits at common law, where the value in controversy shall exceed twenty dollars, the right of trial by jury shall be preserved, and no fact tried by a jury, shall be otherwise reexamined in any Court of the United States, than according to the rules of the common law." Nowhere, however, does the United States Constitution guarantee legal representation for civil cases. Instead, we must depend on our private resources to hire civil legal counsel, which for many, is unaffordable. As a result, *all* our rights stand in jeopardy to the extent that they are subject to civil infringements, which we are not all able to remedy properly in court. Without civil legal representation, we lack adequate means to protect our property, our families, our homes, our jobs, our political rights, and our environment.

We may hope that the Sixth Amendment secures us proper legal counsel at least in criminal cases, but in reality, we do not enjoy equal criminal legal assistance. Those who cannot afford to hire criminal lawyers must depend upon pro bono legal assistance, which may not be available to all, or public Legal Aid clinics and court appointed lawyers, whose conditions of practice put their clients at a disadvantage.

Pro bono legal assistance, where private law firms offer free service as a part of their practice, suffers from the contingency of all private charity, which never can be counted on to offer aid to everyone who needs it. Public assistance must supplement what pro bono work does not provide, but the form public legal assistance takes in our country is notably deficient.

Due to strained public financing, Legal Aid lawyers typically have crushing caseloads and comparatively meager resources to investigate and prepare their clients' defense. According to a 2007 US Department of Justice report, nearly ¾ of county public defenders shoulder caseloads surpassing the maximum recommended annual limit of 150 felonies and 400 misdemeanors. For example, the annual individual caseload of legal aid attorneys in Florida in 2009 was more than 500 felonies and 2,225 misdemeanors. In Washington State, where misdemeanor caseloads recently reached 1,000 per legal aid lawyer per year, clients received less than an hour of time each from their publicly appointed defense attorneys. As a result, fair investigation of the facts of accusations is sorely lacking and plea bargaining ends more than 95% of criminal cases, leaving clients condemned with no proper public scrutiny in court.[229]

Court appointed lawyers, for their part, are paid relatively little for their services, undercutting their ability and incentive to devote sufficient time and energy as a public defender. Whereas in 2016 the median income of all attorneys was $118,160, public defenders fell deep into the lowest quartile of attorney income.[230] A 2015 study of court appointed attorneys in Michigan found that they averaged $580 in earnings per case, whereas criminal lawyers made $222 per hour on average in private practice.[231] Public defenders rarely put up a protracted fight on behalf of their clients, in no small part because they receive too little to fund the effort. Only 1.6% of their cases even went to trial. In only 2% of cases did public defenders hire an outside expert or investigator on behalf of their client. Public defenders filed motions contesting the prosecution in only 8% of cases, and in 22% of the cases, the client met the court appointed attorney for the first time as the trial began in court.[232]

On top of these deficiencies, as if to add insult to injury, 43 states bill clients of legal aid attorneys and court appointed lawyers for the services of their public defenders! In flagrant travesty of our Sixth Amendment, these states saddle indigent clients typically with two charges: an application fee to hire their defender, ranging from $10 to $400, and reimbursement fees running into the thousands of dollars. If these clients cannot pay their bills, they often face interest payments, further fines, confiscation of driver licenses, and incarceration.[233]

Affluent clients, by contrast, can afford to hire their dream team of criminal lawyers, who can marshal far greater resources than their underpaid and overworked public counterparts. So long as this situation persists, we are not equal before the law. In our land of extreme wealth inequality, money still fatefully conditions the quality and extent of our legal representation in the one sphere in which we enjoy constitutionally guaranteed legal assistance. It can be no surprise that the poor disproportionately succumb to plea bargaining and pack our prisons. Insofar as poverty weighs most heavily upon historically discriminated groups, the inequity in criminal legal representation compounds racial disadvantage by facilitating the imprisonment of people of color, which dismembers families and undermines their livelihoods, while disenfranchising those who languish in prison.

The deprivation of fair legal representation is all the more dire in civil cases, given the absence of *any* constitutional guarantee of an assistance of counsel. Individuals may benefit from some pro bono assistance from private law firms and from the help of non-profit organizations like Legal Services, which offer civil representation to some of those who cannot afford to hire lawyers on their own. This assistance, however, is much more limited in scope than that providing criminal representation through Legal Aid clinics and court appointed lawyers.

The Legal Services Corporation, which is the largest funder of non-profit civil legal assistance in the United States, documented in its *2017 Justice Gap Report* that 86% of Americans who need civil legal assistance received none.[234] Of those who approached the Legal Services Corporation for civil legal representation, nearly two thirds failed to get adequate aid for their legal needs due to lack of sufficient resources at its disposal.[235] These unmet needs are pervasive, as indicated by the fact that nearly three fourths of low-income households face a civil legal problem during the year, most often concerning health care, consumer and finance problems, and employment, in that order of frequency.[236]

The failure to obtain civil legal representation has catastrophic results for those facing wrongs that jeopardize their employment, retirement income, health care, education, disability and veteran benefits, housing, child custody, and defense against spousal abuse, sexual harassment, discrimination, and disenfranchisement. In all these cases, the absence of any guarantee of proper civil legal assistance leaves millions virtually powerless to uphold their basic family, social, and political rights. While exposing many to eviction and foreclosure, job loss, denial of retirement income, deprivation of needed health care, and family disruptions, lack of civil counsel further accelerates growing wealth inequality, deepens racial disadvantage, and intensifies the stress that takes a physical and psychological toll on individuals and their dependents.

A telling example concerns how civil legal assistance bears upon tenant rights. Whereas 90% of landlords have legal counsel, 90% of tenants have none. In New York City, when tenants have legal representation they win their civil cases 90% of the time, whereas when they go to court with no attorney, they end up facing eviction half the time.[237] A similar fate awaits homeowners whose lack of legal assistance leaves them all too vulnerable to foreclosure. Our homelessness epidemic is due not just to the lack of affordable housing. It also reflects how the inequity in civil representation tips the scales of justice to rob many of the roof above their heads.

On their own, civil plaintiffs lack the legal expertise to defend their rights adequately in court. Burdened with work and family responsibilities, they also lack the time to prepare their case and even go to court to take the legal measures to which they are entitled. Admittedly, they may not face the wrongful imprisonment that threatens criminal defendants lacking adequate legal assistance. Potential civil plaintiffs are, however, in peril of wrongfully losing their jobs, their homes, their children, their healthcare, their educational opportunities, their retirement and veterans benefits, and their voting rights, while being subject to abuse and discrimination for which they have no remedy.

The social rights agenda remains fundamentally incomplete so long as there persists a justice gap in both criminal and civil legal representation. Whereas the justice gap in criminal legal assistance puts all too many Americans in jeopardy of fueling our world-leading mass incarceration, the justice gap in civil legal assistance puts all too many more at risk of homelessness, unemployment, ill health, broken families, predation, and destitution. There is no "liberty and justice for all" so long as comparable legal assistance for both criminal and civil cases is unavailable to every resident of our land. The abiding absence of equity in legal representation is a national scandal crying out for a national remedy.

The Case for Legal Care for All

Other nations have attempted to eliminate the lack of affordable civil representation by extending the guarantee of legal assistance to civil as well as criminal cases.[238] An important milestone in this effort is the adoption of Article 47 of the Charter of Fundamental Rights of the European Union, which broadly mandates that "Legal aid shall be made available to those who lack sufficient resources in so far as such aid is necessary to ensure effective access to justice."[239] To apply this mandate to civil representation, many nations have relied on the approach taken by the United States to guarantee legal representation in criminal cases, funding legal aid clinics and publicly appointed attorneys to help clients in civil cases. Although these efforts are considerable improvements upon our failure to guarantee representation in civil matters, they fall prey to the same problems plaguing our approach to criminal legal assistance. Affluent individuals can hire private law firms with fulsome time and resources to devote to their clients, whereas those who cannot afford to do so must rely upon public legal defenders with comparatively restricted budgets and heavier caseloads. Although everyone may have access to legal representation, there remains a divide in legal opportunity between an advantaged group that can afford private representation and a disadvantaged group that must rely upon public legal aid.

This abiding inequity reflects the analogous problems that plague public health systems that guarantee health care to all, but fund public sector health care providers alongside a private sector health industry that offers faster premium services to those with more financial resources. Although everyone has access to health care, individuals with more money still enjoy a privileged level of treatment that undermines equal opportunity to medical well-being. We can readily overcome such inequity in health care by following the approach of a single payer public health insurance program, which allows individuals to seek care at any health provider of their choice, who the common public health insurer will pay. This arrangement gives everyone access to the same level and quality of healthcare, while retaining the established array of healthcare providers, be they for-profit or non-profit private enterprises or public institutions.

A Legal Care for All program, following the approach of a single payer public health insurance, can achieve the same even-handed fulfillment of right in the domain of legal representation. Unlike programs that offer means-tested access to public legal aid clinics and court appointed lawyers, a legal care for all public insurance system will truly level the playing field for legal representation. A public legal insurance fund with no copays and no deductibles allows all individuals to go to any lawyer of their choosing to obtain personal civil or criminal legal advice and/or representation. No longer will clients with less money be shunted to a second tier of legal service providers with less resources than the premium services available to more affluent individuals. No longer will personal wealth condition legal representation, for under Legal Care for All, no matter which attorneys clients hire, the public legal insurance scheme will pay their legal representatives in full.

Moreover, Legal Care for All can keep legal costs in check without undermining the solvency of law firms. Just as a single payer health insurance program has the means to cut our health care costs in half through effective price negotiation with health care providers, so Legal Care for All can contain legal expenditures through similar unified national bargaining that meets the needs of all parties to the legal process. Negotiations between the public legal insurance authority and representatives of lawyers will set common viable rates for different legal services that the public legal insurance program will pay legal practitioners. Since the legal care insurance plan will cover all personal legal advice and representation, lawyers will not have the option to reserve superior services for deeper pockets. Furthermore, Legal Care for All will not cover corporate legal services, leaving law firms free to seek business in that field. Of course, once the fulfillment of the social rights agenda for employee empowerment achieves fair worker representation on corporate boards, corporate law practice will operate with a different concern for the interests of all parties to our economy.

In addition, with a single payer public insurance system in place, Legal Care for All can save considerable administrative costs for both health and legal services by joining the legal insurance program to the public health insurance program in a unified endeavor that guarantees every resident access to both health care and legal representation.

On all counts, the Legal Care for All program will generally increase the business of lawyers who represent individuals in civil and criminal matters, while containing the cost of personal legal services. The vast majority of civil claimants who currently go to court without legal assistance will be able to hire lawyers, who will no longer suffer the overwhelming caseloads and inferior resources of legal aid attorneys and their court-appointed counterparts. Legal Care for All will therefore fulfill the right to legal representation without reducing choice of legal representation or harming the practice of personal criminal and civil legal attorneys.

Why We Should Prohibit Plea Bargaining

The enactment of Legal Care for All eliminates one of the chief factors responsible for the explosion of plea bargaining in criminal cases in the United States, which has provided a fast track to mass incarceration. Under current circumstances, economically disadvantaged individuals who cannot afford private attorneys must rely on legal aid clinics and court appointed lawyers who do not have the resources or time to mount adequate defenses. This situation contributes to the scandalous 95% rate of plea bargaining in criminal cases, which leaves defendants, victims, and the public with no due examination of the facts of the case in court.

The entering of pleas and the cessation of further court investigations upon admission of guilt might ideally involve warranted recognition of the legitimacy of court decisions on the part of defendants. To whatever degree this may occur, it transpires at the expense of an absolute privileging of confessions, as if an admission of guilt trumps all other facts of the case. Obviously, a guilty plea need not be honest or accurate, but may obscure the truth. A defendant may plead guilty to protect others or out of self-deception or a misunderstanding of all circumstances contributing to the crime at issue. Moreover, allowing guilty pleas to end court scrutiny is an invitation to abuse, inciting psychological and physical pressure to get defendants to confess. Furthermore, even when a confession of guilt is honest and accurate, allowing a guilty plea to end court proceedings prevents the public from finding out the facts of the case. This cloaking of the full truth was notoriously present in the trial of the assassin of Martin Luther King, where the guilty plea helped preempt any further criminal investigation of the full story of the assassination.

Even with proper representation by a private attorney of the defendant's choosing, who is fairly compensated by the public legal insurance of Legal Care for All, circumstances can arise where plea bargaining proceeds to the detriment of justice, hobbling the right of the public to know the facts of the case. The imperative for a full impartial investigation is particularly relevant in criminal cases, since crime involves a willing against right and not just harm to a particular individual, which may or may not result from crime.

Other nations have eliminated plea bargaining by eliminating all pleas in criminal cases.[240] We should follow this route. Whenever individuals are indicted with criminal charges, they deserve a proper court investigation of the facts of the case, together with the equitable legal representation Legal Care for All guarantees. Admittedly, courts will have more full trials to handle, but it is our responsibility to fund sufficient court staff and facilities to enable everyone to have their rights legally upheld with due process.

So long as money conditions one's ability to defend one's rights through our legal system, oligarchy taints our democracy, letting wealth dominate at the expense of self-determination. The establishment of Legal Care for All and the abolition of plea bargaining will transform our legal system to the benefit of our freedom, but these measures do not completely prevent differences in private wealth from impeding equal treatment in the legal process. Three practices infecting our legal system still allow money to decide the fate of our rights before the law: cash bail, the creeping metamorphosis of our legal institutions into profit seeking enterprises, and the proliferation of fines and fees within the legal system.

Why We Should Abolish Cash Bail

All legal subjects deserve treatment as innocent until proven guilty with due process. Pre-trial detention is admissible if there are reasonable grounds to fear that the accused is at high risk to abscond or commit crimes jeopardizing public safety, including destruction of evidence and witness tampering. No one, however, should be subject to pre-trial detention without a timely judicial hearing with proper legal assistance, such as Legal Care for All can guarantee.[241] Bail, as traditionally understood, allows an accused to avoid pre-trial detention with some assurance of attending court proceedings and posing no serious threat to public safety. The Eighth Amendment of the United States Constitution affirms that,

"Excessive bail shall not be required, nor excessive fines imposed, nor cruel and unusual punishments inflicted."

The United States is one of only two nations that permits cash bail[242] and no feature of our administration of justice more brazenly makes our legal fate depend upon our wealth. Cash bail violates the Eighth Amendment because any bail is excessive that requires the accused to put up a cash surety that the accused will forfeit upon nonappearance in court. Why this is so is starkly evident.

On the one hand, cash bail is always excessive insofar as it imposes special hardship upon those of lesser wealth. These inequitable hardships are most severe when individuals who cannot pay cash bail suffer the penalty of pre-trial detention despite presumptive innocence. They incur a fundamentally unlawful violation of due process, since they suffer detention with no proper hearing, no right to counsel, and no right to call and question witnesses, let alone any right to appeal their jailing.[243] Moreover, their pre-trial detention, which can drag on for months and years, all too often causes loss of needed income and employment, precipitating evictions and foreclosures, as well as further harm to family welfare, including forfeiture of child custody and disruption of marriage. Significant hardships also apply to those of lesser means who pay cash bail and escape pre-trial confinement. Even if they furnish the entire bail payment on their own and retrieve it when they appear for trial, they must deal with the loss of that money during their wait for court proceedings to begin. The costs deepen their impoverishment further when they must rely on for-profit bail bond companies, which levy non-refundable fees, as well as added interest charges on borrowed bail bond payments. Although these accused avoid jail, cash bail saddles them and their families with new lasting financial burdens that they are least able to afford.

On the other hand, cash bail should never be available when due process hearings have determined the accused to be a serious threat to public safety or liable to abscond. For this determination, relevant factors include the gravity of the alleged crime, the past record of the accused, the prospective strength of evidence, and even the safety of the accused, who may face extra-judicial threats.[244] The relevant court needs to review promptly and duly all these grounds, with adequate legal assistance afforded the accused, who remains presumed innocent. If pre-trial detention then is judged appropriate, there should be no opportunity for anyone having sufficient wealth to post cash bail to escape jail awaiting trial. Money should never buy freedom for anyone when duly conducted legal proceedings mandate detention. We jeopardize both public safety and the public interest to bring an accused to trial when those with greater wealth can use cash bail to walk free and far without firm impediment. Our cash bail policy does just that by enabling half of high-risk defendants to take advantage of the collusion of for-profit bail bondsmen to forestall detention before trial, without any court supervised monitoring.[245] Cash bail thereby imperils public safety and secure court appearance, while imposing undue punishment upon the poor.

The crushing inequities of cash bail take an enormous toll on our people. Those who cannot pay cash bail make up nearly 60%[246] of the nearly half million Americans presumed innocent but awaiting trial in jail.[247] Those detained due to the inability to post cash bail also comprise 95% of jail population growth since 2000,[248] significantly increasing our unparalleled mass incarceration. The cost of jailing these presumed innocents, who are *not* reasonable threats to public safety *nor* likely to abscond, can amount to $120 per day,[249] which we, the public, bear while our jailed fellows and their families suffer an economic calamity of their own. While in jail, these presumed innocents do not have the same opportunity to secure legal assistance and prepare their cases as they would have if released from custody. As their confinement continues, pre-trial detainees are often more and more ready to resort to plea bargaining to escape their indeterminate jailing, submitting to conviction without any public scrutiny of the facts of the case in court.[250] Furthermore, as they languish and their economic and family problems mount, pre-trial detainees understandably suffer depression, which too often leads to suicide, as notorious examples have made newsworthy.[251] As Eric Sterling, executive director of the Criminal Justice Policy Foundation, has said, "A system where you are presumptively jailed unless you can buy your freedom is a form of pretrial punishment",[252] which can amount to capital punishment for unlucky, distressed, and forgotten detainees.

Insofar as African Americans, Native Americans, and Hispanics are disproportionately poor, it can be no surprise that they suffer nearly half of these pre-trial detentions. Not only are they "twice as likely to be stuck in jail because they cannot afford money bail," but, as Cherise Fanno Burdeen reports in *The Atlantic*, they "face higher bail amounts on average than white defendants with similar charges."[253] Minority detentions only further compound their social disadvantage and strangle their political rights to vote, run for office, and support campaigns. All these factors contribute to make them disproportionately liable to share pre-trial detainees' tendency to have a higher rate of conviction than those on bail and to suffer a higher rate of "recidivism".[254]

Meanwhile, our for-profit bond bail industry prospers. Whereas other countries have outlawed any payments for posting bond, we have allowed for-profit bond bail companies to charge non-refundable fees to their clients, who commonly pay 10% of their posted bail to those companies, which receive back the entire cash bail when clients appear in court.[255] To pad their profits further, bond bail companies charge hefty interest to those clients who must borrow from them to pay the non-refundable bail fee. Dominated by less than 10 corporations, the for-profit bail bond industry reaps annual revenues of $14 billion, clearing $2 billion of yearly profit.[256] Meanwhile, we taxpayers spend another $14 billion to fund the jailing of those who cannot afford bail and sit in pre-trial detention.[257] These expenses represent a significant drain upon both the private means of people living on the edge of destitution, who are disproportionately people of color,[258] and public resources that could be promoting equal treatment under the law.

The abolition of cash bail is imperative if we are to prevent wealth from conditioning our legal standing and instead enforce liberty and justice for all. Those properly deemed to pose a high safety or flight risk may warrant detention while awaiting trial. Everyone else should escape the unwarranted punishment of pre-trial detention. Never should one be able to buy one's way out of jail. We can enlist other means than jail to ensure trial appearance, such as regular reporting in person or electronically, including GPS monitoring. If we employ such measures, we should do so without imposing any fees and with least inconvenience so as not to impede livelihood, family welfare, or political involvement.[259] Under these conditions, (non-cash) bail can serve its legitimate aims without subverting justice and accelerating our world-leading mass incarceration.[260]

Why We Should Prohibit For-Profit Prisons

Today, the United States leads the world in not only incarcerating people, but privatizing prisons. Nearly one quarter of the world's imprisoned population languishes in our prisons, in no small part due to War on Crime and War on Drugs policies expanding mandatory minimum sentences, three strike laws imposing life terms, and restrictions on probation, parole, and other alternatives to imprisonment. As our prisons multiply to house our growing incarcerated multitude, more and more operate for-profit. Since 1984,[261] increasing numbers of United States' prisons have become private enterprises, seeking gain. As our prison population has exploded, a growing five billion dollar corrections industry has turned more than 130 prisons into business ventures,[262] housing

7% of state and 18% of federal prisoners, and almost 75% of immigration detainees.[263]

The ostensible rationale for privatizing prisons is that a profit seeking business can most readily reduce the costs of incarceration. Numerous studies spanning three decades have called into question whether private prisons are noticeably lower cost than public penitentiaries. Back in 1996, a General Accounting Office study found no compelling evidence that private prisons were less expensive to operate than government facilities.[264] The verdict was the same in 2011, when both the Arizona Department of Corrections and Policy Matters Ohio issued reports finding private prisons in their respective states to have no demonstrable cost advantages over public prisons.[265] Another survey of twenty-four cost-effectiveness studies found no conclusive difference between private and public prisons.[266] This inability to locate private prison cost savings applies despite the fact that, in comparison to public institutions, private prisons tend to house prison populations requiring less expensive care,[267] tend to be comparatively understaffed with less trained and less well-compensated employees, and tend to offer less extensive services.

Even if private prisons are less expensive to run than their public counterparts, cost efficiency is not the governing principle of the legal administration of punishment. What matters most is the justice of the prison system, which mandates that the fulfillment of right take precedence over all other considerations.

For-profit prisons operate in stark conflict with the impartial implementation of due punishment of criminals. Run as profit seeking enterprises, prisons have a vested interest in incarcerating as many people for as long and cheaply as possible. To fulfill their governing business model, for-profit prisons aim at expanding our world-leading mass incarceration, while subjecting inmates to the most miserly conditions, with the least public oversight. Moreover, private corrections corporations have an economic incentive to spend whatever money they can to pad their profits by influencing government officials and lobbying for legislation to expand prison privatization and increase the numbers of prisoners and the length of their sentences, while decreasing private prison services, staffing, and training, and minimizing their public accountability. Profit maximization is simply not oriented at providing all prisoners adequate legal resources to defend their rights, sufficient mental and physical health care, fair contact with friends and family, and as many highly qualified, adequately trained, well-paid staff as necessary to deliver optimal services. For-profit prisons will reap the greatest revenues by billing the public as much as they can, while spending as little as possible on prison facilities, staffing, and oversight, and charging inmates as much as possible for whatever functions can be levied upon them and their families.

The record of for-profit prisons exhibits all of these predatory practices, which are facilitated by the exemption of private prisons from the open record laws that put government institutions under sweeping public scrutiny.[268] Unencumbered by mandatory transparency and accountability, for-profit corrections facilities can all too easily follow their commercial incentive to cover up problems that threaten their bottom line. Not surprisingly, for-profit detention centers lag behind public facilities in key areas of prison management and inmate welfare.

First, private prisons are significantly more unsafe for inmates and staff alike. For-profit prisons have a noticeably higher rate of violent incidents victimizing both groups.[269] The rate of violent assault in private prisons in Mississippi, for example, is triple the rate in public facilities.[270] On a federal level, a 2004 Federal Probation Journal report states that private prisons have 50% higher inmate-on-inmate and inmate-on-staff assaults than at public facilities.[271] A 2016 United States Department of Justice Report confirms that privately run federal prisons are less safe, less secure, and more punitive than their public counterparts.[272] This situation is hardly accidental. Private prisons suffer from a notably lower ratio of staff to inmates, leaving employees less able to prevent incidents between prisoners, as well as to protect themselves from violence.[273] Exacerbating these problems is that the more thinly stretched employees in for-profit prisons have less training, less experience, and lower qualifications than corrections officers in public facilities. Not surprisingly, they are generally paid less than their public counterparts and lack union organization to defend their welfare against the correction corporation's profit maximization agenda. As a result, private prison staff has a turnover rate of 53%, compared to 16% at public facilities, leaving a less experienced and less stable work force.[274] All these factors weigh against staff well-being and that of their families, as well as against proper care for inmates.

Symptomatic of these deficiencies is the long list of inmate abuse scandals that have plagued the industry.[275] Among the most notorious is that of a Florida for-profit prison, which enlisted juvenile detainees to enforce discipline by manhandling others. As the local Broward County chief assistant public defender declared, "The children are used by staff members to inflict harm on other children."[276]

The greater danger to inmates in private prisons does not just involve higher rates of violence. For-profit prisons also offer inmates less adequate medical care, which can become a death sentence for unlucky prisoners suffering from grave physical or mental problems. In California, to cite one telling case, nurses threatened to strike in protest of "unsafe" substandard health care at a for-profit prison chain.[277] Inadequate medical treatment, however, is not the only threat to the health of private prison inmates. Under the veil of private management, prison food has sometimes been so meager and unhealthy as to imperil the proper nourishment of inmates. In a glaring instance, for-profit prisons reportedly both underfed Michigan inmates and served them rotten, rat-infested food.[278]

Finally, for-profit prisons offer comparatively less drug counseling and job training than public prisons.[279] This is to be expected insofar as private prisons have no incentive to release prisoners or reduce recidivism. Not surprisingly, the highest recidivism rates are in states, such as New Mexico, Alaska, Hawaii, and Vermont, with the highest proportion of privately imprisoned inmates.[280]

Who are the victims of these abuses? Those who suffer directly from prison privatization are people of color, who disproportionately feed the mass incarceration on which for profit prisons prosper. Insidiously, their victimization is further encouraged by the influence peddling, bribery, and lobbying on which private corrections corporations have spent many millions to grow their profits.

On occasion, for-profit prison companies have engaged in blatant corruption. Perhaps the most infamous example is the 2011 "cash for kids" jail scheme where private prison operators bribed the Luzerne County, Pennsylvania, Juvenile Court Judge to fill their facility by imposing harsh punishments on thousands of children.[281]

Legal, but more sweeping in toxic effect, are the broad campaign contribution and lobbying efforts of private corrections corporations. Like any other business that operates under a system permitting corporate money to solicit political support, the private prison industry has an economic incentive to spend many millions of dollars to curry favor that promises to enhance its profits. Since 1989, the two leading for-profit prison companies, the Corrections Corporation of America (CCA) and the GEO Group, have alone contributed over ten million dollars to candidates and lavished twenty five million dollars on lobbying efforts to increase prison sentences, expand the prison population, and extend prison privatization.[282] A significant part of this investment has gone to ALEC (the American Legislative Exchange Council), which has lobbied state legislators to enact laws extending incarceration to nonviolent offenses. Although private prison corporations have denied lobbying on immigration policy, the CCA spent $10,560,000 between 2008 and 2014 to increase immigrant detention, with no small success.[283] All these efforts have encouraged the acceleration of mass incarceration, which serves the business model of for-profit prisons, at the expense of disproportionately ravaging the lives and families of poor people and people of color. Caught in the web of punishment are the more than 2.7 million United States children who have a parent in prison.[284] For their sake and the sake of current and future prisoners whose rights brazen profit maximization imperils, we should abolish the for-profit prison industry.[285]

Why We Should Prohibit For-Profit Probation Services

The prohibition of private prisons will eliminate a shameful stain on our criminal justice system, but the work of securing equity before the law will not be complete without remedying the abuses of for-profit probation services.

Whereas parole consists in early release of prisoners, whose behavior warrants freedom from detention, probation consists in a supervised period during which offenders avoid imprisonment by meeting certain conditions. Both parole and probation serve justice by reducing unnecessary, unwarranted incarceration, which, in the United States, takes a disproportionate toll on the poor and people of color. Four and a half million Americans are currently on probation or parole.[286] If we are to uphold equality before the law, it is not enough to have Legal Care for All, end plea bargaining, abolish cash bail, and prohibit for-profit prisons. We must also insure that neither parole nor probation disadvantage individuals in function of their wealth.

As our exploding mass incarceration has set the stage for the rise of a for-profit prison industry, the parallel growth in our criminal justice expenditures has precipitated the emergence of a for-profit probation service industry. State and municipal governments, which have refused to raise needed funding through fair taxes, have increasingly relied on a for-profit probation industry to extract revenues from offenders. To serve public debt collection on mounting unpaid court fines, private probation companies have offered an "offender-funded" business model, which promises to take all costs off the shoulders of government and place them entirely on the backs of offenders. More than a thousand United States courts have enlisted for-profit probation services to monitor the deferred court payments of offenders, who are on probation because they lack the funds to pay off their fines upon sentencing.[287] Although probation in such cases should pertain only to court imposed fines, private probation companies make their money by charging offenders extra supervision fees, which grow the longer probation lasts. As these "offender-funded" surcharges accumulate, offenders face more debt and longer probation, during which failure to meet added payments threatens further penalties, including possible imprisonment. This arrangement falls heavier upon individuals the poorer they are, for the more those offenders lack funds to pay off fines, the longer time they remain on probation and the heavier charges they accumulate from the supervision fees of their for-profit probation minders.[288] Since the revenues of private probation companies come directly from these extra fees, the business model of the "offender-funded" for-profit probation industry depends upon a continuing supply of poor offenders who it can squeeze for as much and long as possible, while spending as little upon probation services as it can manage. What also helps the bottom line for private probation companies is their exemption from any financial responsibility for the expenses of detaining probationers who fail to pay their supervision fees. Although the "offender-funded" business model purports to free taxpayers of probation expenditures, we end up bearing the cost of imprisonment when private companies jail their charges for inability to pay the added supervision fees.[289]

Since private probation services are exempt from open-records laws that apply to public operations, they, like the for-profit prison industry, benefit from a lack of transparency and accountability. Investigative journalism has exposed some probation industry firms that have extorted high fees from offenders, while offering them scant supervisory services.[290] Maintaining high caseloads at the expense of probationer care, of course, serves the business model of the private probation industry. It is no secret that just as for-profit prisons lag behind public prisons with respect to staff training and experience, so private probation companies require staff to have "less certification, licenses, education, training, and employment recommendations than required of probation officers in the employ of the state."[291]

To secure business, for-profit probation services have followed the lead of for-profit prisons in contributing to political candidates, both local and state-wide, while enlisting lobbyists to their cause.[292] The more private probation companies can extract from poor offenders, the more influence they can peddle to grow their "cash register probation"[293] industry.

For-profit probation companies have mushroomed in many of our states, collecting deferred court fines from probationers to hand over to local government, while taking in from these poor offenders tens of millions of dollars of additional fees that often far exceed the original penalty. Georgia has become a leader in enlisting private probation services, after inaugurating the practice through state legislation in 2000.[294] In just this one state, for-profit probation companies have made $40 million yearly from the service fees levied on their misdemeanor offenders.[295] At any given time, more than thirty for-profit probation companies supervise nearly 340,000 Georgia offenders, who make up 80% of the misdemeanor probationers in the state.[296]

The blatant inequity of "offender-funded" probation services has drawn growing criticism, but not court judgments banning the practice.

Instead, in Georgia, the state Supreme Court has ruled private probation supervision to be constitutional, but has declared it illegal to extend a probationer's sentence after sentencing.[297] More recently, the Georgia Supreme Court came close to undermining the "offender-funded" business model by ruling that Sentinel Offender Services violated probationers' rights by imposing "tolls" on top of government fines, with payment schedules for supervision fees that extend well beyond repayment of the original probation fine.[298] Meanwhile, plaintiffs have sued probation service companies, like Sentinel, for unilaterally imposing such "services" as drug tests for which offenders are billed. Although for-profit probation businesses have paid out some large settlements, they continue to operate on the "offender-funded" model.[299] More sweeping lawsuits are in progress, challenging for-profit probation supervision as tantamount to criminalizing poverty by putting people on probation who are too poor to pay off court fines and subjecting them to the further penalty of probation service fees, as well as imprisonment if they fail to pay these extra costs.

For-profit probation services raise the specter of a new introduction of debtor's prison. Back in 1983 the United States Supreme Court had ruled in *Bearden v. Georgia* that an individual cannot have probation revoked and be put in jail due to the inability to pay a fine.[300] Despite that ruling, the current practice of private probation supervision is keeping alive and well the threat of imprisonment for non-payment. We should end this criminalization of poverty and abolish for-profit probation.

Why We Should End the Proliferation of Fines and Fees in the Legal System

There would be little opportunity for the for-profit probation industry to prosper were it not for the proliferation of fees that government at all levels has imposed upon any persons seeking to defend their rights in court. The explosion of fees has not come out of nowhere. In the four decades since the declarations of the War on Crime and the War on Drugs, the population in United States detention increased by 700 percent, while annual state corrections systems costs rose from $6 to $67 billion in 2010.[301] Pandering politicians have been reluctant to use fair taxation to meet the growing costs of enforcing our laws and upholding our legal entitlements. Instead, government has shifted more and more of the growing burden of judicial system expenditures upon those residents who find it necessary to come before the law.

The United States system of justice has become a toll road, requiring personal payments to obtain the legal service to which we are all entitled as equal subjects before the law. A new regime of judicial monetary extraction has arisen, intensifying and supplementing the longstanding use of court fines with an epidemic of fees. Thereby making money an increasingly pervasive condition for the due legal enforcement of rights, our system of justice is imposing hardships that fall disproportionately upon those with less wealth. Proliferating court fines and fees are playing an increasingly significant role in this subversion of legal equity.

Misdemeanor fines might seem to be an innocuous part of the judicial system. They are innocuous for affluent residents, who can pay off these penalties immediately upon sentencing with negligible effect upon their livelihood and welfare. The case is very different for the many Americans who live on the edge of or in poverty. A simple parking ticket can be catastrophic for anyone who lacks the money to pay it, since such an individual may soon face an accumulation of late fees and interest payments that are increasingly difficult to afford. All too many courts are ready to penalize the poor who cannot meet these ballooning debts by suspending their driver's license, canceling benefits like subsidized housing and food stamps,[302] or summoning them to court.[303] Loss of public housing can mean homelessness and all the personal and family traumas this entails. Loss of food stamps can mean malnutrition or starvation, with fatal or lifelong consequences, especially for dependent children. Loss of a driver's license may seem comparatively unimportant, but it can mean the end of a job and of access to childcare, health clinics, food and drug stores, and other crucial services for any American who lives in areas without adequate public transportation. Loss of income can then lead to eviction and foreclosure, as well as family difficulties that threaten marriage and child custody. Finally, driving without a license or failing to pay fines can lead to criminal prosecution and imprisonment, further destroying livelihood and family life. All these consequences entrap the poor in a whirlpool of deepening deprivation that makes it less and less possible to overcome the original court debt that brought on all these complications.[304]

Impositions of misdemeanor fines, as well as arrests, have themselves proliferated in parallel with stop and frisk and "broken window" policing policies that are disproportionately conducted in impoverished minority neighborhoods. The same holds true for fines and arrests for victimless crimes, such as marijuana possession,[305] which predominantly harvest the very communities whose members have least access to quality legal representation.

It may be forgotten, but let us remember again that in 1983 the United States Supreme Court ruled in *Bearden v. Georgia* that nobody unable to pay court debts should be imprisoned or further penalized for their poverty. Instead, our justice system has an obligation to find some alternate resolution, such as replacing a fine with community service.[306] This call to legal equity has fallen on deaf ears, however, as courts throughout our land continue to impose fines and fees and to exact punishment upon failure to pay.

The bill now placed upon the shoulders of legal subjects extends well beyond court fines to include charges for many services formerly provided free by the state as basic fixtures of due process. The list is shocking.

In 43 states and the district of Columbia, defendants are billed for public defender representation; in 41 states, inmates pay for room and board in jail and prison; in 44 states, offenders pay for probation and parole services; and in every state except Hawaii, and the District of Columbia, probationers and parolees pay fees for GPS monitoring devices.[307]

Now fees follow individuals at every step of the legal process. Even before they enter the courtroom, they must pay fees for arrest warrants, DNA sample collection, and public defenders.[308] Then follow "court costs", including not only fees supporting court salaries, utilities, and facilities, but even charges for jury trials.[309] Finally, fees continue to mount after sentencing, through charges for prison services, for probation and parole monitoring, and even for performing community service.

If persons cannot afford to pay for these services, they simply go without them if possible or accumulate further debt that puts them in jeopardy of more costly passage through the tollbooths of our criminal justice system. Moreover, the accrued debt is hardly interest free. Instead, the debt keeps growing, especially when states, such as Washington, charge an average 12% interest rate on felony case defendants.[310]

Perversely, the proliferation of fees and of incarceration for failing to pay them only increases the costs of the legal system, which elicit these tolls in the first place. The expense of jailing and imprisoning debtors quickly outpaces unpaid fines, while imposing vast collateral costs on the welfare of the families and neighborhoods of the unlucky poor who cannot buy their way out of detention.

Whereas the affluent can pay their fines, walk free, and evade all the other justice system tolls, those less fortunate are punished for their poverty with a cavalcade of fees that deepen their deprivation and the racial disadvantage they disproportionately bear. Today, massive numbers of Americans live under the weight of fine and fee debts imposed by our legal process. From 1991 to 2004, the number of prisoners owing fines and fees rose from 25 to 66 percent.[311] Today, nearly 85% of inmates leaving prison remain entrapped in the debt shackles of justice system fines and fees.[312] That these numbers are only the tip of the iceberg is indicated by how, seven years later, in just one American city, Philadelphia, more than 320,000 residents, a fifth of its population, had unpaid court debts.[313]

We need to eliminate the court fines and judicial system fees that are making justice contingent upon how much money a legal subject possesses. If we also institute Legal Care for All, eliminate cash bail, prohibit plea-bargaining, abolish for-profit prisons, and end for-profit probation services, we can ensure that all legal subjects in the United States are free and equal before the law.

We cannot achieve a new birth of freedom if we only implement the social rights agenda and ignore the inequities in our legal system. To realize our freedoms, we must be able to defend them in court, and for this, we must all have equal access to the legal process, irrespective of our wealth. The policies laid out in this chapter show how we can attain legal equity and liberate the administration of law from the hold of money.

8. The Fair Funding of Our Social Rights

The Cost of Social Justice

The fulfillment of social rights is always relative to the level of opportunity a nation can provide in virtue of its production of wealth and geopolitical situation. Social justice never concerns utopian strivings for what a nation cannot implement. Instead, the shared prerogatives of rights always operate with the options that are at hand. The more prosperous a nation and the greater its freedom from foreign interference, the more opportunities it can make commonly available to its members.

We in the United States are fortunate to possess a potential for opportunity that no other country can rival. We have the largest, most productive economy in human history, with an internal market of unmatched size. Our military is the strongest in the world and we face no realistic threats of foreign military occupation or imperial domination that can limit our national prerogatives. Instead, whatever obstacles to opportunity plague our nation are barriers of our own making. We have allowed ourselves to become more unequal than any other developed nation, with the least social mobility of all.[314] Our racial and gender disadvantages remain entrenched and more of our society lives in economic insecurity than ever since the days of the Guilded Age.

If only we mobilize sufficient political will, we can fulfill the social rights agenda that will secure our imperiled freedoms. The investments needed to do so are completely manageable, given the wealth, productivity, and geopolitical advantages at our disposal.

The keystone of our new birth of freedom is the Federal Job Guarantee. It will eliminate unemployment and poverty wages by offering any resident who is willing and able to work a job serving our community at a new fair minimum wage adjusted to inflation and national productivity gains. We should not underestimate the magnitude of this transformative investment. We need to take into account that unemployment levels rise and fall, as well as that official unemployment figures do not include all those individuals who are working part time but desire full time employment, nor the many others who have given up looking for work out of despair. Accordingly, we should be prepared to tackle unemployment levels such as we encountered in the last Great Recession, when 10% of breadwinners could not find employment. On this basis, the Federal Job Guarantee would need to provide jobs to 16,000,000 people, a tenth of the 160 million Americans earning a living. If the new fair minimum wage amounts to $20 per hour and the workweek is limited to 40 hours, the annual wage of each guaranteed job employee comes to $41,600 ($20 per hour x 40 hours per week x 52 weeks). The total annual wages bill of public sector employment to eliminate 10% joblessness would then amount to 16,000,000 x $41,600 = $656,600,000,000. We should add to this total the likely overhead investments of putting these people to work. Comparable WPA projects had overhead expenses of 1/3 of the wages bill. On this basis, the overhead of employing 16,000,000 people would come to $281,866,667,000. The total investment of the Federal Job Guarantee would then amount to $656,600,000,000 + $281,866,667,000 = $938,466,677,000, approximately 5% of the 2018 United States GNP of $18,766,395,000,000.[315]

This investment may appear imposing, even though it comes to only 1/20 of our GNP. It is, however, more than offset by three factors: 1) enormous savings in welfare expenditures that would no longer be necessary, 2) increased tax revenues from the additional income of the 16,000,000 unemployed put to work and from the increased economic activity generated by their spending, and 3) the value of the goods and services that their employment produces.

Currently the Federal government spends $700 billion and state governments spend $300 billion annually on more than 126 welfare programs.[316] Many of these could be largely, if not entirely curtailed, due to the reduction of poverty that enactment of the fair minimum wage that accompanies the Federal Job Guarantee would achieve.[317] In addition, with the full employment of the Federal Job Guarantee, our government could completely suspend annual unemployment insurance payments of $170 billion.

Moreover, guaranteed jobs would have a significant impact upon the rates of recidivism and the level of incarceration in the United States, both of which far exceed those of other developed nations. Currently, we spend on average $33,274 per inmate per year.[318] Now that we have more than 2,300,000 prison inmates, we are spending more than $76,530,200,000 annually on our mass incarceration. If we reduced our world leading incarceration rate (698 per 100,000) to that of Canada (114 per 100,000),[319] we would save $64,109,348,500. The elimination of unemployment and poverty wages achieved by the Federal Job Guarantee could contribute to a good part of these savings.

Secondly, we can deduct from the cost of the Federal Job Guarantee that portion of its wages bill that goes to taxes. These include not only federal and state income taxes, but property taxes and sales taxes. If the total amount of tax revenue generated by Federal Job Guarantee wages came to 20% of gross income, those additional tax payments would offset the Federal Job Guarantee investment by another $131,320,000,000.

Finally, the goods and services produced by those employed by the Federal Job Guarantee program will add vast amounts of value to our national infrastructure and human capital. There is no reason to expect the work expended to be any less productive than that operating in the private sector. Ordinarily prevailing levels of productivity insure that goods and services have prices no less than the costs of their production, since otherwise a business loses money and goes under. Accordingly, the market value of what Federal Job Guarantee employees contribute to our national endowment should entirely offset their wages bill and overhead costs.

The social rights initiatives to balance work and family and end childhood poverty have a significant cost, but they too are manageable investments. The costs of free public childcare and eldercare are steep, but families who are struggling to keep livelihood and family welfare in harmony are already paying much of these expenses. The cost of full time public childcare is estimated to be around $90 billion,[320] or less than half a percent of our national GNP. Eldercare is much more costly, due to the higher price and higher labor intensity of the varied sorts of assistance that are required. Approximately 12 million Americans are in need of long-term care. The spectrum of the annual costs of elder care services proceed from $17,750 for adult day care, to $40,000 for home care aide, to $42,000 for a home health aide, to $45,000 for assisted living, and to $82,855 for skilled nursing home care.[321] If we take as average a $40,000 annual expense, the total bill for eldercare would come to $480 billion. Together, the expense for public child and elder care comes to $570 billion, only 3% of our national GDP.

The cost of wiping out childhood poverty with a universal child allowance of $900 per month per child is also sizeable. There are approximately 74,000,000 children in the United States.[322] A $900 monthly child allowance would therefore amount to $799,200,000,000 or 4% of US GNP.

Another formidable expense is expanding Social Security Disability and Retirement benefits so that they are comparable to the fair minimum wage of $20/hr. Currently, the 43.1 million Social Security retirees receive a miserly $1,413 monthly benefit, well below the monthly

$3,466.67 income from the fair minimum wage. The 8.7 million recipients of Social Security Disability payments receive even less, averaging $1,198 in monthly benefits.[323] The cost of raising Social Security Retirement benefits to the level of the fair minimum wage requires a monthly supplement of $2,053.67, which, dispensed to the 43,100,000 retirees comes to an additional total monthly expense of $88,513,180,000. We should add to this the monthly supplement of $2,268.67 that is needed to raise disability benefits to the fair minimum level, which, distributed to the 8.7 million disabled beneficiaries, amounts to an additional total monthly expense of $19,737,400,000. Together, the required supplements to Society Security Retirement and Disability Benefits total $108,250,580,000 monthly, or $1,299,007,000,000 annually, which is equivalent to 7% of our GNP. These investments in fair Social Security and Disability benefits will not only curtail poverty and eliminate the need for many welfare programs addressed to impoverished retirees and disabled people, but will increase consumer demand and the investment in increased production to take advantage of the resulting growth in consumer spending. It will therefore also raise tax revenues on the growth of income generated by these "multiplier" effects.

Fulfilling our right to higher education through free tuition and stipends at public colleges and technical schools involves public investments that students and their families are already shouldering. To relieve them of their mounting student debt burden, we need to cover tuition for the approximately 14.8 million students at public colleges and public technical schools.[324] According to the National Center for Education Statistics, the average cost of total tuition, fees, and room and board rates for full time undergraduate students at public institutions was $16,757 per year, as of 2015-16.[325] To cover this expense for all 14.8 million public college students, which include students doing vocational trainings at 2 year public colleges, we need to invest $248 billion each year, or 1.3 % of our annual GNP.

It is difficult to estimate the cost of Legal Care for All. According to the American Bar Association, in 2017 there were 1,335,983 lawyers in the United States. Their average income, according to 2016 figures, was $139,880.[326] The total income of individual lawyers comes to $186,875,000,000, whereas the total earnings of United States law firms come to $274 billion dollars, of which a $100 billion goes to the largest corporate law firms.[327] Legal Services requested $502,700,000 to cover the expense of representing the 20% of civil litigants who they hope to assist.[328] Extrapolating, we should expect at least $2 billion dollars of additional cost to represent the 80% of civil litigants who currently go to court without legal representation. Since a significant part of law firm earnings comes from commercial rather than personal criminal or civil representation, the total legal costs covered by Legal Care for All should fall far below $100 billion.

On the other hand, huge savings come from implementing a public single payer health care insurance program, which can bring our health bills in line with those of other affluent nations. Currently, we spend yearly $3.4 trillion dollars on health care, which amounts to $10,348 per person.[329] That total is double what other comparable nations spend annually per person on health care, all of whom achieve better health outcomes. If we implement single payer public health insurance and negotiate drug and treatment prices in line with international levels, we can save $1.7 trillion dollars every year.

Further, if we complete our social rights agenda, fulfilling our right to fair wages, employee empowerment, fair retirement and disability benefits, healthcare, decent housing, educational opportunity, and legal representation, we are in a position to reap an additional $1 trillion dollars of savings every year from reductions of welfare programs that have become obsolete.

What then, are the net costs of achieving social justice in the United States? The additional expenses of fulfilling the social rights agenda amount to $570 billion for public child and elder care, $799.2 billion for child allowances, $100 billion for Legal Care for All, $248 billion for free higher education at public institutions, and $1,299,007,000,000 for Social Security supplements, for a grand total of $3,005,407,000,000. We can subtract from this gross total the huge savings of $1.7 trillion from reduced health care expenditures and $1 trillion for reductions in welfare programs. The net investment to fulfill our social rights is then no more than $305,407,000,000. If we add the cost of the Federal Job Guarantee ($938,466,677,000) and subtract from that only the $170 billion of superseded unemployment benefits and the $131,320,000,000 of additional tax revenues, ignoring the offsets of the market value of produced goods and services, we have an additional $637,146,677,000 of net investment. The total net investment for achieving the social rights agenda would then amount to $942,553,677,000, which equals just 5% of our annual GNP.

Funding Options of a Sovereign Democracy

Any sovereign nation that has due control over its own currency has three options for funding its programs: issuing money, borrowing, and taxation.

So long as a nation autonomously directs its own fiscal policy, it can increase the supply of its sovereign currency to pay for public expenditures. To do so with maximum latitude, the sovereign currency must be non-convertible and have a floating exchange rate. Then, fiscal policy will not be constrained by the need to maintain sufficient reserves of gold (or some other commodity to which currency is convertible) or foreign currency. Even under these conditions, whatever monetary instruments a government issues will retain real, as opposed to nominal value only in relation to the taxable wealth of the nation, its productivity, its ability to obtain credit from domestic and foreign sources, and the extent to which its economy is affected by international trade and the relative strength of foreign currencies. Under favorable circumstances, inflation may be negligible. Under unfavorable circumstances, expansion of sovereign money supply can lead to hyperinflation, undercutting the ability of fiscal policy to support public spending. As historical examples of hyperinflation indicate, a sovereign currency will be most vulnerable to collapse under very specific conditions, such as when a nation is liable for huge debts paid in gold or foreign currency (e.g. the war reparation burden facing Weimar Germany) or undergoing a precipitous decline in domestic production (e.g. the collapse of agriculture following land reform in Mugabe's Zimbabwe).[330]

The United States has more room than almost any other nation to fund its operations by issuing money. We have the largest and most productive economy, with the largest home market of any nation. Exports and imports do make up a sizeable portion of United States commerce. Our currency can retain domestic stability despite international currency fluctuations due to the enormity of the domestic market, the amount of taxable income, and the unmatched security that investments are recognized to have within our borders. All of these factors further enable the United States to borrow unparalleled amounts of money from foreign investors, which helps support the value and international importance of our sovereign currency. Moreover, the dollar is used in commercial transactions within many other countries to such an extent that the total amount of United States currency in circulation abroad exceeds that used domestically, according to some estimates.[331] With such global trust in and dependence upon our currency, we could conceivably meet the entire cost of fulfilling social justice in the United States by adjusting our money supply, without significant devaluation of the dollar.

We can entirely avoid the risks of devaluation by relying upon the second option of deficit spending. The United States can easily borrow the equivalent of the total net investment of the social rights agenda, which is considerably less than recent federal tax reductions on the wealthy. Foreign lenders remain open to buying large amounts of United States bonds in recognition of the unrivaled security of the American economy. They recognize that deficit spending can foster increased growth, improving productivity, and strengthening the dollar. Compounding the receptivity of foreign lenders to financing American deficit spending is their huge prior investment in United States bonds, whose solvency they need to maintain. With massive bond holdings pitched to the dollar, foreign lenders have a vested interest to prevent any United States default and extend further credit to keep our nation prospering. Much of these foreign bond holdings come from nations that enjoy huge trade surpluses with the United States, such as China, Japan, and Germany. They continue to accumulate vast amounts of American dollars, which they need to invest securely, and whose value they want to maintain, especially when any fall in the dollar's worth will threaten the price competitiveness of their exports.[332] For all these reasons, deficit spending is an attractive option. At a time when interest rates are still near historic lows, we can use borrowing to fulfill our social rights more cheaply than ever, invigorating our economy and rendering debt payments a diminishing part of our growing national wealth.

Resistance to deficit spending remains rampant on both sides of the political spectrum, despite its advantages in the current economic conjuncture. Worries about minting money and borrowing may rarely be decisive,[333] but the third option of taxation has a compelling attraction of its own. Although we may not need to rely upon taxation to fund the social rights agenda, doing so has a distinct advantage over either money supply expansion or deficit spending. Taxation allows us not only to pay for the fulfillment of social freedom, but to channel wealth in ways that promote both equal opportunity and economic vitality. Democracy depends upon a fair tax system that supports the public investments on which family welfare, social autonomy, and political empowerment rest. In turning to taxation to support the social rights agenda, we have an opportunity to reshape our entire tax system so that it fosters the independence and security without which citizens cannot govern themselves.

Freedom and Taxation

Taxation is a partial restriction upon property right insofar as it requires individuals to relinquish a portion of their property to the state to fund its operations. As with any restriction of freedom, taxation has legitimacy to the extent that it is necessary to protect and foster self-determination. The state is entitled to tax its residents insofar as it requires funds to provide the services that uphold their rights, including their right to property.

Taxation for the sake of freedom is also the way of sustaining public services that most respects the autonomy of taxpayers. Taxation avoids requiring individuals to provide specific services or goods. It allows government to operate without confiscating particular items and without requisitioning specific jobs, as was done by *corvée* labor. By taking money instead, taxation gives taxpayers the greatest latitude in deciding how to contribute to public services. Although taxpayers are obliged to part with a certain amount of money, they are otherwise free to go about their business and preside over their property as they see fit. They retain the prerogative to decide what goods to keep or sell and what earning activities to pursue in order to be able to pay their tax bill. Moreover, by relying on tax revenues, government puts itself in the position of having to purchase the goods and services it needs in order to carry out its functions. Whether this involves public or private sector employment, it occurs through the exercise of market freedom by employees and other commodity owners who furnish government with the means to fulfill its tasks.

In addition, taxation can be used to incentivize spending in goods and services that promote our freedoms and to discourage expenditures that jeopardize our environmental and personal health, on which our autonomy depends.[334]

Despite these inherent connections between taxation and the realization of freedom, taxes can conflict with right if they fall upon individuals in ways that obstruct the opportunity of some more than others. The burden of taxes depends on not just the amount of taxes paid, but on how this amount affects the welfare of individuals. If individuals have very different levels of wealth and income, an equal flat tax of $20,000 will impose hardships on some and negligible consequences on others. Less affluent individuals are more likely to suffer impositions that fundamentally change their life prospects, whereas the most affluent individuals will hardly notice any impact upon themselves or their families. Unequal effects on opportunity will also apply when an equal percentage tax applies to spending, income or wealth. In all these cases, an equal percentage tax will disproportionately restrict the options of those of more modest means than those of greater affluence. A 10% sales tax will most constrain the opportunities of those least well off, whereas the same percentage tax will have the least discernible impact on the lifestyle of the most rich. Equal percentage income and wealth taxes will take the same disproportionate tolls on opportunity.

We compound such inequities when our tax rates favor specific types of wealth acquisition that affluent members of society disproportionately enjoy. In the United States, taxes on capital gains and inheritance are significantly lower than general income taxes. Capital gains make up a much larger part of the income of our most economically privileged residents, who disproportionately profit from capital assets such as stocks, bonds, real estate, and other holdings, and disproportionately benefit from inheritance. Consequently, the bargain tax rates on capital gains and inheritance reinforce the privileging and disadvantaging of different parts of our population, to the increasing impairment of equal opportunity. This result also hampers economic growth since the wealthiest individuals can spend much less of their riches in personal consumption than can the less affluent, who must recycle much more of their income to maintain themselves and their families. The more income and wealth inequality is reduced, the more "multiplier" effects are enhanced, triggering more robust economic growth.

Finally, the more complicated and enormous our tax code is, the more difficulty people of modest means have in navigating it to their advantage. The more wealth individuals have, the more able they are to hire tax advisors to ply the tax code and make it serve their interests.

Simplification and guaranteed accessibility of the tax code are imperatives for fair taxation. We must thus address the form as well as the content of tax regulations if taxation is to serve freedom as it should.

Tax Reform and the Fulfillment of the Social Rights Agenda

In 2017, United States public tax revenues totaled $6.08 trillion, of which $3.32 trillion, $1.52 trillion, and $1.24 trillion were collected, respectively, by the Federal Government, state governments, and local governments.[335] This total amounts to 32% of the U. S. GNP. Of the Federal tax total, 49% were individual income taxes, 36% were Social Security, Medicare, Unemployment, and Retirement payroll taxes, 7% were corporate income taxes, and 8% were excise and other special taxes. Of the state tax revenue total, 42% were income taxes, 48% were sales taxes, 6% were license taxes, 2% were property taxes, and other taxes amounted to less than 3%.[336] Of local government taxes, well over 90% were property taxes.[337] These breakdowns are significant because of all the taxes collected, only income taxes predominantly involve significantly graduated rates. Other taxes are primarily flat rate, taking the same percentage no matter how large the amount of spending, income, or wealth may be.

Flat taxes (which impose the same amount on every taxpayer) and flat rate taxes (which impose the same percentage tax on every taxpayer) are regressive in that they deepen disadvantage by disproportionately weighing upon the opportunity of individuals, relative to how much income and wealth they have. Sales taxes, capital gains taxes,[338] and property taxes are the main culprits of regressive taxation in the United States. They impose rates upon taxpayers that do not take into equitable account the wealth at their disposal.

A fair tax system should avoid flat taxes and flat rate taxes and rely as much as possible upon progressive, that is, highly graduated taxes. Highly graduated tax rates rise as the amount that is taxed increases. This graduated increase spreads the burden of taxation so that it falls on those most able to shoulder its weight.

Highly graduated tax rates thereby promote equal opportunity in three respects. First, highly graduated tax rates ensure that taxation does not disproportionately disadvantage those with less means. That would financially penalize the poorest among us, as well as further intensify inequalities in income and wealth that impinge upon equal opportunity. Secondly, highly graduated tax rates reduce income and wealth inequality and thereby level the playing field for all. Thirdly, by reducing income and wealth inequality, highly graduated tax rates promote economic growth and increased tax revenues due to the "multiplier effect" of a fairer distribution of wealth. Increasing income and wealth inequality tends to reduce the level of economic activity because those who dispose of greater concentrations of wealth tend to spend a smaller percentage of their income and wealth on goods and services than those of lesser means, who must use comparatively more of their resources on personal consumption. Since individuals with greater concentrations of wealth tend to hoard most of their money in financial portfolios, despite higher personal expenditures, the more unequal the distribution of wealth, the more economic growth tends to stagnate. This tendency is exhibited by how, as the distribution of wealth in the United States became more and more unequal, our rate of economic growth slowed to half of what it was when wages kept pace with national productivity and maintained their share in national income.[339]

To promote freedom through fair taxation, we should make highly graduated taxes the primary source of public revenues. Great Britain introduced graduated income taxation in 1798 to fund its war against revolutionary France[340] and the United States followed suit in 1862 to help fund the Union war effort. After court challenges led to a suspension of Federal income taxation,[341] the 16th Amendment secured its constitutionality and since 1913, the United States has continuously levied a Federal income tax with varying graduated rates. Federal income tax rates began with a top tax rate of 7% and reached their peak in 1944, when the highest income bracket was taxed at 94%. During the 1950's under President Eisenhower, the top income tax bracket continued to be taxed as high as 92%. Since then Federal income tax rates have become more and more flattened, with Ronald Reagan overseeing tax cuts on the higher income levels that put a cap at 28%.[342] These flattenings of graduated income tax rates have significantly defeated their opportunity enhancement and helped facilitate the vast increase in income and wealth inequality that has since plagued the United States.[343] According to Thomas Piketty, we could raise the top income tax rate to over 80% on incomes over $500,000 or $1,000,000 without reducing our economic growth.[344] Doing so would not only allow many more to benefit from our growing prosperity, but enhance economic expansion by recycling a greater share of income in consumer spending, rather hoarding it in speculative investments.

Several flawed tax policies have further undermined the efficacy of our graduated income taxation. First, current regulations exempt capital gains and inheritance from income tax graduated rate schedules. We instead tax capital gains at a much flatter rate significantly lower than comparable income tax levels. Inheritance, on the other hand, is not taxed at all unless it exceeds a high amount that applies to only a tiny fraction of our population. Inheritances of that magnitude or larger are taxed at a largely flat rate.[345] Secondly, our tax code allows deductions for gifts up to a certain level as well as myriad other deductions, all of which exempt large portions of received wealth from graduated income taxation. Finally, we allow a battery of regressive taxes, such as flat rate sales taxes, to burden disproportionately those who can least afford to contribute.

We can uphold the opportunity enhancement of graduated income tax if we eliminate these policies. We should treat capital gains and inheritance as income subject to the same rates as any other earnings. We should abolish all gift deductions and as many other deductions whose rationale has been removed by fulfillment of the social rights agenda.

Eliminating income tax deductions provides a major step towards simplifying our tax code. This provides needed transparency, so that we taxpayers can comprehend just how equitable our tax system is. It also removes the advantage more affluent taxpayers have in being able to afford tax advisors whose mastery of current tax code complexities allows their clients to game the tax system.

Moreover, we should eliminate as many regressive taxes as possible and use federal, state, and local graduated taxes to make up for their contributions. All flat consumption taxes, with the possible exception of "sin taxes" that discourage spending on unhealthy products, warrant abolition. We should also eliminate payroll taxes since these favor non-wage income, more generally accruing to the rich, while encouraging employers to substitute robots for workers.[346]

Much of the resistance to raising taxes has fraudulently rebelled at raising graduated income taxes, while letting regressive sales taxes increase to pay for needed services. We must mobilize the political will to make our tax system fair by shifting the burden as much as possible to highly graduated taxation.

Why We Need Highly Graduated Wealth Taxation

These graduated taxes should not be restricted to income taxation. We cannot have a fair tax system unless we also enact highly graduated wealth taxation. Wealth taxation is a crucial instrument of social freedom in a nation such as ours, where wealth inequality far exceeds income inequality. Today, in the United States, the richest 1% own nearly twice as much wealth as the bottom 90%.[347] By contrast, the 1% most highly paid individuals earn 39% as much as the bottom 90%.[348] The disparity in wealth is a particularly important factor in the disproportionate disadvantage of people of color. Whereas the average household income of African Americans is 63% that of White Americans,[349] the average wealth of an African American household is less than 1/9 that of a White American family.[350] Since many of the richest Americans gain huge increases in the equity value of their wealth while drawing comparatively little taxable income, fair sharing of the burden of taxation depends upon tapping wealth, instead of relying primarily on taxing income.

The United States possesses the largest accumulation of private wealth of any nation in human history. The value of this accumulated wealth reached $94.8 trillion dollars in 2017, more than five times our national income.[351] We can draw far greater tax revenues from wealth than from income and do so at a much lower tax rate than applies to earnings.

Today wealth taxation in the United States predominantly consists in property taxes, which are flat taxes restricted largely to real estate holdings. For most Americans who have any equity, the family residence makes up the primary portion of household wealth. For wealthy individuals, the situation is very different. Even though the very rich may own multiple homes, the value of their financial investments far overshadows the value of their real estate. This situation calls for two basic approaches to wealth taxation.

To begin with, property taxes, targeting real estate, should be highly graduated to fairly shoulder the tax burden and promote more equitable distribution of wealth.

Secondly, wealth taxation should extend beyond real estate to all financial holdings. The means for implementing this extension are readily available. Tax authorities can reliably track financial wealth through compulsory reporting of sales and purchases of stocks and bonds and of bank and investment accounts. Compliance with wealth taxation can then be secured through automatic financial transfers from the financial institutions holding these assets.

Moreover, by imposing wealth taxation on the wealth of individual residents, while applying graduated income tax to all their capital gains, we can mitigate the effect of corporate profits upon income and wealth inequality. We can then entirely eliminate taxes on corporations,[352] removing whatever burdens these impose upon national business competitiveness and economic growth,[353] and lifting the incentive for corporations to keep their profits abroad.[354]

We can escape the specter of capital flight to avoid wealth taxation by applying the same worldwide coverage that the United States currently extends to income taxation. Just as our Federal income tax covers income earned anywhere in the world, so our wealth taxes can apply to any wealth owned by United States residents wherever on the globe it be found.[355]

The vast accumulations of wealth concentrated among our richest 1% offer a painless opportunity to use wealth taxation to pay for the entire additional cost of the social rights agenda without meaningfully impinging upon the opportunity of anyone. As of 2017, the wealthiest 1% in the

United States own nearly $37 trillion. All it would take to pay the additional expense of fulfilling the social rights agenda is $942,553,677,000. A 2.5% wealth tax on the holdings of our richest 1% will raise this amount. Their "pain", if at all noticeable, could be reduced by spreading the wealth tax to a wider section of the richest Americans, using a series of graduated rates.

Wealth taxation can be used to cover not only the new investments fulfilling the social rights agenda, but a sizeable part of public spending that other taxes, including income taxation, currently fund. In 1999, Donald Trump proposed a onetime 14.25% wealth tax on personal fortunes worth $10 million or more to generate $5.7 trillion to wipe out our national debt.[356] A more modest annual wealth tax on the richest 10% (who hold 77.2% of our national wealth)[357] could significantly reduce the tax burden of the rest of our population, sustain current levels of public investment, and enhance wealth equality in behalf of both equal opportunity and economic growth. If we combine wealth taxation with a graduated income tax returning to the upper tax bracket rates of the Eisenhower years, we can meet all our public investment imperatives while radically reducing the entire tax burden weighing upon Americans who fall into the lower 90% of income and of wealth. Fair taxation could then command overwhelming political support by offering a single page simplified tax return and substantial tax relief to the vast majority of residents.[358]

Any national wealth tax might still face legal challenges similar to those that suspended income taxation until the 16th Amendment secured its constitutionality by mandating that "Congress shall have power to lay and collect taxes on incomes, from whatever source derived, without apportionment among the several States, and without regard to any census or enumeration." It is debatable whether a federal wealth tax runs afoul of the Constitution's Article I, Section 9, Clause 4, which reads, "No Capitation, or other direct, Tax shall be valid, unless in Proportion to the Census or enumeration herein before directed to be taken." The current composition of the Supreme Court may well offer a receptive audience to constitutional challenges of a federal wealth tax, despite Donald Trump's earlier onetime wealth tax endorsement. In that case, we may need to ratify another constitutional amendment to guarantee fair taxation. Let a proposed 28th Amendment then read, "Congress shall have power to lay and collect taxes on personal wealth, from whatever source derived, without apportionment among the several States, and without regard to any census or enumeration."

In any event, public investment to fulfill our social rights need not wait for full implementation of a graduated federal wealth tax. Just as Lincoln and Roosevelt did not need tax revenues in hand to make the investments necessary to protect our republic from economic and military collapse, so we should not hesitate to enact the public programs that will secure our household and social freedoms, invigorate our economy, and unchain our democracy.[359]

The Simplicity of Tax Legislation versus the Complexity of Tax Administration

Tax legislation has become a monstrous behemoth. Its staggering proliferation of codicils may enrich a growing army of professional tax advisors and those who can most easily afford to hire them, but otherwise it buries the public in a maze of obscurity. We need to shed light on taxation so that it can be and be known to be fair. The function of legislators is to set down the general standing rules that taxation should follow. How tax rates should be determined to meet the public investment needs of a particular fiscal year is an administrative matter that properly falls to the executive branch. Congress should promulgate the basic ground rules of highly graduated income and wealth taxes, mandate the programs that fulfill our social rights, and leave it to the proper government agencies to determine what specific rates are needed to fund the required public initiatives. No longer should tax law, like so much other legislation, fill massive tomes produced by lobbyists who alone can draft them, as well as know what they are peddling. Instead, law should confine itself to what guides implementation, without preempting the details of executive administration.[360]

Then, it will actually be possible for legislators to draft and read the tax law they consider, as well as for citizens to understand the finished results. Only under these conditions can we insure that fair taxation prevails and that government by, for, and of the people is able to uphold all our rights.

Works Cited

Arendt, Hannah, *Between Past and Future: Eight Exercises in Political Thought* (New York: Viking Press, 1961)

Aristotle, *Nicomachean Ethics* and *Politics*, in *The Complete Works of Aristotle, Volume Two*, ed. Jonathan Barnes (Princeton: Princeton University Press, 1984)

Atkinson, Anthony B., *Inequality: What Can Be Done?* (Cambridge, MA: Harvard University Press, 2015)

Blades, Joan, & Rowe-Finkbeiner, Kristin, *The Motherhood Manifesto: What America's Moms Want and What to Do About It* (New York: Nation, 2006)

Du Bois, W. E. B., *Black Reconstruction in America 1860-1880* (New York: the Free Press, 1998)

Harvey, Philip, "Is there a Progressive Alternative to Conservative Welfare Reform", *Georgetown Journal on Poverty Law & Policy*, Volume XV, Number 2, Summer 2008

Hayek, Friedrich A., *The Constitution of Liberty* (Chicago: University of Chicago Press, 1960)

Hayek, F. A., *The Road to Serfdom* (Chicago: University of Chicago Press, 2007)

Hegel, G. W. F., *Elements of the Philosophy of Right*, trans. by H. B. Nisbet (Cambridge: Cambridge University Press, 1991)

Hegel, G. W. F., *Philosophy of Mind: Part Three of the Encyclopaedia of the Philosophical Sciences (1830)*, trans. William Wallace (Oxford: Oxford University Press, 1971)

Hobbes, Thomas, *Leviathan*, ed. C. B. Macpherson (Harmondsworth, UK: Penguin Books, 1968)

Jacobs, Jane, *The Death and Life of Great American Cities* (New York: Random House, 1961)

Jonas, Hans, *The Imperative of Responsibility: In Search of an Ethics for the Technological Age* (Chicago: The University of Chicago Press: 1984)

King, Jr., Martin Luther, *The Radical King*, ed. by Cornell West (Boston: Beacon Press, 2015)

King, Jr., Martin Luther, *Where Do We Go From Here: Chaos or Community?* (New York: Harper & Row, 1967), pp. 197-8.

Kojève, Alexandre, *Tyranny and Wisdom*, trans. Michael Gold, in Strauss, Leo, *On Tyranny*, Revised and Enlarged Edition (Ithaca, NY: Cornell University Press, 1975)

Kostzer, Daniel, "Argentina: A Case Study on the *Plan Jefes y Jefas de Hogar Desocupados*, or the Employment Road to Economic Recovery",

Working Paper No. 534, The Levy Economics Institute of Bard College, May 2008

Levine, David P., *Economic Theory- Volume One: The elementary relations of economic life* (London: Routledge & Kegan Paul, 1978)

Levine, David P., *Economic Theory- Volume Two: The system of economic relations as a whole* (London: Routledge & Kegan Paul, 1981)

Locke, John, *Second Treatise on Government*, ed. Thomas P. Peardon (Indianapolis: Bobbs-Merrill, 1952)

Marx, Karl, *Capital: A Critique of Political Economy, Volume I,* trans. Samuel Moore and Edward Aveling (New York: International Publishers, 1967)

Marx, Karl, *Capital - Volume III: The Process of Capitalist Production as a Whole*, ed. by Frederick Engels (New York: International Publishers, 1967)

Marx, Karl, *Early Political Writings*, ed. & trans. by Edward O'Malley (Cambridge: Cambridge University Press, 1994)

Marx, Karl, *Economic and Philosophical Manuscripts of 1844*, trans. Martin Milligan (New York: International Publishers, 1964)

Marx, Karl & Engels, Friedrich, *The German Ideology: Parts I & III*, ed. R. Pascal (New York: International Publishers, 1963)

Morsink, Johannes, *The Universal Declaration of Human Rights: Origins,*

Drafting, and Intent (Philadelphia, University of Pennsylvania Press, 1999)

Nietzsche, Friedrich, *On the Genealogy of Morality*, trans. Carol Diethe (Cambridge, UK: Cambridge University Press, 1994)

Pateman, Carol, *Participation and Democratic Theory* (New York: Cambridge University Press, 1970)

Picketty, Thomas, *Capital in the Twenty-First Century* (Cambridge, MA: Harvard University Press, 2014)

Plato, *Republic*, in *Complete Works*, ed. by John M. Cooper (Indianapolis: Hackett, 1997)

Polanyi, Karl, *The Great Transformation* (Boston: Beacon Press, 1957)

Ricardo, David, *The Principles of Political Economy and Taxation* (London: Dent Everyman's Library, 1969)

Roosevelt, Franklin D., *The Public papers and Addresses of Franklin D. Roosevelt: 1944-45 Volume*, compiled by Samuel I. Rosenman (New Yorker: Harper & Brothers Publishers, 1950)

Rothstein, Richard, *The Color of Law: A Forgotten History of How Our Government Segregated America* (New York: Liveright, 2018)

Smith, Adam, *An Inquiry into the Nature and Causes of the Wealth of Nations* (New York: The Modern Library, Random House, 1937)

Stern, Andy, *Raising the Floor: How a universal basic income can renew our economy and rebuild the American dream* (New York: Public Affairs, 2016)

Taylor, N., *American-Made: The Enduring Legacy of the WPA: When FDR Put the Nation to Work*, (Tantor Media, 2008)

Winfield, Richard Dien, *Autonomy and Normativity: Investigations of Truth, Right and Beauty* (Aldershot, UK: Ashgate, 2001)

Winfield, Richard Dien, *From Concept to Objectivity: Thinking Through Hegel's Subjective Logic* (Aldershot, UK: Ashgate, 2006)

Winfield, Richard Dien, *Hegel and the Future of Systematic Philosophy* (Houndmills, UK: Palgrave Macmillan, 2014)

Winfield, Richard Dien, *Hegel's Phenomenology of Spirit: A Critical Rethinking in Seventeen Lectures* (Lanham, MD: Rowman & Littlefield, 2013)

Winfield, Richard Dien, *Hegel's Science of Logic: A Critical Rethinking in Thirty Lectures* (Lanham, MD: Rowman & Littlefield, 2012)

Winfield, Richard Dien, *Law in Civil Society* (Lawrence, Kansas: University Press of Kansas, 1995)

Winfield, Richard Dien, *Modernity, Religion, and the War on Terror* (London: Ashgate, 2007)

Winfield, Richard Dien, *Reason and Justice* (Albany, NY: State University of New York Press, 1988)

Winfield, Richard Dien, *Rethinking Capital* (Cham, Switzerland: Palgrave Macmillan, 2016)

Winfield, Richard Dien, *Stylistics: Rethinking the Art Forms After Hegel* (Albany, NY: State University of New York Press, 1996)

Winfield, Richard Dien, *Systematic Aesthetics* (Gainesville, FL: University Press of Florida, 1995)

Winfield, Richard Dien, *The Intelligent Mind: On the Genesis and Constitution of Discursive Thought* (Houndmills, UK: Palgrave Macmillan, 2015)

Winfield, Richard Dien, *The Just Economy* (London: Routledge, 1988)

Winfield, Richard Dien, *The Just Family* (Albany: State University Press of New York, 1998)

Winfield, Richard Dien, *The Just State: Rethinking Self-Government* (Amherst, NY: Humanity Books, 2005)

Winfield, Richard Dien, *The Living Mind: From Psyche to Consciousness* (Lanham, MD: Rowman & Littlefield, 2011)

Wray, L. Randall, *Modern Money Theory, Second Edition* (Houndmills, UK: Palgrave Macmillan, 2015)

Endnotes

1. As John Locke and Thomas Hobbes both recognized, the civil government established by social contract need not be democratic, since individuals may consent to rule by a monarch or a select few, who may just as well uphold everyone's person and property as rule by the many. See Hobbes, Thomas, *Leviathan*, ed. C. B. (Harmondsworth, UK: Penguin Books, 1968), p. 239; Locke, John, *Second Treatise on Government*, ed. Thomas P. Peardon (Indianapolis: Bobbs-Merrill, 1952), Sections 131-132, pp. 73-74.
2. For a powerful examination of these social inequalities, see Andy Stern, *Raising the Floor: How a universal basic income can renew our economy and rebuild the American dream* (New York: Public Affairs, 2016).
3. For a riveting and detailed account of how freed slaves pushed for the establishment of public schools in the South, see W. E. B. Du Bois, *Black Reconstruction in America 1860-1880* (New York: The Free Press, 1998), Chapter XV, "Founding the Public School", pp. 637-669.
4. All citations of Roosevelt's January 11, 1944 "Message to the Congress on the State of the Union" are from the text contained in *The Public papers and Addresses of Franklin D. Roosevelt: 1944-45 Volume*, compiled by Samuel I. Rosenman (New Yorker: Harper & Brothers Publishers, 1950), pp. 32-42. The "second Bill of Rights" is on p. 41.
5. Admittedly, "the right to a useful and remunerative job" and "the right to earn enough to provide adequate food and clothing and recreation" should already remove the need for income replacement when jobs are lost. With the employment right recognized and actually enforced, any individuals who become unemployed will have a job waiting for them. Replacement income will, however, be called for when old age, illness, or

accident make it impossible to continue earning a living.

6. This was particularly true of New Deal public housing initiatives, which explicitly excluded African Americans, and Social Security, whose coverage excluded many occupations, such as domestic work and farm labor, in which people of color were disproportionally employed. For an examination of the overt racial discrimination practiced by New Deal public housing policies, see Richard Rothstein, *The Color of Law: A Forgotten History of How Our Government Segregated America* (New York: Liveright, 2018).
7. The only nations attending the United Nations General Assembly meeting on December 10, 1948, who voted, but did not support adoption of the Universal Declaration of Human Rights, were the Union of South Africa, Saudi Arabia, and the Soviet Union and its satellite regimes, who all abstained for obvious reasons.
8. All citations of "the Universal Declaration of Human Rights" are taken from the text as found in Morsink, Johannes, T*he Universal Declaration of Human Rights: Origins, Drafting, and Intent* (Philadelphia, University of Pennsylvania Press, 1999), pp. 329-336.
9. Articles 1 through 15 and 17 through 21 uphold our basic civil and political freedoms "without distinction of any kind, such as race, color, sex, language, religion, political or other opinion, national or social origin, property, birth or other status" (Article 2). Articles 13-15 uphold our rights to leave any country, to seek asylum from persecution, and to have a nationality of which we cannot be "arbitrarily deprived" or "denied the right to change" (Article 15). Articles 17-21 affirm the rights to property (Article 17), freedom of thought, conscience, and religion (Articles 18 and 19), the right to peaceful assembly and association (Article 20), and the right to participate in government (Article 21).
10. Article 16 does not specify whether the right to marry extends to same sex as well as heterosexual unions, but nothing about it blocks that due extension.
11. Martin Luther King, Jr., *The Radical King*, ed. By Cornel West (Boston: Beacon Press, 2015), p. 241.
12. In a 1968 essay, published shortly after his assassination in Look Magazine, Martin Luther King wrote, "We need an economic bill of rights. This would guarantee a job to all people who want to work and are able to work. It would also guarantee

an income for all who are not able to work." See Martin Luther King, "We need an economic bill of rights", *The Guardian*, April 4, 2018 (https://www.theguardian.com/commentisfree/2018/apr/04/martin-luther-king-jr--economic-bill-of-rights)

13. For an account of Coretta Scott King's role in this campaign, see David Stein, "Why Coretta Scott King Fought for a Job Guarantee", *Boston Review*, May 17, 2017 (http://bostonreview.net/class-inequality-race/david-stein-why-coretta-scott-king-fought-job-guarantee).
14. David Stein, "Why Coretta Scott King Fought for a Job Guarantee", *Boston Review*, May 17, 2017 (http://bostonreview.net/class-inequality-race/david-stein-why-coretta-scott-king-fought-job-guarantee).
15. The call for full employment finally was removed from the Democratic Party platform under Bill Clinton's presidency.
16. "Until philosophers rule as kings or those who are now called kings and leading men genuinely and adequately philosophize, that is, until political power and philosophy entirely coincide, while the many natures who at present pursue either one exclusively are forcibly prevented from doing so, cities will have no rest from evils, Glaucon, nor, I think, will the human race. And, until this happens, the constitution we've been describing in theory will never be born to the fullest extent possible or see the light of the sun." Plato, *Republic*, Book V, 473c-e, Plato, *Complete Works*, ed. John M. Cooper (Indianapolis: Hackett Publishing Company, 1997), p. 1100.
17. Prime examples are the philosophical contributions of St. Augustine and St. Thomas Aquinas to Christianity, Nagarjuna to Buddhism, Shankara to Vedanta Hinduism, Al-Farabi and Ibn Rushd to Islam, and Maimonides to Judaism.
18. As Kojève observes, in entering politics, the philosopher faces a twofold dilemma. On the one hand, engaging in philosophy's search for truth is just as much a full-time endeavor as attempting to steer government to do what is right. Given our finite mortality, we must suspend, if not abandon, one activity in taking up the other. Moreover, if we come to politics for the sake of realizing philosophical principle, we face another hurdle, that of bridging the gap between the universality of the concepts of right and the individuality of the actual situation in which we live. In other words, we must formulate the concrete policies with which the universal norms of conduct

can be implemented in our unique historical conjuncture. Producing this formulation can easily be an all-consuming activity in its own right. If that leaves us forsaking participation in governing to giving mere advice to those who rule, we risk the impotence of remaining within the "republic of letters". See Kojève, Alexandre, *Tyranny and Wisdom*, trans. Michael Gold, in Strauss, Leo, *On Tyranny, Revised and Enlarged Edition* (Ithaca, NY: Cornell University Press, 1975), pp. 173-177.

19. In Hegel's *Phenomenology of Spirit: A Critical Rethinking in Seventeen Lectures* (Lanham, MD: Rowman & Littlefield, 2013), I have attempted to show that Hegel has succeeded in undermining the dogma that knowing always rests on foundations, a dogma that bars the way to autonomous reason. In *Hegel's Science of Logic: A Critical Rethinking in Thirty Lectures* (Lanham, MD: Rowman & Littlefield, 2012) and *From Concept to Objectivity: Thinking through Hegel's Subjective Logic* (London: Ashgate, 2006) I have tried to confirm how Hegel has largely succeeded in presenting the autonomous development of the categories of thought, with which truth can be grasped. In two connected works, *Conceiving Nature after Aristotle, Kant, and Hegel: the Philosopher's Guide to the Universe* (Houndmills, UK: Palgrave Macmillan, 2017) and *Universal Biology after Aristotle, Kant, and Hegel: the Philosopher's Guide to Life in the Universe* (Houndmills, UK: Palgrave Macmillan, 2018) I have attempted to show how nature can give rise to rational animals. In *The Living Mind: From Psyche to Consciousness* (Lanham, MD: Rowman & Littlefield, 2011) and *The Intelligent Mind: On the Origin and Constitution of Discursive Thought* (Houndmills, UK: Palgrave Macmillan, 2015) I have tried to establish how our psychology and linguistic interaction enable individuals to think and act freely. In *Reason and Justice* (Albany: State University of New York Press, 1988) and the essay collections, *Overcoming Foundations: Studies In Systematic Philosophy* (New York: Columbia University Press, 1989), *Freedom and Modernity* (Albany: State University of New York Press, 1991), and *Autonomy and Normativity: Investigations of Truth, Right and Beauty* (London: Ashgate, 2001), I outline the different practices and institutions that constitute the reality of freedom. I develop in detail how family relations can constitute an association of self-determination in *The Just Family* (Albany: State University Press of New York, 1998). *The Just Economy* (New York: Routledge, 1988), *Law in Civil*

Society (Lawrence, Kansas: University Press of Kansas, 1995), and *Rethinking Capital* (Houndmills, UK: Palgrave Macmillan, 2016) together provide a systematic account of social freedom as realized in a genuinely civil society. Finally, in *The Just State: Rethinking Self-Government* (Amherst, NY: Humanity Books, 2005), I conceive the institutions of political freedom.

20. Charlotte Norsworthy & Savannah Peat, "Clarke County leans Democratic in Republican state", *The Red and Black*, November 9, 2016 (https://www.redandblack.com/athensnews/clarke-county-leans-democratic-in-republican-state/article_78aaacc8-a63d-11e6-8c1f-d37f20964c1c.html).
21. Whereas Hice and Broun ran unopposed in 2016 and 2012, respectively, in 2014, Hice defeated his Democratic challenger, Kenneth Dious, with 66.52% of the vote, whereas in the 2010 and 2008 elections in which Broun had Democratic opponents, Broun won 67.4% (against Russell Edwards) and 60.7 % (against Bobby Saxon) of the vote. See "Georgia's 10th Congressional District", Ballotpedia (https://ballotpedia.org/Georgia%27s_10th_Congressional_District).
22. In the 2016 elections, the rate of uncontested state House seats was 83%, the highest in the nation. Republican incumbents held the overwhelming majority of most of these uncontested seats. See Greg Bluestein, "Georgia House had nation's highest rate of uncontested seats in 2016", *Atlanta Journal Constitution*, June 26, 2017 (https://politics.myajc.com/blog/politics/georgia-house-had-nation-highest-rate-uncontested-seats-2016/sKANodoik9Xv7qOmoY2zXN/).
23. A few states still maintain caucuses in which groups of party members meet to decide who will be the nominee.
24. If we take the United States' minimum wage at its maximum real value, attained in 1968 with a nominal rate of $1.60 per hour, and adjust it for inflation and productivity gains, the fair minimum wage would start at more than $22 per hour. See Caroline Fairchild, "Minimum Wage Would be $21.72 if It Kept Pace with Increases in Productivity: Study", *Huffington Post*, 02/13/2013, and John Schmitt, "Minimum Wage: Catching up to Productivity", *Democracy*, Summer 2013, No. 29.
25. Nietzsche develops this mistaken view in *On the Genealogy of Morality*, trans. Carol Diethe (Cambridge, UK: Cambridge University Press, 1994).

26. Individuals with less wealth spend a higher percentage of their income than the wealthy, engendering a greater multiplier effect, where their purchases lead to greater investment and enhanced economic growth. Consequently, extreme income and wealth inequality is a damper on economic vitality.
27. According to the 2010 Census, the residents of Georgia's 10th Congressional District are 69.1% White, 24.5% Black, 2.2% Asian, and 0.3% Native American. See "Georgia's 10th Congressional District", Ballotpedia (https://ballotpedia.org/Georgia%27s_10th_Congressional_District). By 2016, the interim Census the population breakdown became 68.71% White, 24.86% Black, 5.87% Hispanic, 2.14% Asian, and 0.1% Native American (https://www.census.gov/mycd/?st=13&cd=10).
28. I resided during my first nine years in an apartment in Fresh Meadows, Flushing, Queens, New York City.
29. According to the Georgia Secretary of State Office report, "General Election Turnout By Demographics May 2018", the 2018 Georgia 10th District Democratic primary had 20,296 voters identified as African American (51.62% of total votes cast) and 15,668 voters identified as White (39.85% of total votes cast).
30. I want to thank David Herald, Arvin Alaigh, Sanjna Bhatnagar, Nenne Onyioha-Clayton, and Chris Townsend for serving, respectively, as Campaign Manager, Campaign Assistant, Campaign Treasurer, Volunteer Coordinator, and Outreach Coordinator.
31. This was Tyrone Brooks.
32. David Dayen, "Meet the First 2018 Candidate to Run on a Federal Jobs Guarantee: And he's doing it in deep-red rural Georgia", *The Nation*, January 12, 2018.
33. The East Metro for Social Justice is a political action social justice group active in Covington, GA.
34. Attending the forum were members of the United Steelworkers of America Local 486G, CWA Local 3203, CWA Local 3204, CWA Local 3265 (United Campus Workers of Georgia), SAG-AFTRA, and the Amalgamated Transit Union Local 732.
35. An exception is Athens' WXAG, which caters to the African American community in the surrounding area. Although WXAG has a variety of talk shows that host

in-depth discussions with political candidates and community leaders, its audience is restricted to the region around Athens, leaving most of the 10th Congressional District beyond its range.

36. According to the Bureau of Labor Statistics report, "The Employment Situation – April 2017", of total April 2017 employment of 153,262,000, only 2,587,000 employees worked in agriculture, that is, only 1.69 %.
37. According to the Bureau of Labor Statistics report, "The Employment Situation – April 2017", of total April 2017 employment of 153,262,000, only 19,795,000 employees worked in goods-producing industries (12.9%), of which 12,333,000 employees worked in manufacturing proper (only 8%).
38. According to the Bureau of Labor Statistics report, "The Employment Situation – April 2017", of total April 2017 employment of 153,262,000, non-producing service employees amounted to 133,467,000 people (87 %).
39. Andy Stern, *Raising the Floor: How a universal basic income can renew our economy and rebuild the American dream* (New York: Public Affairs, 2016), p. 88.
40. This is according to the 2015 report by the International Labor Organization, cited by Stern, *Raising the Floor*, p. 77.
41. Stern, *Raising the Floor*, p. 76.
42. Stern, *Raising the Floor*, p. 88.
43. Economic Policy Institute, State of Working America Data Library, "The Productivity-Pay Gap," 2017.
44. Stern, *Raising the Floor*, p. 36.
45. "Nearly half of children in the United States live dangerously close to the poverty line, according to new research from the National Center for Children in Poverty (NCCP) at Columbia University's Mailman School of Public Health", https://www.mailman.columbia.edu/public-health-now/news/nearly-half-american-children-living-near-poverty-line.
46. This is according to the 2015 annual Global Wealth Report released by Credit Suisse.
47. US Census Bureau, "Income distribution to $250,000 or More for Households: 2013" (https://www.census.gov/hhes/www/cpstables/032014/hhinc/hinc06.xls).
48. In 2016, the median wealth of an African American family ($13,460) was 9.5% of a

White American family ($142,180), and the mean wealth of an African American family ($102,477) was 11% of a White American family ($935,584). See Angela Hanks, Danyelle Solomon, and Christian E. Weller, "Systematic Inequality: How America's Structural Racism Helped Create the Black-White Wealth Gap", Center for American Progress, February 21, 2018 (https://www.americanprogress.org/issues/race/reports/2018/02/21/447051/systematic-inequality/).

49. As the Nation reported (David Dayen, "Meet the First 2018 Candidate to Run on a Federal Jobs Guarantee", *The Nation*, January 12, 2018), I was the first candidate for Congress to advocate a Federal Job Guarantee.

50. As Andy Stern recounts, in 1918 Bertrand Russell wrote in his book, Roads to Freedom, "that a certain small income, sufficient for necessaries, should be secured to all, whether they work or not." See Stern, *Raising the Floor*, p. 173.

51. Martin Luther King, Stern notes, expressed his reasons for supporting a basic income in his 1967 book, *Where Do We Go From Here: Chaos or Community*, writing, "the solution to poverty is to abolish it directly by a now widely discussed measure: the guaranteed income." See Stern, *Raising the Floor*, p. 175.

52. See Robert Reich, "Why We'll Need a Universal Basic Income", http://robertreich.org/post/151111696805.

53. Stern lays out his argument for UBI in *Raising the Floor*.

54. So Marx writes in Volume III of *Capital*, "In fact, the realm of freedom actually begins only where labour which is determined by necessity and mundane considerations ceases; thus in the very nature of things it lies beyond the sphere of actual material production. Just as the savage must wrestle with Nature to satisfy his wants, to maintain and reproduce life, so must civilized man, and he must do so in all social formations and under all possible modes of production. With his development this realm of physical necessity expands as a result of his wants; but, at the same time, the forces of production which satisfy these wants also increase. Freedom in this field can only consist in socialised man, the associated producers, rationally regulating their interchange with Nature, bringing it under their common control, instead of being ruled by it as by the blind forces of Nature; and achieving this with the least expenditure of energy and under conditions most favourable to, and worthy of, their human

nature. But it nonetheless still remains a realm of necessity. Beyond it begins that development of human energy which is an end in itself, the true realm of freedom, which, however, can blossom forth only with this realm of necessity as its basis." See Karl Marx, *Capital: Volume 3: The Process of Capitalist Production as a Whole*, ed. by Frederick Engels (New York: International Publishers, 1967), p. 820.

55. Karl Marx and Frederick Engels, *The German Ideology: Parts I & III*, ed. R. Pascal (New York: International Publishers, 1963), p. 22.
56. Plato, *Republic*, in Plato, *Complete Works*, ed. John Cooper, trans. G. M. A. Brube, rev. C. D. C. Reeve (Indianapolis: Hackett Publishing Company, 1997), Book VIII, 561b, c-d, p. 1172.
57. Karl Marx, *Capital: Volume 1: A Critical Analysis of Capitalist Production*, ed. by Frederick Engels (New York: International Publishers, 1967), p. 168.
58. The following discussion of the Speenhamland experiment draws upon Karl Polanyi's account in *The Great Transformation: The Political and Economic Origins of Our Time* (Boston: Beacon Press, 1957), pp. 77-102.
59. Although, according to figures for 2016, the number of "small businesses", enterprises employing fewer than 500 employees, in the United States is 30 million, 82% of these "enterprises" (24.8 million) employ no one. They are in fact contract employees, providing goods and services on a piecework basis. See "Facts & Data on Small Business and Entrepreneurship", 2018, Small Business and Entrepreneurship Council, (https://sbecouncil.org/about-us/facts-and-data/).
60. As King stated less than a month before his assassination, "if a man does not have a job or an income at that moment, you deprive him of life. You deprive him of liberty. And you deprive him of the pursuit of happiness." See Martin Luther King, Jr., *The Radical King*, ed. by Cornel West (Boston: Beacon Press, 2015), p. 241.
61. Hegel, G. W. F., *Elements of the Philosophy of Right*, trans. H. B. Nisbett (Cambridge, UK: Cambridge University Press, 1991), §245, p. 267.
62. "The Productivity-Pay Gap", Economic Policy Institute, August 2018, (https://www.epi.org/productivity-pay-gap/).
63. See L. Randall Wray, *Modern Money Theory, Second Edition*, pp. 250-251.
64. A fair minimum wage, under current conditions, should start at no less than $20 per

hour. The United States' minimum wage attained its maximum real value in 1968 with a nominal rate of $1.60 per hour, which is more than $10 per hour given inflation. If we adjust that figure for productivity gains as well, the fair minimum wage would actually begin at more than $22 per hour. See Caroline Fairchild, "Minimum Wage Would be $21.72 if It Kept Pace with Increases in Productivity: Study", Huffington Post, 02/13/2013, and John Schmitt, "Minimum Wage: Catching up to Productivity", *Democracy*, Summer 2013, No. 29.

65. See Chapter 3 for a discussion of how a public single payer health insurance scheme can entirely relieve businesses of health care costs and save our nation $1.7 trillion dollars in health expenses each year.
66. See Wray, *Modern Money Theory, Second Edition*, p. 239.
67. Taylor, N., *American-Made: The Enduring Legacy of the WAP: When FDR Put the Nation to Work*, Tantor Media, 2008, pp. 523-24
68. See U.S. Census Bureau and Kimberly Amadeo, "U.S. GDP by Year Compared to Recessions and Events", in *The Balance*, April 19, 2017.
69. As Stern notes, the WPA constructed "650,000 miles of new or improved roads, 124,000 new or improved bridges", and "1,100,000 new or improved culverts". It further "improved or repaired 39,000 schools" and built "85,000 public buildings", "8,000 new or improved parks", and "18,000 new or improved playgrounds and athletic fields". See Stern, *Raising the Floor*, p. 156.
70. As Taylor writes, "The New Deal jobs programs ... took a broken country and in many important respects helped to not only revive it, but to bring it into the twentieth century. The WPA built 650,000 miles of roads, 78,000 bridges, 125,000 civilian and military building, 700 miles of airport runways; it fed 900 million hot lunches to kids, operated 1,500 nursey schools, gave concerts before audiences of 150 million, and created 475,000 works of art." Taylor, *American-Made: The Enduring Legacy of the WAP: When FDR Put the Nation to Work*, pp. 523-24.
71. Philip Harvey, "Is There a Progressive Alternative to Conservative Welfare Reform?", *Georgetown Journal on Poverty Law & Policy*, Volume XV, Number 2, Summer 2008, p. 187. Wray suggests a lower overhead, writing, "In direct job creation programs, an amount equal to 25 percent of the wage bill has been common." See Wray, *Modern*

Money Theory, Second Edition, p. 233.

72. The same is true of Argentina's Plan Jefes y Jefas, which responded to the 2001 Argentine financial crisis with a guaranteed job program for poor heads of households, providing 2 million new jobs. It was rescinded once economic recovery was achieved. See Wray, *Modern Money Theory, Second Edition*, pp. 236-7, and Daniel Kostzer, "Argentina: A Case Study on the Plan Jefes y Jefas de Hogar Desocupados, or the Employment Road to Economic Recovery", Working Paper No. 534, The Levy Economics Institute of Bard College, May 2008.
73. As David Stein recounts in his *Boston Review* (Spring, 2017) article, "Why Coretta Scott King Fought for a Job Guarantee", "In 1974, Scott King co-founded the National Committee for Full Employment/Full Employment Action Council (NCFE/FEAC) to fight for legislation that guaranteed jobs for all Americans." The effort culminated in the passage of the Humphrey-Hawkins full Employment Act of 1978, which, however, did not guarantee jobs for anyone who wanted one, but instead encouraged limited reductions in unemployment primarily through fiscal policy. The campaign for full employment then faded away.
74. Article 23 of the Universal Declaration of Human Rights begins by declaring, "1. Everyone has the right to work, to free choice of employment, to just and favourable conditions of work and to protection against unemployment."
75. If we take the United States' minimum wage at its maximum real value, attained in 1968 with a nominal rate of $1.60 per hour, and adjust it for inflation and productivity gains, the fair minimum wage would actually start at more than $22 per hour. See Caroline Fairchild, "Minimum Wage Would be $21.72 if It Kept Pace with Increases in Productivity: Study", *Huffington Post*, 02/13/2013, and John Schmitt, "Minimum Wage: Catching up to Productivity", *Democracy*, Summer 2013, No. 29.
76. The total investment would come to $938,466,677,000, approximately 5% of the 2018 United States GNP of $18,766,395,000,000. See "United States Gross National Product 1950-2018, Trading Economics, (https://tradingeconomics.com"/united-states/gross-national-product).
77. For a more detailed discussion of these savings, see Chapter 8.
78. For a discussion of this maximal fiscal policy room, see Wray, *Modern Monetary*

Theory, Second Edition, Chapter 4: Fiscal Operations in a Nation That Issues Its Own Currency, pp. 103-136.

79. Stern, *Raising the Floor*, p. 42. According to the Federal Reserve, whereas the richest 1% possess 38.6% of US wealth in 2016, the bottom 90% control just 22.8%, down from 33% in 1989. See Matt Egan, "Record inequality: The top 1% control 38.6% of America's wealth", CNN, September 27, 2017 (https://money.cnn.com/2017/09/27/news/economy/inequality-record-top-1-percent-wealth/index.html).
80. As Wray notes, Keynes rejected this Phillips Curve idea. Keynes writes, "The Conservative belief that there is some law of nature which prevents men from being employed, that it is "rash" to employ men, and that it is financially "sound" to maintain a tenth of the population in idleness for an indefinite period, is crazily improbable .... To set unemployed men to work on useful tasks does what it appears to do, namely, increases the national wealth; and that the notion, that we shall, for intricate reasons, ruin ourselves financially if we use this means to increase our well-being, is what it looks like – a bogy". See Wray, *Modern Money Theory, Second Edition*, p. 234.
81. As Wray explains, the Federal Job Guarantee/Employer of Last Resort program "will act as an automatic stabilizer as employment in the program grows in recession and shrinks in economic expansion, counteracting private sector employment fluctuations.... Furthermore, the uniform basic wage will reduce both inflationary pressure in a boom and deflationary pressure in a bust. In a boom, private employers can recruit from the program's pool of workers, paying a markup over the program wage. The pool acts like a "reserve army" of the employed, dampening wage pressures as private employment grows. In recession, workers downsized by private employers can work at the JG/ELR wage, which puts a floor on how low wages and income can fall." Wray, *Modern Monetary Theory, Second Edition*, p. 223.
82. Even if the resulting increase in consumer income were to increase imports, our government retains the policy tools to overcome any significant economic damage. As Wray notes, "it can still use trade policy, import substitution, luxury taxes, capital controls, interest rate policy, turnover taxes, and so on, if desired to minimize pressures on exchange rates should they rise." Wray, *Modern Money Theory, Second Edition*, p. 225.

83. Martin Luther King, Jr., *Where Do We Go From Here: Chaos or Community?* (New York: Harper & Row, 1967), pp. 197-8.
84. Wray suggests such direct payment "using something like a Social Security number, and paying directly into a bank account much as Social Security programs pay retirement pensions." See Wray, *Modern Money Theory, Second Edition*, p. 233.
85. A few prominent elected officials have begun to advocate a Federal Job Guarantee. These include Senators Bernie Sanders and Kirsten Gillibrand, and Alexandria Ocasio-Cortez, newly elected to the House of Representatives. Meanwhile, in academia, a small, but growing cohort of economists and other thinkers have been forcefully arguing in behalf of the FJG. Prominent among these is law professor Philip L. Harvey (Rutgers) and economists William A. Darity, Jr. (Duke University), Darrick Hamilton (Ohio State University), Stephanie A. Kelton (Stony Brook University), Pavlina R. Tcherneva (Bard College), and L. Randall Wray (Bard College).
86. Philip Bump, "Black and Hispanic unemployment rates have never been below those for whites", Washington Post, May 5, 2017 (https://www.washingtonpost.com/news/politics/wp/2017/05/05/black-and-hispanic-unemployment-has-never-been-below-that-for-whites/?utm_term=.b40f57e4eac4).
87. Adam Smith, *An Inquiry into the Nature and Causes of the Wealth of Nations* (New York: The Modern Library, 1937), pp. 15-16, 22, and Karl Marx, *Capital: A Critique of Political Economy, Volume I*, trans. Samuel Moore and Edward Aveling (New York: International Publishers, 1967), pp. 73-75.
88. For a detailed examination of the dynamic of competition that arises from market activity, see Richard Dien Winfield, *Rethinking Capital* (Cham, Switzerland: Palgrave Macmillan, 2016).
89. Although, according to figures for 2016, the number of "small businesses", enterprises employing fewer than 500 employees, in the United States is 30 million, more 82% of these "enterprises" (24.8 million) employ no one. They are in fact contract employees, providing goods and services on a piecework basis. See "Facts & Data on Small Business and Entrepreneurship", 2018, Small Business and Entrepreneurship Council, (https://sbecouncil.org/about-us/facts-and-data/).
90. It is thus no accident that worker cooperatives in the United States number only

about 300 and employ merely 7,000 workers. (See Cathy Albisa and Ben Palmquits, A New Social Contract: Collective Solutions Built By and For Communities, NES-RI {National Economic & Social Rights Initiative}, May 24, 2018, p. 47; https://www.nesri.org/news/2018/05/a-new-social-contract-collective-solutions-built-by-and-for-communities). Given the limitations of their capital, worker cooperatives are fated by the dynamic of competition to be a peripheral form of enterprise in a market dominated by corporate capital.

91. Marx, Karl, *The Economic and Philosophic Manuscripts of 1844*, trans. Martin Milligan (New York: International Publishers, 1964), pp. 65, 106, 121, 122.
92. Marx, Karl, *Introduction to Critique of Hegel's Philosophy of Right*, in Marx, *Early Political Writings*, ed. & trans. Joseph O'Malley (Cambridge: Cambridge University Press, 1994), pp. 67, 69.
93. Karl Marx, *Capital: A Critique of Political Economy, Volume 1*, p. 168.
94. For an extended discussion of how and why political freedom involves a mediated, rather than immediate relation of the individual will of each citizen to the universal will of the state, see Winfield, *The Just State*, pp. 199-208.
95. The endemic expansion and concentration of private enterprises engenders monopolies that also restrict the options of consumers, while wielding vast economic power that can threaten equal political opportunity and the autonomy of government. Government should step in to break up monopolies and shield the political process from the private concentrations of wealth. Although anti-monopoly initiatives may divide huge enterprises, they will not remove the underlying disparity in the economic power and opportunity of employers and of employees.
96. Stern, *Raising the Floor*, p. 15.
97. Stern, *Raising the Floor*, p. 15.
98. Stern, *Raising the Floor*, p. 37.
99. Stern, *Raising the Floor*, p. 15.
100. As David Merrill has pointed out in conversation, factions of the British Labour Party have suggested reserving 10% of corporate stock for employees. Such a minority stake can hardly give employees much clout. On the other hand, larger requirements would hamper further stock offerings, leaving the enterprise at a

competitive disadvantage.

101. "The top of the supply chain must be held accountable to buying only from suppliers that provide decent working conditions and pay prices that allow those conditions to exist." Cathy Albisa and Ben Palmquits, A New Social Contract: Collective Solutions Built By and For Communities, NESRI (National Economic & Social Rights Initiative), May 24, 2018, p. 43 (https://www.nesri.org/news/2018/05/a-new-social-contract-collective-solutions-built-by-and-for-communities).

102. Article 165 of the Weimar Constitution mandates that "Workers and employees shall, for the purpose of looking after their economic and social interests, be given legal representation in Factory Workers Councils, as well as in District Workers Councils organized on the basis of economic areas and in a Workers Council of the Reich. District Workers Councils and the Workers Council of the Reich shall meet with representatives of employers and other interested population groups as District Economic Councils and as an Economic Council for the Reich for the purpose of performing economic functions and for cooperation in the execution of the laws of socialization. District Economic Councils and the Economic Council of the Reich shall be constituted so that all important economic groups shall be represented therein proportionately to their economic and social importance. The National Ministry shall, before proposing drafts of politico-social and politico-economic bills of fundamental importance, submit them to the Economic Council of the Reich for consideration. The Economic Council of the Reich shall itself have the right to initiate drafts of such bills. If the National Ministry fails to assent, it shall nevertheless present the draft to the Reichstag accompanied by an expression of its views. The Economic Council of the Reich may designate one of its members to appear before the Reichstag in behalf of the proposal. Powers of control and administration may be conferred upon Workers and Economic Councils within the spheres assigned to them. The regulation of the development and functions of Workers and Economic Councils, as well as their relations with other administratively autonomous social bodies shall be exclusively a matter for the Reich." Wikisource.org/wiki/Weimar_Constitution, p. 23.

103. For a more extended critique of economic democracy, see Richard Dien Winfield,

Autonomy and Normativity: Investigations of Truth, Right and Beauty (Aldershot, UK: Ashgate, 2001), Chapter Twelve: "Should the Economy be Democratized?", pp. 141-151.

104. Carol Pateman makes this erroneous claim in her book *Participation and Democratic Theory* (New York: Cambridge University Press, 1970), p. 110.

105. For a systematic critique of corporate representation, see Richard Dien Winfield, *The Just State: Rethinking Self-Government* (Amherst, NY: Humanity Books, 2005), pp. 208-219.

106. It would be a mistake to impose a general carbon tax, since that would penalize bio-fuels. Their combustion may emit carbon, but it does not increase net carbon discharges into the atmosphere, since the plants from which biofuels are produced withdraw as much carbon during their growth. Any carbon tax should instead apply exclusively to fossil fuels.

107. See Hans Jonas for a discussion of how socialist regimes can just as readily imperil our biosphere as unregulated, laissez-faire markets. See Jonas, Hans, *The Imperative of Responsibility: In Search of an Ethics for the Technological Age* (Chicago: The University of Chicago Press, 1984), pp. 142-177.

108. Bradley Sawyer & Cynthia Cox, "How does health spending in the U.S. compare to other countries?", Kaiser Family Foundation, February 13, 2018 (https://www.healthsystemtracker.org/chart-collection/health-spending-u-s-compare-countries/).

109. Bradley Sawyer & Cynthia Cox, "How does health spending in the U.S. compare to other countries?", Kaiser Family Foundation, February 13, 2018 (https://www.healthsystemtracker.org/chart-collection/health-spending-u-s-compare-countries/). Taiwan's health care system has the world's lowest administrative costs at 2% of total expenditures. See "Taiwan Takes Fast Track to Universal Healthcare", All Things Considered, NPR. 2008-04-15.

110. Bradley Sawyer & Cynthia Cox, "How does health spending in the U.S. compare to other countries?", Kaiser Family Foundation, February 13, 2018 (https://www.healthsystemtracker.org/chart-collection/health-spending-u-s-compare-countries/).

111. Robin A. Cohen, Michael E. Martinez, and Emily P. Zammitti, Health Insurance Coverage: Early Release Estimates from the National Health Interview Survey, January-March 2017 (Hyattsville, MD: National Center for Health Statistics, August 2017).
112. Diane Archer, "Medicare Is More Efficient Than Private Insurance", September 20, 2011, Health Affairs Blog (https://www.healthaffairs.org/do/10.1377/hblog20110920.013390/full/).
113. Bradley Sawyer & Cynthia Cox, "How does health spending in the U.S. compare to other countries?", February 13, 2018, Kaiser Family Foundation (https://www.healthsystemtracker.org/chart-collection/health-spending-u-s-compare-countries/#item-start). As the authors report, the average health care expenditure per person in comparable countries is $4,908, less than half the US per capita average of $10,348. These figures are based on 2016 data.
114. For a more complete account of how market competition makes the employer-employee relation the anchor on which livelihood depends, see Richard Dien Winfield, *Rethinking Capital* (Cham, Switzerland: Palgrave Macmillan, 2016), pp. 287-421,
115. See the "2018 Small Business Profile", Office of Advocacy, U. S. Small Business Administration.
116. Admittedly, this problem is mitigated if the retirees have paid into a social security system that can support them in the years to come with the accrued payments they have already made.
117. "America's Families and Living Arrangements: 2011", United States Census Bureau, 15 November 2012; Angela Stringfellow, "The State of Caregiving 2018", 3/23/18, Caregiver Homes (https://blog.caregiverhomes.com/stateofcaregiving).
118. Kimberly Amadeo, "Medical Bankruptcy and the Economy: Do Medical Bills Really Devastate America's Families?", May 16, 2018, *The Balance* (https://www.thebalance.com/medical-bankruptcy-statistics-4154729).
119. Private elementary school and private high school average annually $9,398 and $14,205, respectively. See PrivateSchoolReview.com, "Average Private School Tuition Cost (2017-2018)".
120. Brian Manning, "Total Household Debt Rises for 16th Straight Quarter", Federal

Reserve Bank of New York, August 14, 2018 (https://www.newyorkfed.org/newsevents/news/research/2018/rp180814).

121. The total receiving no civil legal help rises to 87% for the disabled and 88% for veterans. See Legal Services Corporation, 2017 Justice Gap Report.

122. See International Labor Organization (2014), Maternity and Paternity at Work: Law and Practice Across the World (https://www.ilo.org/wcmsp5/groups/public/---dgreports/---dcomm/---publ/documents/publications/wcms_242615.pdf)

123. http://www.lex.bg/laws/ldoc/1594373121, 2/7/2017.

124. See *Fősäkringskassan*, August 9, 2016.

125. Blades, Joan; Rowe-Finkbeiner, Kristin, *The Motherhood Manifesto: What America's Moms Want and What to Do about It* (New York: Nation, 2006).

126. *The World Factbook* (https://www.cia.gov/library/publications/the-world-factbook/rank order/2091rank.html), 3/21/2015.

127. Chatterji, Pink; Markowitz, Sara, "Does the Length of Maternity Leave Affect Maternal Health?", *Southern Economic Journal* 72 (1): 16-41.

128. "In the U.S. 85.8 per cent of males and 66.5 percent of females work more than 40 hours per week". See "The U.S. is the Most Overworked Developed Nation in the World", G. E. Miller, 1/2/2018, 20 Something Finance, https://20something finance.com/American-hours-worked-productivity-vacation/.

129. See "The U. S. is the Most Overworked Developed Nation in the World", G. E. Miller, 1/2/2018, *20 Something Finance*, https://20something finance.com/American-hours-worked-productivity-vacation/.

130. The productivity of American workers has increased 400% since 1950. See "The U. S. is the Most Overworked Developed Nation in the World", G. E. Miller, 1/2/2018, *20 Something Finance*, https://20something finance.com/American-hours-worked-productivity-vacation/.

131. Niall, McCarthy, *Forbes*, June 26, 2017, www.forbes.com/sites/nialmccarthy/2017/06/26/american-workers-have-a-miserable-vacation-allowance-infographical/#7be54656126d.

132. Rebecca Ray, Milla Sanes, & John Schmitt, "No-Vacation Nation Revisited", Center for Economic and Policy Research, May 2013, www.cepr.net.; See also Abigail

Hess, "Here's how many paid vacation days the typical American worker gets", CNBC, July 6, 2018, https://www.cnbc.com/2018/07/05/heres-how-many-paid-vacation-days-the-typical-american-worker-gets-html.

133. Tim Parker, "The Cost of Raising a Child in America", April 25, 2017, https://www.investop4dia.com/articles/personal0finance/090415/cost-raising-child-america.asp.

134. See www.payingforseniorcare.com/longtermcare/costs.html#title2.

135. See Mark Lino, Kevin Kuczynski, Nestor Rodriguez, and TusaRebecca Schap, Expenditures on Children by Families, 2015, United States Department of Agriculture, Center for Nutrition Policy and Promotion, Miscellaneous Report No. 1528-2015, January 2017, Revised March 2017. All the cited statistics on expenditures on children come from this report.

136. Child Trends. (2018). "Number of Children". Bethesda, MD (https://www.childtrends.org/indicators/number-of-children).

137. By contrast, the 1919 Weimar Constitution mandates the "right to a healthy dwelling". See "Public Housing - Germany", Wikipedia (https://en.wikipedia.org/wiki/Public-housing).

138. Constitutional enactment, of course, is not enough. Section 26 of Chapter Two of the Constitution of South Africa declares that "everyone has the right to have access to adequate housing", but nearly 200,000 homeless live on its streets (2015 data; see http://wp.wpi.edu/capetown/projects/p2015/service-dining-rooms/background/homelessness-in-south-africa/), while 3.6 million others live in shacks (2013 data; see http://www.thehda.co.za/uploads/files/HDA_South_Africa_Report_lr.pdf).

139. See "HUD 5th Annual Homelessness Assessment Report to Congress" (http://www.huduser.org/publications/pdf/5thHomelessAssessmentReport.pdf). According to a 2000 study of the Urban Institute, the homeless totaled between 2.3 and 3.5 million. See "A New Look at Homelessness in America, Urban Institute, February 1, 2000 (http://www.urban.org/publciations/9000366.html). A 2009 study estimates that 1.5 million children in the United States are homeless each year. See "Facts and Figures: The Homeless", PBS, June 26, 2009 (http://www.pbs.org/now/shows/526/homeless-facts.html). Meanwhile, Amnesty International USA

estimates that we have five times as many vacant houses as homeless people. See "Vacant Houses Outnumber Homeless People in U.S. (http://www.truthdig.com/eartotheground/item/more-vacant-homes-than-homeless-in-us-20111231#).

140. "According to the U.S. Department of Housing and Urban Development (HUD), there were roughly 554,000 homeless people living somewhere in the United States on a given night last year. A total of 193,000 of those people were "unsheltered", meaning that they were living on the streets and had no access to emergency shelters, transitional housing, or Safe Havens." Kizley Benedict, "Estimating the Number of Homeless in America", *The DataFace*, January 21, 2018 (http://thedataface.com/2018/public-health-/american-homelessness).

141. "30 million houses in the U.S. have serious health and safety hazards, such as gas leaks, damaged plumbing, and poor heating. About 6 million of those have structural problems. Another 6 million have lead paint." See Alexia Fernandez Campbell, "Gas Leaks, Mold, and Rats: Millions of Americans Live in Hazardous Homes", *The Atlantic*, July 25, 2016 (https://www.theatlantic.com/business/archive/2016/07/gas-leaks-mold-and-rats-millions-of-americans-live-in-hazardous-homes/492689/).

142. Rent burdened households, of which 64% have less than $400 in cash savings, are overwhelmingly (84%) African-American. See American Families Face a Growing Rent Burden, a report from the Pew Charitable Trusts, April 2018, p. 5.

143. "While wage growth has remained flat for the past 20 years, the median rent for a vacant home or apartment has doubled over the same period, to about $910 in 2017." See "America's Homelessness Crisis", The Week Staff, The Week, March 11, 2018 (http://the week.com/articles/759683/Americas-homelessness-crisis).

144. These aims follow the general lines of the "Principles of Intelligent Urbanism", which was anticipated by Jane Jacobs in *The Death and Life of Great American Cities* (New York: Random House, 1961), and underlies such movements in city planning as the "New Urbanism", "Walkable Urbanism", "Sustainable Urbanism", "Transit-Oriented Development", and "Smart Development". *The Charter of the New Urbanism* (http:www.cnu.org/charter) opens with the following declaration: "We advocate the restricting of public policy and development practices to support the following principles: neighborhoods should be diverse in use and population; communities should

be designed for the pedestrian and transit as well as the car; cities and towns should be shaped by physically defined and universally accessible public spaces and community institutions; urban places should be framed by architecture and landscape design that celebrate local history, climate, ecology, and building practice."

145. *American Families Face a Growing Rent Burden*, A report from the Pew Charitable Trusts, April 2018, p. 8.

146. *American Families Face a Growing Rent Burden*, The Pew Charitable Trusts, April 2018, p. 4. Since 2001 the share of households living in rental homes has increased by 10% or more for all age groups. As of 2015 the number of renting households amounted to 43 million, increasing by 9.3 million in little more than a decade. See *American Families Face a Growing Rent Burden*, A report from the Pew Charitable Trusts, April 2018, p. 5.

147. *American Families Face a Growing Rent Burden*, The Pew Charitable Trusts, April 2018, p. 4. "Since 2001, gross rent has increased 3 percent a year, on average, while income has declined by an average of 0.1 percent annually, falling from $56,531 in 2001 to $56,516 in 2015. This widening gap between rent and income means that after paying rent, many Americans have less money available for other needs than they did 20 years ago." *American Families Face a Growing Rent Burden*, A report from the Pew Charitable Trusts, April 2018, p. 5.

148. For a survey of the history of rent control, and its two "generations", see Satvik Dev, "Rent Control Laws in India: A Critical Analysis", Centre for Civil Society Sir Ratan Tata Trust, July 17, 2006 (https://papers.ssrn.com/sol3/papers.cfm?abstract_id=926512).

149. Anyone familiar with the housing situation in Kolkata, where strict rent control has reigned, has seen the widespread dilapidation of the exteriors, hallways, and stairways of apartments, which landlords are hard pressed to maintain, given low rent control ceilings and rising maintenance costs.

150. Whether in New York City or Delhi, tenants who might benefit from rent control instead all too often find it impossible to obtain decent apartments without having to make unrecorded, "black" money payments to secure their units.

151. See "This is the staggering amount Americans paid in rent in 2017", Maria

LaMagna, *MarketWatch*, January 11, 2018 (http://marketwatch.com/story/this-is-the-staggering-amount-american-renters-paid-in-2017-2017-12).

152. *American Families Face a Growing Rent Burden*, The Pew Charitable Trusts, April 2018, p. 8.
153. See https://www.hud.gov/program_offices/comm_planning/affordablehousing/, 8/8/2018.
154. "Minimum wage doesn't cover the rent anywhere in the U.S.", Kate Gibson, *MoneyWatch*, June 14, 2018 (https://www.cbs.news.com/news/minimum-wage-doesnt-cover-the-rent-anywhere-in-the-u-s/)
155. See "This is the staggering amount Americans paid in rent in 2017", Maria LaMagna, *MarketWatch*, January 11, 2018 (http://marketwatch.com/story/this-is-the-staggering-amount-american-renters-paid-in-2017-2017-12).
156. See https://www.hud.gov/program_offices/comm_planning/affordablehousing/, 8/8/2018.
157. See https://www.hud.gov/program_offices/comm_planning/affordablehousing/, 8/8/2018.
158. American Families Face a Growing Rent Burden, The Pew Charitable Trusts, April 2018, p. 4.
159. American Families Face a Growing Rent Burden, The Pew Charitable Trusts, April 2018, p. 4.
160. See https://www.brookings.edu/blog/the-avenue/2017/12/19/is-the-rent-too-damn-high-or-are-incomes-too-low/.
161. See https://www.brookings.edu/blog/the-avenue/2017/12/19/is-the-rent-too-damn-high-or-are-incomes-too-low/.
162. See https://www.brookings.edu/blog/the-avenue/2017/12/19/is-the-rent-too-damn-high-or-are-incomes-too-low/.
163. See https://www.brookings.edu/blog/the-avenue/2017/12/19/is-the-rent-too-damn-high-or-are-incomes-too-low/.
164. See https://www.brookings.edu/blog/the-avenue/2017/12/19/is-the-rent-too-damn-high-or-are-incomes-too-low/.
165. See https://www.brookings.edu/blog/the-avenue/2017/12/19/

is-the-rent-too-damn-high-or-are-incomes-too-low/.

166. See https://www.brookings.edu/blog/the-avenue/2017/12/19/is-the-rent-too-damn-high-or-are-incomes-too-low/.
167. See https://www.brookings.edu/blog/the-avenue/2017/12/19/is-the-rent-too-damn-high-or-are-incomes-too-low/.
168. See https://www.brookings.edu/blog/the-avenue/2017/12/19/is-the-rent-too-damn-high-or-are-incomes-too-low/.
169. Due to the collapse of the housing bubble during the Great Recession of 2008, "real net household wealth fell by 57 percent from 2006 to 2011. This decline hit low-income and minority households especially hard because home equity accounts for a larger share of their wealth." See "The State of the Nation's Housing", The Joint Center for Housing Studies of Harvard University, 2012, p. 14. Cited in "Paths to Homeownership for Low-Income and Minority Households", Evidence Matters, Fall 2012 (https://www.huduser.gov/portal/periodicals/em/fall12/highlight1.html).
170. "Federal Reserve report shows homeowner equity dipping below 50 percent, lowest on record", SignOnSanDiego.com, December 28, 2008 (http://www.signonsandiego.com/news/business/20080306-0926-homeequity.html).
171. Patrick Sisson, "Why buying a house today is so much harder than in 1950", Curbed, April 10, 2018 (https://ww.curbed.com/2018/4/10/17219786/buying-ahouse-mortgage-government-gi-bill).
172. Nela Richardson, "Priced Out: The Housing Affordability Gap in America's Largest Metros", Redfin, May 31, 2017 (https://www.redfin.com/blog/2017//05/priced-out-the-housing-affordability-gap-in-amercas-largest-metros.html).
173. Rakesh Kochhar and Anthony Cilluffo, "Income Inequality in the U.S. is Rising Most Rapidly Among Asians", Pew Research Center, July 12, 2018 (http://www.pewsocialtrends.org/2018/07/02/income-inequality-in-the-u-s-is-rising-most-rapidly-among-asians/).
174. Rakesh Kochhar and Anthony Cilluffo, "How wealth inequality has changed in the U.S. since the Great Recession, by race, ethnicity and income", Pew Research Center, November 1, 2017 (http://www.pewresearch.org/fact0tank/2017/11/01/

how-wealth-inequality-has-changed-in-the-u-s-since-the-great-recession-by-race-ethnicity-and-income).

175. Nela Richardson, "Priced Out: The Housing Affordability Gap in America's Largest Metros", Redfin, May 31, 2017 (https://www.redfin.com/blog/2017//05/priced-out-the-housing-affordability-gap-in-amercas-largest-metros.html).
176. Nela Richardson, "Priced Out: The Housing Affordability Gap in America's Largest Metros", Redfin, May 31, 2017 (https://www.redfin.com/blog/2017//05/priced-out-the-housing-affordability-gap-in-amercas-largest-metros.html).
177. Nela Richardson, "Priced Out: The Housing Affordability Gap in America's Largest Metros", Redfin, May 31, 2017 (https://www.redfin.com/blog/2017//05/priced-out-the-housing-affordability-gap-in-amercas-largest-metros.html).
178. Nela Richardson, "Priced Out: The Housing Affordability Gap in America's Largest Metros", Redfin, May 31, 2017 (https://www.redfin.com/blog/2017//05/priced-out-the-housing-affordability-gap-in-amercas-largest-metros.html).
179. Benjamin Feldman, "Unison Home Affordability Report 2018", Unison, April 4, 2018 (https://www.unison.com/blog/home-affordability-2018).
180. "The US homeownership rate has lost ground compared with other developed countries", Laurie Goodman, Christopher Mayer, and Monica Clodius, Urban Institute, March 21, 2018 (https://www.urban.org/urban-wire/us-homeownership-rate-has-lost-ground-compared-other-developed-countries)
181. "The US homeownership rate has lost ground compared with other developed countries", Laurie Goodman, Christopher Mayer, and Monica Clodius, Urban Institute, March 21, 2018 (https://www.urban.org/urban-wire/us-homeownership-rate-has-lost-ground-compared-other-developed-countries)
182. The 1944 GI Bill (the Serviceman's Readjustment Act) empowered the Veterans Administration to guarantee mortgages for veterans under favorable terms, fueling post-war suburbanization. See "Urban Renewal – United States", Wikipedia (https://en.wikipedia.org/wiki/Urban-renewal).
183. "Home-ownership in the United States", Wikipedia (https://en/wikipedia.org/wiki/Home-owernship_in_the United-States)
184. Patrick Sisson, "Why buying a house today is so much harder than in 1950",

Curbed, April 10, 2018 (https://ww.curbed.com/2018/4/10/17219786/buying-ahouse-mortgage-government-gi-bill).

185. Patrick Sisson makes proposals along these lines, writing, "Converting the MID into a 15 per cent tax credit would reduce cost of this subsidy and free up federal funds for downpayment and mortgage assistance to qualified families. The government could also limit the number of mortgages for which a household could deduct interest to just their primary residence, preventing vacation homes from offering a tax benefit. It could also reduce the amount of eligible mortgage to $500,000 instead of the current 1 million, limiting the amount of interest that the very wealthiest Americans can deduct." See Patrick Sisson, "Why buying a house today is so much harder than in 1950", Curbed, April 10, 2018 (https://ww.curbed.com/2018/4/10/17219786/buying-ahouse-mortgage-government-gi-bill).
186. Patrick Sisson, "Why buying a house today is so much harder than in 1950", Curbed, April 10, 2018 (https://www.curbed.com/2018/4/10/17219786/buying-a-house-mortgage-government-gi-bill)
187. The rate of home ownership increased from 40% to 60%. See Patrick Sisson, "Why buying a house today is so much harder than in 1950", *Curbed*, April 10, 2018 (https://www.curbed.com/2018/4/10/17219786/buying-a-house-mortgage-government-gi-bill).
188. Patrick Sisson, "Why buying a house today is so much harder than in 1950", *Curbed*, April 10, 2018 (https://www.curbed.com/2018/4/10/17219786/buying-a-house-mortgage-government-gi-bill)
189. Patrick Sisson, "Why buying a house today is so much harder than in 1950", *Curbed*, April 10, 2018 (https://www.curbed.com/2018/4/10/17219786/buying-a-house-mortgage-government-gi-bill)
190. Esterl, Mike, "In this Picturesque Village, the Rent Hasn't Been Raised Since 1520", *The Wall Street Journal*, December 26, 2008. See also the Fuggerei's official website: http://www.fuggerei.de/.
191. Habitat for Humanity Annual Report FY2017: July 1, 2016-June 30, 2017, (https://www.habitat.org/multimedia/annual-report-2017/).
192. Grounded Solutions Network, 2017 Member Report (January 2018), p. 8, cited

in Cathy Albisa and Ben Palmquits, A New Social Contract: Collective Solutions Built By and For Communities, NESRI (National Economic & Social Rights Initiative), May 24, 2018, p. 38 (https://www.nesri.org/news/2018/05/a-new-social-contract-collective-solutions-built-by-and-for-communities).

193. "Public Housing – Sweden", Wikipedia (https://en.wikipedia.org/wiki/Public-housing).

194. Alexia Fernandez Campbell, "Gas Leaks, Mold, and Rats: Millions of Americans Live in Hazardous Homes", *The Atlantic*, July 25, 2016 (https://www.theatlantic.com/business/archive/2016/07/gas-leaks-mold-and-rats-millions-of-americans-live-in-hazardous-homes/492689/).

195. Schwartz, A. F., *Housing Policy in the United States* (2010), cited in Wikipedia, "Housing quality and health outcomes in the United States" (https://en.wikipedio.ord/wiki/Housing-quality-and-health-outcomes-in-the-United-States)

196. Schwartz, A. F., *Housing Policy in the United States* (2010), cited in Wikipedia, "Housing quality and health outcomes in the United States" (https://en.wikipedio.ord/wiki/Housing-quality-and-health-outcomes-in-the-United-States)

197. Alana Semuels, "Good School, Rich School; Bad School, Poor School: the inequality at the heart of America's education system", *The Atlantic*, August 25, 2018 (https://www.theatlantic.com/business/archive/2016/08/property-taxes-and-unequal-schools/497333/).

198. For an account of how public education arose in the South under Reconstruction, see W. E. B. Du Bois, *Black Reconstruction in America 1860-1880* (New York: Free Press, 1998), Chapter XV, "Founding the Public School", pp. 637-669.

199. Alana Semuels, "Good School, Rich School; Bad School, Poor School", *The Atlantic*, August 25, 2016 (https://www.theatlantic.com/business/archive/2016/08/property-taxes-and-unequal-schools/497333/).

200. Hegel repudiates the substitution of play for instruction of children, maintaining that, "in passing from play to the seriousness of learning ... the main thing is awakening feeling in them that as yet they are not what they ought to be ... This striving after education on the part of children themselves is the immanent factor in all education... For this reason, we must describe as completely preposterous the pedagogy

which bases itself on play, which proposes that children should be made acquainted with serious things in the form of play and demands that the educator should lower himself to the childish level of intelligence of the pupils instead of lifting them up to an appreciation of the seriousness of the matter in hand ... Children must, of course, be roused to think for themselves; but the worth of the matter in hand should not be put at the mercy of their immature, vain understanding." See Hegel, G. W. F., *Philosophy of Mind: Part Three of the Encyclopaedia of the Philosophical Sciences (1830)*, trans. William Wallace (Oxford: Oxford University Press, 1971), pp. 59-60.

201. This involves accommodating what is particular to the student, at the expense of focusing on the common concerns around which democratic education revolves. Hegel, according to his students' lecture transcripts, inveighs against this tendency, stating: "the assertion that the teacher should carefully adjust himself to the individuality of each of his pupils, studying and developing it, must be treated as idle chatter. He has simply no time to do this. The peculiarities of children are tolerated with the family circle; but at school there begins a life subject to general regulations, to a rule which applies to all; it is the place where mind must be brought to lay aside its idiosyncrasies, to know and to desire the universal, to accept the existing general culture. This reshaping of the soul, this alone is what education means. The more educated a man is, the less is there apparent in his behavior anything peculiar only to him, anything therefore that is merely contingent." See Hegel, *Philosophy of Mind*, pp. 51-52.

202. As Socrates argues in the *Republic*, Book VII, 536e, "no free person should learn anything like a slave. Forced bodily labor does no harm to the body, but nothing taught by force stays in the soul ... Then don't use force to train the children in these subjects; use play instead. That way you'll also see better what each of them is naturally fitted for." See Plato, *Complete Works*, ed. John M. Cooper (Indianapolis: Hackett Publishing Company, 1997), p. 1151.

203. Hannah Arendt criticizes these "democratizing" tendencies in teacher training and classroom operation in her essay, "The Crisis in Education", in Hannah Arendt, *Between Past and Future: Eight Exercises in Political Thought* (New York: Viking Press, 1961), pp. 173-196.

204. Sylvia Allegretto and Lawrence Mishel, "The teacher pay penalty has hit a new high: Trends in the teacher wage and compensation gaps through 2017", Economic Policy Institute, September 5, 2018 (epi.org/153196).
205. In fact, "the teacher work force is becoming more female: 77 percent of teachers in public and private elementary and high schools are women, up from 71 percent three decades ago." See "Students Thrive When teachers Are Their Race" by Clare Cain Miller, *The New York Times*, Tuesday, September 11, 2018, p. 1.
206. Sylvia Allegretto and Lawrence Mishel discuss these points in their report, "The teacher pay penalty has hit a new high: Trends in the teacher wage and compensation gaps through 2017", Economic Policy Institute, September 5, 2018 (epi.org/153196).
207. Bruce J. Biddle and David C. Berliner, "A Research Synthesis: Unequal School Funding in the United States, Beyond Instructional Leadership, May 2002, Volume 59, Number 8, pp. 48-59.
208. According to the 2016 Annual Survey of School System Finances by the U.S. Census Bureau, 8.1% of public school funding was supplied by the Federal Government, 47.4% was supplied by state governments, and 44.5% was supplied by localities.
209. Without adjustment for the highly differing cost of living between states, the highest nominal 2016 average teacher salary is $77,957 (New York State) and the lowest nominal 2016 average teacher salary is $42,025 (North Dakota). See Cory Turner, "The Fight Over Teacher Salaries: A Look At The Numbers", NPR, March 16, 2018 (https://www.npr.org/sections/ed/2018/03/16/592221378/the-fight-over-teacher-salaries-a-look-at-the-numbers).
210. Cory Turner, "The Fight Over Teacher Salaries: A Look At The Numbers", NPR, March 16, 2018 (https://www.npr.org/sections/ed/2018/03/16/592221378/the-fight-over-teacher-salaries-a-look-at-the-numbers).
211. Alana Semuels, "Good School, Rich School; Bad School, Poor School: The inequality at the heart of America's education system", *The Atlantic*, August 25, 2016 (https://theatlantic.com/business/archive/2016/08/property-taxes-and-unequal-schools/497333/).
212. See U. S. Census Bureau 2016 Annual Survey of School System Finances.

213. Alana Semuels, "Good School, Rich School; Bad School, Poor School: The inequality at the heart of America's education system", *The Atlantic*, August 25, 2016 (https://theatlantic.com/business/archive/2016/08/property-taxes-and-unequal-schools/497333/).
214. Alana Semuels, "Good School, Rich School; Bad School, Poor School: The inequality at the heart of America's education system", *The Atlantic*, August 25, 2016 (https://theatlantic.com/business/archive/2016/08/property-taxes-and-unequal-schools/497333/).
215. "A 20 percent increase in per-pupil spending a year for poor children can lead to an additional year of completed education, 25 percent higher earnings, and a 20 percentage point reduction in the incidence of poverty in adulthood, according to a paper from the National Bureau of Economic Research," Alana Semuels, "Good School, Rich School; Bad School, Poor School: The inequality at the heart of America's education system", *The Atlantic*, August 25, 2016 (https://theatlantic.com/business/archive/2016/08/property-taxes-and-unequal-schools/497333/).
216. California did so after the 1971 Serrano vs. Priest court decision, and Vermont followed suit in 1997 with its Act 60. See Alana Semuels, "Good School, Rich School; Bad School, Poor School: The inequality at the heart of America's education system", *The Atlantic*, August 25, 2016 (https://theatlantic.com/business/archive/2016/08/property-taxes-and-unequal-schools/497333/).
217. See Kacey Guin, Betheny Gross, Scott Deburgomaster, and Marguerite Roza, "Do Districts Fund Schools Fairly?", *Education Next*, Fall 2007, Vol. 7, No. 4.
218. Alana Semuels, "Good School, Rich School; Bad School, Poor School: The inequality at the heart of America's education system", *The Atlantic*, August 25, 2016 (https://theatlantic.com/business/archive/2016/08/property-taxes-and-unequal-schools/497333/).
219. Alana Semuels, "Good School, Rich School; Bad School, Poor School: The inequality at the heart of America's education system", *The Atlantic*, August 25, 2016 (https://theatlantic.com/business/archive/2016/08/property-taxes-and-unequal-schools/497333/).
220. Alana Semuels, "Good School, Rich School; Bad School, Poor School: The

inequality at the heart of America's education system", *The Atlantic*, August 25, 2016 (https://theatlantic.com/business/archive/2016/08/property-taxes-and-unequal-schools/497333/).

221. Alana Semuels, "Good School, Rich School; Bad School, Poor School: The inequality at the heart of America's education system", *The Atlantic*, August 25, 2016 (https://theatlantic.com/business/archive/2016/08/property-taxes-and-unequal-schools/497333/).

222. According to the U.S. Department of Education report, Education in the United States: A Brief Overview, September 2005, p. 13, "Compulsory schooling ends by law at 16 in 30 states, at age 17 in nine states, and at age 18 in 11 states plus the District of Columbia."

223. Scott Fullwiler, Stephanie Kelton, Catherine Ruetschlin, and Marshall Steinbaum, The Macroeconomic Effects of Student Debt Cancellation, February 2018, Levy Economics Institute Report, Bard College, p. 6.

224. Scott Fullwiler, Stephanie Kelton, Catherine Ruetschlin, and Marshall Steinbaum, The Macroeconomic Effects of Student Debt Cancellation, February 2018, Levy Economics Institute Report, Bard College, p. 7.

225. Scott Fullwiler, Stephanie Kelton, Catherine Ruetschlin, and Marshall Steinbaum, The Macroeconomic Effects of Student Debt Cancellation, February 2018, Levy Economics Institute Report, Bard College, p. 6.

226. A principal reason for the limited impact of a government assumption of student loan forgiveness is that "because the loans made by the Department of Education – which make up the vast majority of student loans outstanding – were already funded when the loans were originated, the new costs of cancelling these loans are limited to the interest payments on the securities issued at that time." See Scott Fullwiler, Stephanie Kelton, Catherine Ruetschlin, and Marshall Steinbaum, The Macroeconomic Effects of Student Debt Cancellation, February 2018, Levy Economics Institute Report, Bard College, p. 7.

227. Scott Fullwiler, Stephanie Kelton, Catherine Ruetschlin, and Marshall Steinbaum, The Macroeconomic Effects of Student Debt Cancellation, February 2018, Levy Economics Institute Report, Bard College, p. 6.

228. The total of disenfranchised current and former incarcerated felons in the United States is 6.1 million. See Christopher Uggen, Ryan Larson, & Sarah Shanno, "6 Million Lost Voters: State-Level Estimates of Felony Disenfranchisement, 2016", October 6, 2016, The Sentencing Project (https://www.sentencingproject.org/publications/6-million-lost-voters-state-level-estimates-felony-disenfranchisement-2016/). These numbers will be reduced thanks to the Florida ballot initiative that was passed in the 2018 election and will restore voting rights to more than a million former felons.
229. Alexa Van Brunt, "Poor people rely on public defenders who are too overworked to defend them", *The Guardian*, Wednesday, June 17, 2015.
230. Wilhelm Schnotz, "The Average Salary of a Court Appointed Attorney", Bizfluent, September 26, 2017 (https://bizfluent.com/info-7742979-average-salary-court-appointed-attorney.html).
231. Justin A. Hinkley and Matt Mencarini, *Lansing State Journal*, November 3, 2016.
232. Justin A. Hinkley and Matt Mencarini, *Lansing State Journal*, November 3, 2016.
233. Joseph Shapiro, "As Court Fees Rise, The Poor Are Paying the Price", NPR, May 19, 2014.
234. The total receiving no civil legal help rises to 87% for the disabled and 88% for veterans. See Legal Services Corporation, 2017 Justice Gap Report.
235. Legal Services Corporation, 2017 Justice Gap Report.
236. The rate goes up to 80% for low-income households with someone disabled, 80% for low-income households with children, and 97% for low-income households with victims of spousal and/or sexual abuse. See Legal Services Corporation, 2017 Justice Gap Report.
237. Lauren Sudeall Lucas and Darcy Meals, "Every year, millions try to navigate US courts without a lawyer", *The Conversation*, September 21, 2017.
238. For example, Article 39A of the Constitution of India proclaims that, "The State shall secure that the operation of the legal system promotes justice, on a basis of equal opportunity, and shall, in particular, provide free legal aid, by suitable legislation or schemes or in any other way, to ensure that opportunities for securing justice are not denied to any citizen by reason of economic or other disabilities."

See https://www.india.gov.in/my-government/constitution-india/constitution-india-full-text.

239. Official Journal of the European Communities, 18.12.2000, C364/20.

240. John H. Langbein explains how the German legal system operates without plea bargaining in his essay, "Land Without Plea Bargaining: How the Germans Do It", *Michigan Law Review*, Vol. 78:204, pp. 204-225.

241. The United States Bail Reform Act of 1984, which the Supreme court upheld in United States v. Salerno, duly required "a hearing on a motion to detain, and gave the defendant a right to counsel at the hearing, a right to call and cross-examine witnesses, and a right to appeal the decision of the court if it ruled in favor of detainment." See Caitlin Hill, "A Brief History of Cash Bail", ACLU Ohio, December 12, 2017 (https://www.acluohio.org/archives/blog-posts/a-brief-history-of-cash-bail).

242. The Philippines is our one accomplice in this practice, reflecting our former colonial rule. All other nations outlaw cash bail. See Adam Liptak, "Illegal Globally, Bail for Profit Remains in the U.S.", *The New York Times*, January 28, 2008, and John Murphy, "Revision of State Bail Laws", Ohio State Law Journal, 1971, Volume 32: pp. 451-486.

243. Caitlin Hill makes these points in her piece, "A Brief History of Cash Bail", ACLU Ohio, December 12, 2017 (https://www.acluohio.org/archives/blog-posts/a-brief-history-of-cash-bail).

244. Such grounds are duly specified in the United Kingdom Bail Act of 1976, Schedule 1 (http://www.statutelaw.gov.uk/legResults.aspx?ActiveTextDocld=1341710).

245. Cherise Fanno Burdeen, "The Dangerous Domino Effect of Not Making Bail", *The Atlantic*, April 12, 2016 (http://www.theatlantic.com/politics/archive/2016/04/the-dangerous-domino-effect-of-not-making-bail/477906).

246. Teresa Wiltz, "Locked Up: Is Cash Bail on the Way Out?", *Stateline*, March 1, 2017.

247. Udi Ofer, "We Can't End Mass Incarceration Without Ending Money Bail", American Civil Liberties Union, 2018 (https://www.aclu.org/blog/smart-justice/we-cant-end-mass-incarceraton-without-ending-money-bail)

248. Teresa Wiltz, "Locked Up: Is Cash Bail on the Way Out?", *Stateline*, March 1, 2017.

249. This is the rate for jail inmates in Philadelphia. See Teresa Wiltz, "Locked Up: Is

Cash Bail on the Way Out?", *Stateline*, March 1, 2017.

250. Teresa Wiltz, "Locked Up: Is Cash Bail on the Way Out?", *Stateline*, March 1, 2017.

251. Sandra Bland is a sad example: too poor to post bail for a traffic stop, she hanged herself in 2015 in a jail in Texas. See Teresa Wiltz, "Locked Up: Is Cash Bail on the Way Out?", *Stateline*, March 1, 2017. Others whose pre-trial detention due to failure to afford cash bail led to their death include Jeffrey Pendleton (remanded for a marijuana possession misdemeanor charge) and Kalief Browder. See Cherise Fanno Burdeen, "The Dangerous Domino Effect of Not Making Bail", *The Atlantic*, April 12, 2016 (http://www.theatlantic.com/politics/archive/2016/04/the-dangerous-domino-effect-of-not-making-bail/477906).

252. Teresa Wiltz, "Locked Up: Is Cash Bail on the Way Out?", *Stateline*, March 1, 2017.

253. Cherise Fanno Burdeen, "The Dangerous Domino Effect of Not Making Bail", *The Atlantic*, April 12, 2016 (http://www.theatlantic.com/politics/archive/2016/04/the-dangerous-domino-effect-of-not-making-bail/477906).

254. "A 2016 Columbia University report found that defendants who've been charged bail have a 12 percent higher chance of being convicted and are 6 to 9 percent more likely to be charged with another crime." See Teresa Wiltz, "Locked Up: Is Cash Bail on the Way Out?", *Stateline*, March 1, 2017. Another study "showed that the non-felony conviction rate jumps from 50 percent to 92 percent for those jailed pretrial. For felony cases, the rate jumps from 59 percent to 85 percent." See Udi Ofer, "We Can't End Mass Incarceration Without Ending Money Bail", American Civil Liberties Union, 2018 (https://www.aclu.org/blog/smart-justice/we-cant-end-mass-incarceraton-without-ending-money-bail). As Udi Ofer points out, this higher conviction rate reflects how "people become desperate to leave jail and agree to plea deals." See Udi Ofer, "We Can't End Mass Incarceration Without Ending Money Bail", American Civil Liberties Union, 2018 (https://www.aclu.org/blog/smart-justice/we-cant-end-mass-incarceraton-without-ending-money-bail).

255. Udi Ofer, "We Can't End Mass Incarceration Without Ending Money Bail", American Civil Liberties Union, 2018 (https://www.aclu.org/blog/smart-justice/we-cant-end-mass-incarceraton-without-ending-money-bail).

256. Udi Ofer, "We Can't End Mass Incarceration Without Ending Money Bail",

American Civil Liberties Union, 2018 (https://www.aclu.org/blog/smart-justice/we-cant-end-mass-incarceraton-without-ending-money-bail).

257. Cherise Fanno Burdeen, "The Dangerous Domino Effect of Not Making Bail", *The Atlantic*, April 12, 2016 (http://www.theatlantic.com/politics/archive/2016/04/the-dangerous-domino-effect-of-not-making-bail/477906).

258. As Udi Ofer writes, "In Maryland, for example, the state's Office of the Public Defender found that over a five-year period, more than $75 million in bail bond premiums were charged in cases that were resolved without finding of any wrong-doing. Overall, for-profit bond premiums cost families in the state more than $250 million over five years, and that does not include interest or other fees. When you take a deeper look, as we have, you'll see that these predatory loan practices are often concentrated in the poorest communities and are disproportionately paid by Black people. We're seeing hundreds of millions of dollars drained from our most under-served communities into the hands of the bail bond industry and multinational corporations." See Udi Ofer, "We Can't End Mass Incarceration Without Ending Money Bail", American Civil Liberties Union, 2018 (https://www.aclu.org/blog/smart-justice/we-cant-end-mass-incarceraton-without-ending-money-bail)

259. Bernie Sanders' proposed No Money Bail Act, which forbids "payment of money as a condition of pre-trail release with respect to a criminal case", would be a great step forward (See Lauren Gambino and Ben Jacobs, *The Guardian*, Wednesday, July 2018). Any such legislation needs to insure that alternative surety measures, such as GPS monitors and pre-trial supervision, operate without charge so that the non-cash bail system does not disadvantage those with less wealth.

260. As Caitlin Hill observes, "It's crucial that courts prioritize release by turning away from secured money bonds and instead use the least restrictive means necessary to ensure public safety and appearance." See Caitlin Hill, "A Brief History of Cash Bail", ACLU Ohio, December 12, 2017 (https://www.acluohio.org/archives/blog-posts/a-brief-history-of-cash-bail).

261. In 1984, the Corrections Corporation of America (CCA) became the nation's first private company to take over complete operation of a jail, which occurred at a

facility in Shelby County, Tennessee. See Philip Mattera and Mafruza Khan with Greg Leroy and Kate Davis, "Jail Breaks: Economic Development Subsidies Given to Private Prisons", Good Jobs First, October 2001, p. 2.

262. Sean Bryant, "The Business Model of Private Prisons", *Investopedia*, June 22, 2015 (https://www.investopedia.com/articles/investing/062215/business-model-private-prisons.asp).
263. See ACLU, "Private Prisons", American Civil Liberties Union (https://aclu.org/issues/smart-justice/mass-incarceration/private-prisons), and Lauren-Brooke Eisen, "Private Prisons Lock Up Thousands of Americans With Almost no Oversight", Time, November 8, 2017.
264. U.S. General Accounting Office, Private and Public Prisons: Studies Comparing Operational Cost and/or Quality of Service, GAO/GGD-96-158, August 1996.
265. American Bar Association, "Prisons for Profit: Incarceration for Sale", *Human Rights Magazine*, Summer 2011, Volume 38, March 7, 2012.
266. See Maahs, J. and Pratt, T. "Are Private Prisons More Cost-Effective than Public Prisons? A Meta-Analysis of Evaluation Research Studies", Crime and Delinquency, 1999, No. 45 (3): pp. 358-371.
267. A 2001 study unveils the tendency to send less costly inmates to private prisons, inflating their cost savings. See *Policy Matters Ohio*, "Selective Ceiling: Inmate Population in Ohio's Private Prisons", May 2001.
268. This exemption applies to private state prisons as well as private federal immigration detention facilities. See Lauren-Brooke Eisen, "Private Prisons Lock Up Thousands of Americans With Almost no Oversight", *Time*, November 8, 2017.
269. A notorious example is CCA's for-profit Northeast Ohio Correctional Facility in Youngstown, Ohio, which had 13 stabbings, 2 murders, and 6 escapes during its first fourteen months of operation, leading the city to file a lawsuit to make CCA meet minimum security standards. See American Bar Association, "Prisons for Profit: Incarceration for Sale", *Human Rights Magazine*, Summer 2011, Volume 38, March 7, 2012.
270. Bernie Sanders, "We Must End For-Profit Prisons", *Politico*, February 26, 2016 (http:www.politico.com/sponsor-content/2016/02/we-must-end-for-profit-prisons).

271. American Bar Association, "Prisons for Profit: Incarceration for Sale", *Human Rights Magazine*, Summer 2011, Volume 38, March 7, 2012.
272. See Oliver Laughland, "Private federal prisons more dangerous, damning Department of Justice investigation reveals", *The Guardian*, August 12, 2016 (https://www.theguardian.com/us-news/2016/aug/12/private-federal-prisons-more-dangerous-justice-department)
273. In the for-profit Walnut Grove Correctional Facility, where the ratio of staff to prisoners was 1 to 120, overwhelmed staff did not intervene in a prison riot sending six inmates to the hospital. See Newkirk, M., and Selway, W., "Gangs ruled Prison as For-Profit Model Put Blood on Floor", *Bloomberg News*, July 11, 2013.
274. American Bar Association, "Prisons for Profit: Incarceration for Sale", *Human Rights Magazine*, Summer 2011, Volume 38, March 7, 2012.
275. For an inventory of notorious examples, see Philip Mattera and Mafruza Khan with Greg Leroy and Kate Davis, "Jail Breaks: Economic Development Subsidies Given to Private Prisons", *Good Jobs First*, October 2001, pp. 5-6.
276. In a notorious case at a Florida for-profit prison, juvenile detainees were enlisted to beat up others. As the local Broward County chief assistant public defender declared, "The children are used by staff members to inflict harm on other children."
277. Bernie Sanders, "We Must End For-Profit Prisons", *Politico*, February 26, 2016 (http:www.politico.com/sponsor-content/2016/02/we-must-end-for-profit-prisons).
278. Bernie Sanders, "We Must End For-Profit Prisons", *Politico*, February 26, 2016 (http:www.politico.com/sponsor-content/2016/02/we-must-end-for-profit-prisons).
279. American Bar Association, "Prisons for Profit: Incarceration for Sale", *Human Rights Magazine*, Summer 2011, Volume 38, March 7, 2012.
280. American Bar Association, "Prisons for Profit: Incarceration for Sale", *Human Rights Magazine*, Summer 2011, Volume 38, March 7, 2012.
281. American Bar Association, "Prisons for Profit: Incarceration for Sale", *Human Rights Magazine*, Summer 2011, Volume 38, March 7, 2012.
282. This is according to the Washington Post. Bernie Sanders, "We Must End

For-Profit Prisons", *Politico*, February 26, 2016 (http:www.politico.com/sponsor-content/2016/02/we-must-end-for-profit-prisons).

283. As reported by Grassroots Leadership. See Bernie Sanders, "We Must End For-Profit Prisons", *Politico*, February 26, 2016 (http:www.politico.com/sponsor-content/2016/02/we-must-end-for-profit-prisons).

284. Bernie Sanders, "We Must End For-Profit Prisons", *Politico*, February 26, 2016 (http:www.politico.com/sponsor-content/2016/02/we-must-end-for-profit-prisons).

285. In support of abolishing for-profit prisons, Israeli Supreme Court President Dorit Beinisch said what a United States Supreme Court Chief Justice should one day declare, that "when the power to incarcerate is transferred to a private corporation whose purpose is making money, the act of depriving a person of liberty loses much of its legitimacy. Because of this loss of legitimacy, the violation of the prisoner's right to liberty goes beyond the violation entailed in the incarceration itself." See Tomer Zarchin, "International Legal Precedent: No Private Prisons in Israel", *Haaretz*, November 20, 2009.

286. Wendy Sawyer and Wanda Bertram, "New reports show probation is down, but still a major driver of incarceration", *Prison Policy Initiative*, April 26, 2018 (https://www.prisonpolicy.org/blog/2018/04/26/probation_update-2/).

287. Chris Albin-Lackey, "Profiting From Probation: America's "Offender-Funded" Probation Industry", *Human Rights Watch*, February, 2014, p. 1.

288. Chris Albin-Lackey, "Profiting From Probation: America's "Offender-Funded" Probation Industry", *Human Rights Watch*, February, 2014, p. 3.

289. James Salzer, "Court rules private probation legal but extending sentences is not", *The Atlanta Journal-Constitution*, November 24, 2014.

290. See James Salzer, "Court rules private probation legal but extending sentences is not", *The Atlanta Journal-Constitution*, November 24, 2014.

291. "Private Probation", July 12, 2018, Wikipedia (https://en.wikipedia.org/w/index/php?title+Private_probation&oldid=849892975).

292. James Salzer, "Court rules private probation legal but extending sentences is not", *The Atlanta Journal-Constitution*, November 24, 2014.

293. This is the phrase used by a probationers' lawyer to describe the for-profit probation business. See James Salzer, "Court rules private probation legal but extending sentences is not", *The Atlanta Journal-Constitution*, November 24, 2014.
294. Beth Schwartzapfel, "Probation-for-Profit Just Got Less Profitable", The Marshall Project, April 13, 2007.
295. James Salzer, "Court rules private probation legal but extending sentences is not", *The Atlanta Journal-Constitution*, November 24, 2014.
296. James Salzer, "Court rules private probation legal but extending sentences is not", *The Atlanta Journal-Constitution*, November 24, 2014.
297. James Salzer, "Court rules private probation legal but extending sentences is not", *The Atlanta Journal-Constitution*, November 24, 2014.
298. James Salzer, "Supreme Court: Private probation legal, but not drawn-out sentences", *The Atlanta Journal-Constitution*, November 24, 2014.
299. Beth Schwartzapfel, "Probation-for-Profit Just Got Less Profitable", The Marshall Project, April 13, 2007.
300. Chris Albin-Lackey, "Profiting From Probation: America's "Offender-Funded" Probation Industry", *Human Rights Watch*, February, 2014, p. 4.
301. Joseph Shapiro, "As Court Fees Rise, The Poor Are Paying The Price", All Things Considered, NPR, May 19, 2014.
302. Joseph Shapiro, "As Court Fees Rise, The Poor Are Paying The Price", All Things Considered, NPR, May 19, 2014.
303. According to the Equal Justice Under Law civil rights non-profit organization, 38 states suspend drivers' licenses for non-payment of court debt, which may have nothing to do with driving violations. See "3. Suspended Drivers Licenses", https://equaljusticeunderlaw.org/overview/.
304. See Equal Justice Under Law, "8. Examples of How America's Legal System Punishes People Who Are Poor", https://equaljusticeunderlaw.org/overview/.
305. See Equal Justice Under Law, "8. Examples of How America's Legal System Punishes People Who Are Poor", https://equaljusticeunderlaw.org/overview/.
306. Equal Justice Under Law, "8. Examples of How America's Legal System Punishes People Who Are Poor", https://equaljusticeunderlaw.org/overview/.

307. Joseph Shapiro, "As Court Fees Rise, The Poor Are Paying The Price", All Things Considered, NPR, May 19, 2014.
308. Joseph Shapiro, "As Court Fees Rise, The Poor Are Paying The Price", All Things Considered, NPR, May 19, 2014.
309. As Joseph Shapiro reports, in Washington state, defendants are charged $250 for a 12 person jury and $125 for a 6 person jury. In Allegan County, Michigan, he reports, court officials testified that defendants paid court cost fees intended for covering "salaries of court employees, for heat, telephones, copy machines, and even to underwrite the cost of the county employees' fitness gym." See Joseph Shapiro, "As Court Fees Rise, The Poor Are Paying The Price", All Things Considered, NPR, May 19, 2014.
310. Joseph Shapiro, "As Court Fees Rise, The Poor Are Paying The Price", All Things Considered, NPR, May 19, 2014.
311. Joseph Shapiro, "As Court Fees Rise, The Poor Are Paying The Price", All Things Considered, NPR, May 19, 2014.
312. Joseph Shapiro, "As Court Fees Rise, The Poor Are Paying The Price", All Things Considered, NPR, May 19, 2014.
313. Joseph Shapiro, "As Court Fees Rise, The Poor Are Paying The Price", All Things Considered, NPR, May 19, 2014.
314. Rakesh Kochhar & Anthony Cilluffo, "Income Inequality in the U.S. Is Rising Most Rapidly Among Asians, Asians displace blacks as the most economically divided group in the U.S.", Pew Social Trends, July 12, 2018 (http://www.pewsocialtrends.org/2018/07/12/income-inequality-in-the-u-s-is-rising-most-rapidly-among-asians/).
315. "United States Gross National Product 1950-2018, Trading Economics, (https://tradingeconomics.com"/united-states/gross-national-product).
316. Andy Stern, *Raising the Floor: How a universal basic income can renew our economy and rebuild the American dream* (New York: Public Affairs, 2016), p. 201.
317. The Federal Job Guarantee cost would be offset by $436.67 billion alone due to the following programs it would make largely unnecessary: unemployment insurance ($170 billion), SNAP food aid ($82 billion), the Earned Income Tax Credit ($82

billion), the Child Nutrition Program ($20.8 billion), the WIC and CSFP Feeding Programs ($6.67 billion), the TANF support payments to states ($20.8 billion), and the Low Income Home Energy Assistance program ($3.7 billion). See Andy Stern, Raising the Floor, p. 212.

318. "The Price of Prisons", Vera (https://www.vera.org/publications/price-of-prisons-2015-state-spending-trends/).
319. Peter Wagner & Wendy Sawyer, "States of Incarceration: The Global Context 2018", Prison Policy Initiative, June 2018 (https://www.prisonpolicy.org/global/2018.html).
320. Washington Post, 4/16/2016.
321. "Senior Care Costs/Aging Care Calculator", August, 2017, Paying For Senior Care, (https://www.payingforseniorcare.com/longtermcare/costs/html).
322. Child Trends. (2018). "Number of Children". Bethesda, MD (https://www.childtrends.org/indicators/number-of-children).
323. "Fact Sheet: Social Security", June 2018, Social Security Administration (https://www.ssa.gov/news/press/factsheets/basicfact-alt.pdf).
324. This is the estimate for 2018. See "U.S. college enrollment statistics for public and private colleges from 1965 to 2016 and projections up to 2027", Statista, https://www.statista.com/statistics/183995/us-college-enrollment-and-projections-in-public-and-private-institutions/.
325. "Tuition Costs of Colleges and Universities", National Center for Education Statistics, https://nces.ed.gov/fastfacts/display.asp?id=76.
326. *US News & World Report*, 2018 (https://money.usnews.com/careers/best-jobs/lawyer/salary).
327. "Largest law firms by revenue", February, 2018, Wikipedia (https://en.wikipedia.org/wiki/List_of_largest_law_firms_by_revenue).
328. Legal Services Corporation, "2017 Justice Gap Report" (https://www.lsc.gov/media-center/publications/2017-justice-gap-report).
329. Bradley Sawyer & Cynthia Cox, "How does health spending in the U.S. compare to other countries?", February 13, 2018, Kaiser Family Foundation (https://www.healthsystemtracker.org/chart-collection/

health-spending-u-s-compare-countries/#item-start).

330. See Wray, *Modern Money Theory, Second Edition*, pp. 261-2, for a discussion of how these special circumstances contributed to hyperinflation.

331. L. Randall Wray, *Modern Money Theory, Second Edition* (Houndmills, UK: Palgrave Macmillan, 2015), p. 43.

332. David Merrill has suggested in conversation that if China, for example, were not to renew its United States Bond holdings, it would be left with no alternative than to leave its dollars at the Federal Reserve Bank, suffering the loss of bond interest earnings. China could, however, convert these dollars into investments in other nations, as well as into productive investments at home. Nonetheless, the security of United States Bonds and the importance of sustaining the strength of the dollar give China ample reasons for maintaining, as well as increasing, its United States Bond portfolio.

333. L. Randall Wray maintains in *Modern Money Theory, Second Edition* (p. 2), that a "sovereign government cannot become insolvent in its own currency; it can always make payments as they come due in its own currency." Yet, as Wray admits, this ability is not completely unlimited, for, as he quotes his mentor, Hyman Minsky, noting, "Anyone can create money", but "the problem lies in getting it accepted" (*Modern Money Theory, Second Edition*, p. 6). As history has shown, economic crises can lead to situations where the domestic, not to mention foreign value of a sovereign national currency plummets as prices rise in hyperinflation. Then, even if taxes must be paid in the sovereign currency, which Wray maintains is the basis for acceptance of that currency (*Modern Money Theory, Second Edition*, p. 49), the "money of account" may become so devalued that other means of exchange get employed, including more stable foreign currencies.

334. As David Merrill has pointed out in conversation, this use of taxation can be a key element in promoting public health, more energy efficient housing sizes and densities, and other consumer purchases that advance the transition away from fossil fuel dependency.

335. "Current Government Revenue in the U.S.", USGovernmentRevenue, 11/1/2018, https://www.usgovernmentrevenue.com/total_revenue.

336. "State Tax Collections by State: 2016-17", U. S. Census Bureau, 2017 Annual Survey of State Tax Collections.
337. Extrapolating from the "Quarterly Summary of State and Local Government Tax Revenue for 2017: Q4", United States Census Bureau.
338. Capital gains have had some degree of graduated rates, but these are significantly lower than those that apply to income taxes, which privileged the wealthy who most benefit from capital gains. For figures of recent capital gains tax rates, see Lowrey, Annie, "Tax code May Be the Most Progressive Since 1979", *The New York Times*, January 4, 2013 (https://www.nytimes.com/2013/01/05/business/after-fiscal-deal-tax-code-may-be-most-progressive-since-1979.html).
339. Andy Stern, *Raising the Floor: How a universal basic income can renew our economy and rebuild the American dream* (New York: Public Affairs, 2016), pp. 30ff.; "United States GDP Annual Growth Rate", Trading Economics, 2018 (https://tradingeconomics.com/united-states/gdp-growth-annual).
340. Clark, Gregory, "The Annual RPI and Average Earnings for Britain, 1209 to Present (New Series), 2017 (https://measuringworth.com/ukearncpi/).
341. In the 1895 Pollock v. Farmer's Loan & Trust co. decision, the United States Supreme Court deemed income tax to be unconstitutional on the grounds that it was a direct tax that violated Article I, Section 9, Clause 4, which reads, "No Capitation, or other direct, Tax shall be valid, unless in Proportion to the Census or enumeration herein before directed to be taken." See Chief Justice Fuller's opinion, 158 U. S. 601, 634 http://www.let.rug.nl/usa/D/1876-1900/reform/pollock.htm).
342. "Personal Exemptions and Individual Income Tax Rates: 1913-2002", Internal Revenue Service (https://www.irs.gov/pub/irs-soi/02inpetr.pdf).
343. As Piketty points out, these flattenings and reductions in graduated income tax rates have contributed to the "explosion of executive salaries" that has played a significant role in advancing income and wealth inequality in the United States and, to a lesser extent, in much of the developed world. See Piketty, *Capital in the Twenty-First Century*, pp. 508 ff.
344. Piketty, *Capital in the Twenty-First Century*, pp. 513.
345. As of 2018, there is a lifetime inheritance tax exclusion of $5.6 million, above which

beneficiaries pay a 40% inheritance tax on whatever exceeds that total. Any lifetime inheritance below $5.6 million pays no inheritance tax. See Dan Caplinger, "2018 Estate Tax Rates", The Motley Fool, Occtober 25, 2017 (https://www.fool.com/taxes/2017/10/25/2018-estate-tax-rates.aspx). As Piketty points out, between 1937 and 1939, United States estate taxes had rates above 70 percent, which would serve to discourage the perpetuation of huge estates without any expropriation or prohibition. See Thomas Piketty, *Capital in the Twenty-First Century*, trans. Arthur Goldhammer (Cambridge, MA: Harvard University Press, 2014), p. 505.

346. For further discussion of why consumption, payroll, and corporate income taxes are bad taxes, see Wray, *Modern Money Theory, Second Edition*, pp. 153-6.
347. According to the Federal Reserve, whereas the richest 1% possess 38.6% of US wealth in 2016, the bottom 90% control just 22.8%, down from 33% in 1989. See Matt Egan, "Record inequality: The top 1% control 38.6% of America's wealth", CNN, September 27, 2017 (https://money.cnn.com/2017/09/27/news/economy/inequality-record-top-1-percent-wealth/index.html)
348. According to 2015 Federal Income Tax Data, the top 1% of income came to 20.65% of total personal income, the top 10% of income came to 47.36% of total personal income, leaving 52.64% of total personal income to the lowest 90% of earners. See Erica York, "Summary of the Latest Federal Income Tax Date 2017 Update", Tax Foundation, January 17, 2018 (https://taxfoundation.org/summary.federal-income-tax-data-2017/).
349. US Census Bureau, "Income distribution to $250,000 or More for Households: 2013" (https://www.census.gov/hhes/www/cpstables/032014/hhinc/hinc06.xls).
350. In 2016, the median wealth of an African American family ($13,460) was 9.5% of a White American family ($142,180), and the mean wealth of an African American family ($102,477) was 11% of a White American family ($935,584). See Angela Hanks, Danyelle Solomon, and Christian E. Weller, "Systematic Inequality: How America's Structural Racism Helped Create the Black-White Wealth Gap", Center for American Progress, February 21, 2018 (https://www.americanprogress.org/issues/race/reports/2018/02/21/447051/systematic-inequality/).
351. Tim Worstall, "Us Household Wealthy ticks Up $2.3 Trillion to $94.8T – But This

Is Wrong, Entirely Wrong", *Forbes*, June 8, 2017 (https://www.forbes.com/sites/timworstall/2017/06/08/us-household-wealth-ticks-up-2-3-trillion-to-94-8t-but-this-is-wrong-entirely-wrong/#7c38ded7621a)

352. As Wary notes (*Modern Money Theory, Second Edition*, p. 144), the elimination of corporate income tax was advocated by New Dealer, Beardsley Ruml, chairman of the New York Federal Reserve Bank during the 1940's and, more recently, by Hyman Minsky.

353. Piketty presents a wealth taxation plan that targets capital in general, which then, as he points out, may adversely affect businesses, particularly when they are in the red. He attempts to mitigate this problem by accompanying tax on capital stock with tax on the revenue streaming from capital. So he writes, "A tax system based solely on the capital stock (and not on realized profits) would put disproportionate pressure on companies in the red, because their taxes would be as high when they were losing money as when they were earning high profits, and this could plunge them into bankruptcy. The ideal tax system is therefore a compromise between the incentive logic (which favors a tax on the capital stock) and an insurance logic (which favors a tax on the revenue stream stemming from capital)." See Piketty, *Capital in the Twenty-First Century*, p. 527.

354. Wray, *Modern Money Theory, Second Edition*, pp. 155-6.

355. Piketty promotes this policy on an international scale, arguing, "if democracy is to regain control over the globalized financial capitalism of this century, it must also invent new tools, adapted to today's challenges. The ideal tool would be a progressive global tax on capital, coupled with a very high level of international financial transparency." See Piketty, *Capital in the Twenty-First Century*, p. 515. We can lead the way with highly graduated wealth taxation on the global wealth of U.S. residents. Moves to increase international financial transparency will facilitate our own administration of wealth taxation.

356. "Trump proposes massive onetime tax on the rich", CNN, November 9, 1999 (http://articles.cnn.com/1999-11-09/politics/trump.rich-1-donald-trump-trump-said-trump-trump-said-the).

357. Matt Egan, "Record inequality: The top 1% control 38.6% of America's wealth",

CNN, September 27, 2017 (https://money.cnn.com/2017/09/27/news/economy/inequality-record-top-1-percent-wealth/index.html).

358. For example, we could come up with a simple single page tax filing form by dispensing with all deductions, treating all sizeable gifts, capital gains, and inheritance as income, eliminating all income and wealth taxation on the lower 90%, and raising graduated income and wealth tax rates to whatever levels are required to fund our public investment needs.
359. David Merrill suggested these parallels in conversation.
360. At my 50th Roslyn High School Reunion, I spoke with a classmate law school graduate who had spent his career as a Congressional legislative advisor, helping legislators craft laws. He acknowledged the need to simplify legislation, but maintained that legislators were unwilling to leave details to the administrators due to widespread suspicion that the executive branch was too politicized to apply the law with impartial discretion. The prevailing view in Congress was that the law would have to specify its own application, as much as possible.

Index

D

E

F

G

H

I

J

K

L

M

N

O

P

R

S

T

U

W

Y

About the Author

Richard Dien Winfield is Distinguished Research Professor of Philosophy at the University of Georgia, where he has taught since 1982. He is married to Sujata Gupta Winfield, an immigration attorney, and has three grown children. Winfield is also the author of 21 previous books of philosophy. In 2018 he ran unsuccessfully for US Congress in the Democratic Primary in Georgia's 10th District. He has entered the 2020 special US Senate election in Georgia.

CPSIA information can be obtained
at www.ICGtesting.com
Printed in the USA
BVHW070925190123
656605BV00007B/411